JB JOSSEY-BASS

THE BATTLE OVER THE MEANING OF EVERYTHING

Evolution, Intelligent Design,
and a School Board in Dover, PA

Gordy Slack

BICENTENNIAL

1807

WILEY

2007

BICENTENNIAL

John Wiley & Sons

Published by Jossey-Bass
A Wiley Imprint
989 Market Street, San Francisco, CA 94103-1741   www.josseybass.com

Library of Congress Cataloging-in-Publication Data

Slack, Gordy.
  The battle over the meaning of everything: evolution, intelligent design, and a school board in Dover, PA / Gordy Slack.
     p. cm.
  Includes bibliographical references and index.
  ISBN-13: 978–0–7879–8786–2 (cloth)
  ISBN-10: 0–7879–8786–7 (cloth)
  ISBN-13: 978–04703–7931–8 (paperback)
  ISBN-10: 0–4703–7931–6 (paperback)
  1. Kitzmiller, Tammy—Trials, litigation, etc. 2. Dover Area School District (Dover, Pa.)—Trials, litigation, etc. 3. Evolution (Biology)—Study and teaching—Law and legislation—Pennsylvania—Dover. 4. Intelligent design (Teleology)—Study and teaching—Law and legislation—Pennsylvania—Dover. I. Title.
  KF228.K589S59 2007
  344.748'41077—dc22   2007005825

Printed in the United States of America
FIRST EDITION
HB Printing   10 9 8 7 6 5 4 3 2 1
PB Printing   10 9 8 7 6 5 4 3 2 1

CONTENTS

iii

FOR MY SONS LEO AND JONAH: MAY YOU CONTINUE TO
JOYOUSLY PURSUE THE TRUTH AND TO REGARD WITH SKEPTICAL
RESPECT THOSE WHO SWEAR TO HAVE FOUND IT

PROLOGUE

The intelligent design movement had taken the nation by storm, and in the process I had lost a bet. Sort of.

In January 1998, my father and I had marched down Berkeley's College Avenue, overdressed in suits and sweating like Mormons at the equator. It was extraordinarily hot, and the midday sun raised bubbles in the asphalt. We were arguing about evolution, as usual, as we raced toward Boalt Hall, the University of California at Berkeley's law school. We were going there to meet Phillip Johnson, professor of law, author of a book called *Darwin on Trial,* and the founding father of what my dad described as the "neo-creationist" intelligent design (ID) movement.

I was an editor at a natural history magazine, and the theme of my work was evolutionary biology. That fact was a big bee in the bonnet of my dad, a Princeton-trained experimental psychologist who, to my dismay, had recently turned super-Christian anti-evolution neo-creationist proponent of ID. He'd been corresponding with Phil Johnson and had somehow talked him, and me, into having lunch together.

When we burst into his office ten minutes late, breathless and hot, Johnson offered us each a glass of water. I would have much preferred a double scotch. What the hell was I doing here? Why had I, a science writer and evolutionist, agreed to have lunch with a crusading creationist lawyer? How could this possibly turn out well?

Johnson, at fifty-six, looked older than his years. He was a short, squarish person with mischievous crinkly eyes and a thin wisp of gray hair that breached the top of his shiny head. He expressed lots of both confidence and humility, and they commingled disarmingly. Despite his mission, he had none of the fundamentalist preacher about him. He was urbane, articulate, and smart as a whip; not at all what I expected to find in the guy who'd resurrected creationism from the dung heap of America's really bad twentieth-century ideas.

We walked the short distance to the comfortable, redwood-shaded Berkeley Faculty Club. Once we settled in to our meal, Johnson and I argued intensively, ceaselessly, but civilly for an hour and a half, taking turns so we could eat our chicken and mashed potatoes between bursts of rhetoric.

Though the intelligent design movement was still an infant, all of its basic arguments were already in place. Johnson argued that evolution was an ideology, not a science; that what passed for scientific proof in evolutionary biology was neither scientific nor proof but rather rhetoric resting on bad philosophy. Evolution was bad science, he said, but what this debate was really about was neither evolution nor ID, but the worldviews they enabled. Evolution, he said, permits a relativistic, purposeless, Godless view of the world, in which self-aggrandizement and pleasure are sufficient ends in themselves, and the only objective measure of goodness is reproductive fitness.

I stood up for evolution, citing the ever-stronger evidence found in the fossil record, the avalanche of new genetic evidence, and lab work directly observing evolution not only in microorganisms but in big ones such as fruit flies. Natural selection had not only helped create a coherent narrative about the source of life, I said, but also helped create drug-resistant pathogens and the new medicines used to treat them.

Johnson shook his head. No, he said, and cited a new book in which Lehigh University biochemist Michael Behe allegedly took apart each of Darwin's claims. In addition to revealing Darwin's fallacies, Behe also showed that the biological world was riddled with structures which were complex in a way that Darwin's step-by-step natural selection couldn't begin to explain. Design—intelligent design—was the only other explanation, Behe and Johnson said.

If there's any evidence for natural selection, Johnson said, it is only for minor changes within a species. The big stuff, evolution of new kinds of life from old ones, complex ones from simple ones, birds from dinosaurs, just doesn't fly, he said. It couldn't. You don't find an organism with half a lung, half an eye, half a flagellum, he said.

"What about lungfish?" I asked. "Aren't they a likely candidate for the ancestor to all terrestrial vertebrates? Don't they have something like half a lung?"

"No," he said.

"Yes," I said.

"No," he said.

Neither Johnson, the lawyer, nor I, the science writer, could settle the question there. Although we were both better equipped with facts and theoretical understanding than most people having this debate, it still boiled down to a basic difference. I believed in evolution, he did not.

Darwin's theory of evolution was, for me, a fundamental belief. If natural selection couldn't explain some irreducibly complex structure now, I said, one day either it, or some other natural process, would be able to. I just knew it.

"Okay!" he said, as if crying Eureka! "You've said it! You assume that even if Darwin's theory is wrong, that one day there will be some other natural, mindless, unintentional explanation of life's history . . . that's exactly the assumption that props up the whole materialistic view of the world. It locks intelligent design out of science by definition, whether there is evidence for design or not. And that's exactly the view of the world that ID is going to bring down like a house of cards," he said, not even trying to suppress his impish smile.

Just like a kid, I reached out to shake his hand, saying, "Want to bet?"

He ignored my hand. "Give us five or ten years, and you'll see scientific breakthroughs biologists hadn't dreamed of before ID," he said. "Today science can't follow the evidence where it leads. If data points toward ID, scientists have to ignore it. But people can't do that forever. And when they accept the evidence for design, there won't just be a new scientific paradigm. The cultural legacies of materialism will implode as well."

"That's a bold prediction," I said. "We'll see."

"Yes, we'll see," he said.

We finished our coffee, exchanged business cards, agreed that it had been interesting, and said goodbye.

My dad and I walked out of the shady redwood grove that surrounds the Faculty Club and back into the afternoon sun. I felt like I was leaving Alice's Wonderland, where I'd been talking to a mad genius, one whose paranoia and craving for meaning led him to a view of the world that, while internally coherent, was completely out of whack with the real world as I knew it.

I still haven't bought ID, even in its most discounted versions. But since that lunch with Johnson, I no longer see the debate as open and shut. It is more nuanced, philosophical, and complex—in a word, it is more *fascinating*—than I ever could have imagined before that meeting, which is what makes this story so much fun to tell and what will make it so surprising and perhaps compelling to read.

In addition to giving me a crash course in the craziest theory since cold fusion, Johnson taught me something I'd not known about myself: I had a deep attachment to a world run by atoms and their properties, a world free from God and His personality. My bias was informed by data, experience, and a lot of presumably well-placed faith in the scientific establishment. But beneath all that I had to admit an inclination, a proclivity, a prejudice, an assumption that the world was ultimately, in itself, without meaning.

Johnson was wrong about evolution, I was sure, but he was a provocative lunch date. As my creationist dad and I walked home, I wondered if I'd ever see or hear anything about Johnson again.

I did, and in spades. He has become an icon among neo-creationists; the George Washington of ID.[1]

But it isn't until September 2005, when I am assigned to cover *Kitzmiller* v. *Dover Area School District* in Dover, Pennsylvania, for *Salon.com,* that I look back at the notes I'd written after the lunch with Johnson eight years before. Eight years! Right in the sweet zone, between the five and ten years Johnson had predicted it would take for ID to fly. I know we never shook hands on the bet, but still, what better chance to test his claims than to put them before a federal judge and have the world's authorities on both sides of the issue hold forth?

Time and again, as the story of this remarkable trial unfolds, I will think of Johnson and his prediction that intelligent design would bring about great scientific innovations and then, after it had decapitated evolution, catalyze an implosion of what he calls the "cultural legacies of materialism"— in other words, the modern world as we know it.

Of course, there's much more at stake in the Dover trial than the status of my almost-bet with Johnson. For one, there are the First Amendment rights of Dover High's students; if ID is a religious view and not a science, as the parents bringing the suit against the school board argue, then teaching it would be promoting religion, a constitutional no-no. Second, there are all the school boards across the country ready to introduce ID into their curriculums if it passes the Constitutional hurdle in Dover. Third, every advancement of ID, and its perceived status as science, is a big political boon to the conservative Christian wing of the Republican Party. Lending the authority of science, even marginal science, to the evangelical-driven political right could influence battles over everything from abortion and stem cell research to preemptive military strikes in places such as Iran and Korea. This is a metaphysical debate, but it has extremely practical consequences. Proponents and opponents of ID are on opposite sides of just about every hot-button political issue in America. They are almost certain to disagree about welfare, climate change, nuclear power, government regulation, environmental conservation, birth control, taxes, and America's right to launch preemptive wars.

And finally, underlying it all, the trial will be a head-on match between the two most competitive philosophical strains in the history of Western civilization.

For now, let's call the worldviews clashing in Dover the theistic view and the materialistic one. The theistic view holds that purpose and design are present in the universe, probably put there by a designing, creative, and intentional God. This view, roughly associated with all religions, today finds its most straightforward expression in the intelligent design movement. Intelligent design's special contribution to the theistic view, and just what it needs to really get some political traction, is the belief that a new kind of science can identify proof of that design, and thus a designer, in nature itself.

The second of these warring worldviews, materialism, holds that the universe is the unplanned product of matter and the forces that have governed it over the long history of time. Although as an idea materialism dates back millennia, it is today broadly pinned to the coattails of the nineteenth-century naturalist Charles Darwin and his theory of evolution. That's because Darwin made materialism credible by giving a plausible nature-only explanation for how the forms of life abroad today could have come into being without the aid of a God. Although evolution doesn't prove the universe a purely material place, it does supplant the most compelling reason for believing in God: the apparent miracle of life.

Many of us, maybe most, are happy enough to hold one view or the other at any given time, or to juggle both of these views of the world, depending on what we're trying to do or think about. That includes a lot of religious scientists who are hard-line materialists at work but who are comfortable thinking in terms of God and higher purposes once they shed their lab coats and enter the civilian world.[2] Many will argue that the theistic and materialistic views are not mutually exclusive, that they can be practically woven together into a nuanced view of the world.

But even if most of us can stand the dissonance of these incompatible views in our culture or our selves—wanting, as good Americans, to have our cake and eat it, too—that still leaves the question unanswered: Which one is right? Were we and the rest of the universe created by a God, or by the unfolding ramifications of mere matter? Although *Kitzmiller* will not directly address the question of God's existence—in fact it will try to avoid it like the plague—it definitely will have to address the question of whether science has anything to say on the subject.

By arguing for the inadequacy of evolution, and the necessity of an intelligent designer, a God, and for a fundamental redefinition of science, the advocates of ID are not only promoting a different worldview, they are promoting a different world, one where God's existence and His will are considered objective facts. On one hand, for the growing number of radical theists in the United States that vision of a new America—one that embraces the existence of God and asserts the ultimate reality of His moral authority above all others, and its appropriateness in civic life—is hopeful and bright. For many materialists, on the other hand, it portends a nightmarish return to the Dark Ages.

All these years after that encounter with Johnson, I am thrilled to get an assignment to cover this trial. It's not only my chance to see how ID's progress measures against Johnson's prediction, but also a chance for me to work my way closer to an understanding and appreciation of what my father's conversion, and his worldview, are really all about.

CHAPTER ONE

THE TAKEOVER

JULIE SMITH: "My daughter came home from school, and she says to me, 'Mom, evolution is a lie. What kind of Christian are you, anyway?'"

he town of Dover looks like any of its dozen neighboring communities in the bucolic rolling hills of southern central Pennsylvania. Its neat wooden homes and sprawling cornfields, its little shops and churches, remind me of an earlier America. If you swap those hills and farms for desert, forest, or mountains, it could be any of a thousand wholesome, conservative, and religious communities struggling to survive across the country. Dover is like these American towns, and like much of America, in another way: a deep but invisible faultline of divided beliefs runs right down the middle.

In Dover, that fault suddenly gave way in October 2004 when the local school board proposed a slight alteration to the high school biology curriculum. The rush of pent-up energy released shook this little town to its core, turning neighbor against neighbor, pupil against teacher, and parishioner against pastor. Many regarded those on the opposite side of the divide with disbelief: How on earth they could have lived so close to and so peacefully with people whose fundamental worldview was so different from their own? Others had one foot on each side, and struggled to decide which way to go. Accusations flew, threats were made, and lies were told. Slowly, the fault grew deeper and longer, spreading outward across the nation, polarizing citizens far from Dover and exposing the deep differences in the ways Americans conceive of God and see the world and our place in it—in short, everything.

There is an old Dover and a new Dover. The old one is rooted in Revolutionary War history and the conservatism of multigeneration farms and family trades. The new one is conservative, too, but more educated, more urbane, and, well, less old. As the nearby towns of Harrisburg to the north and York to the south grow, Dover has taken on the role of a suburb; the locals may grudgingly appreciate some of the economic benefits of the newcomers, but their urban attitudes are a less welcome currency.

The old Dover has also been undergoing a religious conversion. Its established, mainline Protestant denominations are being joined by more fundamentalist evangelical churches, intent on spreading their Good News. The new Dover is predominantly Christian, too, but is far more diverse, tolerant, and, on the whole, embracing of modernity. And though there is a rough correlation between the side of the fault you live on and whether you are old or new Dover, it is not that simple. Denomination weighs in heavily, too. Evangelicals and fundamentalists are far more likely to be on one side; more moderate, less vocal believers (as well as agnostics and atheists) are more likely to be on the other. But even that's too simple.

What determines which tectonic plate you're riding depends, more than anything else, on what you believe God is like: Does He prefer Americans? Christians? Republicans? Does He send those who disobey His Word to Hell? Does He hate the ACLU, or does He love it? Is He the kind of God who checks the "no specific preferences" box?

Finally, it depends on whether you are fundamentally certain that God exists, He has a plan, and that's the end of the story, or you're willing to entertain a range of other possibilities. In this regard, Dover's story reflects the tensions growing in the nation as a whole, and it foreshadows the bigger battles to come.

Barrie Callahan is new Dover. She is an attractive, compact, and energetic woman in her mid-fifties. She reminds me a little of Sally Struthers, the actress who played Gloria in the 1970s sitcom *All in the Family*. Her wild, curly blond hair seems out of place in this conservative town. In fact, she is an outsider, having grown up in a suburb of Philadelphia, one hundred miles to the east. Culturally and politically, that one hundred miles might as well be a thousand. As political analyst James Carville quips, Pennsylvania has Philly on the east, Pittsburgh on the west, and Alabama in between.

Barrie's husband, Fred, is also considered an outsider, though he grew up in nearby West York—just six miles to the east, and still in "Alabama"—where he has spent his adult life running a successful paper products business started by his father. Barrie and Fred have lived in the hills of Dover for thirty years, but like other relative newcomers they still wouldn't feel welcome at the suppers at the Dover Fire Hall, where the old Dover families gather weekly. Some of those old families have been in the area "since before America was America," says Joel Lieb, a local teacher who traces his own Dover ancestors back to the 1600s. "Their graves are right here in the cemetery," says Lieb, "I couldn't forget them if I wanted to."

Despite her outsider status, Barrie Callahan was elected to the Dover Area School Board in 1993, after being a stay-at-home mom throughout her older daughter's childhood. She'd majored in psychology at Ursinus College, a small, exclusive liberal arts college near Philadelphia, and she wanted to put her education, energy, and brains to use helping to raise the community's education standard.

It was sometime in the late 1990s, she says, that she first began to notice religious rhetoric creeping onto the stage of school board meetings. "I tried to ignore it," she says. "I just thought it was eccentric. I didn't think it would get out of hand."

The twice-monthly board meetings, held in the cafeteria at the elementary school, were generally modest affairs with the nine board members joined by a reporter or two from the local papers and sometimes a couple of parents with a gripe or an axe to grind. But as the months went on, says Callahan, those meetings grew stranger, more divisive, and more intense.

At first, the zealous chief agent of this new direction was Alan Bonsell, the owner of a car radiator repair shop in town. Bonsell is a large man with a robust goatee and mustache, and short reddish hair that exaggerates the size of his forehead, giving him a playful, bear cub look. He'd been elected to the board in 2001 on a slate with three other conservative candidates who were all campaigning against the school board's plan to overhaul the aging high school building. Though he was new to the board, Bonsell was old Dover through and through.

Shortly after taking office, Bonsell began voicing his concerns about the state of morality among Dover students. He said that he wanted to "bring prayer and faith back into the schools." He frequently mentioned the Bible and creationism. He had a cocksure attitude, and his religious opinions were often colored by a passionate patriotism.

Bonsell's feelings were shared by another vocal board member, Bill Buckingham. Buckingham, also an old-time Dover resident and super-Christian, echoed and sometimes amplified Bonsell's concerns. He also spoke out about America's primacy, its exceptional role in world history and its favored status in the mind of God, the threats posed by secular liberalism, and the arrogance of science—particularly evolutionary biology. Soon many in the old Dover community began to line up behind Bonsell and Buckingham, particularly members of their conservative evangelical churches, Church of the Open Door and Harmony Grove Church.

At first, Callahan says, "I refused to recognize it. I had friends who said they thought it was a religious takeover of the board of education. That whole idea in this day and age seemed just too preposterous to me. But they were right. I didn't keep track," she says, "and I didn't write things down, but the frequency of religious remarks just kept climbing."

She recalled a number of events that at the time seemed isolated and merely quirky, but now, in hindsight, clearly indicated the controversy to come. For instance, at the board's annual retreat in 2002, shortly after he joined the board, Bonsell said his highest priority was "creationism" and his second highest "school prayer." He spoke frankly about wanting to put the historic role of faith in the founding of America back into the curriculum.

At subsequent retreats and meetings, Bonsell had a clear and simple message: America is God's country, those legal American citizens who accept Jesus into their hearts are God's people, and the students of Dover should be taught as much. "It wasn't just Bible talk," says Callahan. "It was the Bible *and* the founding fathers." Dissenters who felt uncomfortable with the message were considered both atheists and unpatriotic.

At one school board meeting someone suggested that if the Christian creation story were told in science class, so should be those of other religions. Another community member was heard commenting after the meeting, "There is only one religion: Christianity. The rest are atheism."

"They were so absolutely sure they were right, beyond question," says Callahan, shaking her head of curls in disbelief.

And then came the burning of Zach Strausbaugh's mural.

A few years earlier, in 1998, Strausbaugh, a high school senior, spent an entire semester painting a four-foot-high, sixteen-foot-long depiction of the evolution of prehuman hominids into more-modern types, the kind of "ape evolving into upright human" that often illustrated old-fashioned science texts. Strausbaugh's mural was part of his senior-year project, and he worked on it under the sanction of two teachers, one representing the art department and the other the science department.

"For a whole semester I worked on it in my art class, at lunch, and before school. I put a lot of time into it," said Strausbaugh, who went on to graduate from the local Penn State campus and to become a designer at a local sheet-metal shop. The mural, which was painted directly on two eight-foot pieces of plywood, wasn't a work of high art, but it was very good for a high school project. It showed nine nearly life-size bipedal figures running across the savanna, from left to right on the mural, representing different stages of early hominid evolution. The figure furthest to the left is hairy and long-armed and the one at the right relatively clean-cut and more upright. It's a take-off on the classic evolutionary progression image, but in this case it's showing only *micro*-evolution—no evolution from one species or kind of animal into another is going on here—no monkey-to-man imagery. Any one of the figures could easily be a brother of its neighbor, but the overall effect of nine generations is significant enough that there is no way the first and ninth figures could be siblings. The evolutionary principle illustrated by the painting is that over time, nearly imperceptible changes add up to notable and significant ones.

At the end of the year, Strausbaugh finished his painting and gave it to the school's science department. No one complained at all. In fact, he got an A for the project and a lot of attention and appreciation from both the art teacher he'd worked with and the science teacher who inherited the mural and mounted it in his biology lab. For five years, the painting hung in the science classroom, a fixture of the school.

Then, on a Monday in August 2003, Bertha Spahr came to school and found that Strausbaugh's painting had disappeared. Spahr, a veteran science teacher at Dover High and the director of the school's science department, called the assistant principal and asked what had happened. He told her that Larry Reeser, who was then head of the Dover High building and grounds department, had come in over the weekend and removed the mural from the classroom. The sixty-eight-year-old Reeser later told *York Daily Record* reporter Lauri Lebo that the painting offended his faith, was obscene, and was full of lies. Furthermore, he said, his granddaughter was entering ninth grade the following year and he didn't want her to be exposed to its "graphic nature." The nakedness. The animality. So he burned it.

Spahr was alarmed and outraged. She called the district superintendent, Richard Nilsen, who told her that Reeser had burned the painting for religious reasons and assured her that he'd been reprimanded and disciplined and a memo had been added to his personnel file. Apparently, though, rumors of Reeser's reprimand were greatly exaggerated. In fact, not only had the board not punished Reeser for burning Strausbaugh's mural, one board member later told Spahr that he was there for the purge and that he "gleefully watched it burn."

When I called Reeser and asked him what had really happened, he told me that he'd been sworn to secrecy, that he could not tell me who had put him up to the affair. He said he was at work on his own book about it and I should leave him alone. Then he hung up.

"I was amazed that someone would do something like that, so blatantly and so disrespectful. I thought it was ignorant and very inappropriate," says Strausbaugh today.

To many in the Dover community, the self-righteous cremation of "objectionable" artwork was a sign, recognizable from other ominous moments in history, that something was going terribly wrong in the power structure of the Dover schools.

The strange thing is, the mural wasn't scientifically controversial. Many old-time creationists, and most intelligent designers of any scientific sophistication, accept the basic evolutionary principle illustrated in Strausbaugh's painting. There really is no choice, if you want to retain a modicum of scientific credibility. Evidence of this kind of micro-evolutionary change is everywhere. Viruses do it virtually before our eyes; and variation among dog breeds, say, or subspecies of frogs, is uncontroversial. Where IDers draw the line, however, is at Darwin's original inference, that those small changes within a species will eventually add up to the creation of altogether new forms and the evolution of new species. Creationists from William Jennings Bryan on up have derisively called this process of incremental change "monkey to man" evolution.

But Strausbaugh's painting doesn't make that inference. If it had shown finches whose beaks changed size over time, for example, Reeser likely wouldn't have paid it much attention, and it wouldn't have been controversial. Most intelligent design proponents readily acknowledge those small changes in the famous Galápagos finches, which played a key role in the development of Darwin's theory of natural selection.[1] In fact, if beak changes were illustrated in proportion to the changes in the hominids in the mural, it would probably take an ornithologist with calipers to detect them, they would be so subtle; much more subtle, for instance, than the difference between the species of Darwin's famous finches. From this perspective, the mural should have been acceptable even to IDers. To the degree that it expressed an evolutionary concept at all, it promoted the least controversial one around.

The reason the mural rubbed some people the wrong way probably has less to do with their intellectual and heartfelt objections to the idea of small evolutionary changes occurring over time, though, than to the fact that the running proto-men were buck naked. If they'd been wearing Scout uniforms, or even just fig leaves, they might have been fine. What is so threatening, so offensive, is the idea that humans are right in there with the rest of the animal kingdom. Beasts. Monkeys. Naked apes. There is no idea more objectionable to certain religious viewpoints than the one that humans are merely animals and subject to the same natural forces as the birds and the bees.

For many, including the old Doverians on the new Dover school board, this is the crux of the battle. Are we special? Are we each a product of a thought of God, and each a part of His plan? Are our lives intrinsically meaningful? Do we possess God-given free will, or is our sense of freedom just another biological adaptation, an illusion of independence from the causal, mechanistic world that defines the materialist's reality? Are we God's creatures, different from the rest of the biological world, or are we simply smarter animals, hunting, grunting, and inventing gods for no purpose but merely to survive and reproduce?

What I found most amazing about the mural story when I first heard it is how little was the splash it made. A few people complained, others shook their heads, but most did nothing.

"If a big deal had been made about the burning of that mural, if the board had looked further into it, made it public, and taken some responsibility, maybe things would have stopped there," says Callahan. But they didn't.

A few months later, in the 2003 election, Callahan was voted off of the board, which then became dominated by a more conservative and more evangelical old-Dover majority. Callahan was ambivalent about giving up her seat. She hadn't campaigned at all, she says. If the people of Dover wanted her to represent them, she was willing; yet after an increasingly ugly and stressful decade of service, she was also ready to step down. But leaving the board didn't end her involvement. She was off the board, but she was still a concerned mom.

Callahan's younger daughter, Katie, was still in high school, and she and her classmates were suffering from a paucity of biology textbooks, a problem that had frustrated Callahan for more than a year. So, despite her lack of an official role, she kept attending board meetings "to find out why they weren't ordering the books."

The biology book in question is one of the country's most popular high school textbooks, and Dover had long used earlier editions. Titled *Biology: A Living Science,* its many editions are authored by the well-known Brown University biologist Kenneth Miller and Joseph Levine. *Biology* is generally considered by teachers and school boards around the country to be the gold standard for basic high school biology texts.

By the June 7, 2004, meeting Callahan had sensed that the board's reluctance to buy books was fueled by more than money concerns. She asked Dover old-timer Bill Buckingham, then chairman of the board's curriculum committee, if he would be leading a vote on whether to authorize the new textbooks.

No, he said, they were not ready to vote on the acquisition. Callahan asked why not? If they didn't order the books soon, another school year would begin with no biology texts. Buckingham paused a moment, looked right at Callahan, and told her that he didn't like the textbook because it was "laced with Darwinism." He wasn't going to proceed with the acquisition until he found a way to balance the teaching of Darwinism with the teaching of creationism, he said. "It's inexcusable to teach from a book that says man descended from apes and monkeys," he was quoted as saying in the *York Daily Record* the next day. "We want a book that gives balance to education."

Callahan couldn't believe her ears.

Then a recent graduate of Dover High School, Max Pell, took the floor. He said that any book that taught creationism would probably violate the constitutionally mandated separation of church and state, and that it would be unfair to students of other faiths. Plus, Pell said, it would be inviting a lawsuit because it's unconstitutional to teach creationism in public school.

Callahan watched as Buckingham and Bonsell came down on Pell like a ton of bricks. They accused the young man of having been brainwashed at university, of being Godless, and of being un-American.

The separation of church and state was never intended by the founding fathers, anyway, said Buckingham. The separation, he said, was a myth invented and propounded by atheists.

The rabbit was out of the hat. "This country wasn't founded on Muslim beliefs or evolution," Buckingham said. "This country was founded on Christianity, and our students should be taught as such."

And look, Buckingham continued, he wasn't being exclusive or unreasonable. He didn't want to teach just creationism. There are two, and only two, viable theories that can explain the history of life, he said, and they are creationism and evolution. He wanted to teach both.

"My jaw dropped," said Callahan. "I couldn't believe it. They wanted to teach creationism. That's what this whole textbook delay was about!"

And then things popped into high gear. Reporter Heidi Bernhard-Bubb, working on a story for the *York Dispatch*, called the American Civil Liberties Union in Harrisburg to get their take on the constitutionality of the board's proposal. The lawyer who took the call, Paula Knudsen, immediately contacted Pennsylvania's ACLU legal director. "I knew it was a constitutional case," she said. "If what the reporter told me was right, it was a clear violation of the First Amendment."

The ACLU got many other calls about the board's decision. One of the first was from Callahan. Another was from long-time high school math teacher Steve Stough. School board members Casey and Jeff Brown called the ACLU, too, and so did parent Cyndi Sneath. She directed the ACLU to her neighbor Tammy Kitzmiller—whose name became attached to the eventual court case-because Kitzmiller's daughter Jessica was going into ninth grade at the high school and would be directly affected by a curriculum change.

The very next day, June 8, 2004, the school board received a notice from the ACLU threatening legal action if they tried to put creationism into their science curriculum. "The case law was pretty clear about this," says Knudsen.

The next school board meeting took place a week later, on June 14. It drew a hundred people from the community, an unheard of number for Dover. Whatever denial or avoidance had kept the religious debate simmering below ground gave way, and the battle over whether to teach creationism alongside of evolution erupted into the open.

Buckingham was quoted in the two daily York newspapers as saying that his generation had prayed and read from the Bible during school, and that ever since, liberals in "black robes" had been taking away such rights of Christians. "Two thousand years ago, someone died on a cross," Buckingham said. "Can't someone take a stand for Him?"

Soon after this meeting, Buckingham upped the ante by announcing that he wanted the board to consider purchasing another textbook: *Of*

Pandas and People: The Central Question of Biological Origins. This was an intelligent design textbook that had been recommended to him by Richard Thompson, president of the Thomas More Law Center. Thompson, a former prosecutor from Michigan, whose Center was funded by Tom Monaghan, the ultra-conservative and religious founder of Domino's Pizza, had also offered to represent the school board free of charge in any legal battles that might come from the teaching of *Pandas.*

At the board's next meeting, and after further consultation with Thompson, Buckingham suddenly shifted gears. For one thing, he stopped—or at least tried to stop—using the word *creationism,* substituting the words *intelligent design.* Second, he abandoned the idea of using *Of Pandas and People* as the main biology text, and argued instead for buying copies of *Pandas* as a "curricular supplement." In fact, he refused to authorize the purchase of *Biology* unless the board also bought *Pandas.*

But Buckingham was losing traction with the board as the book came to a vote. Jane Cleaver, one of his supporters on the nine-member board, was home sick that night, and without her, the vote on authorizing *Biology* split 4 to 4. Now it was up to Angie Yingling, another Buckingham ally. But her support was wearing thin and, worried that the school would have to start another year without any textbooks, she switched her vote. Finally, *Biology* was approved, with no money set aside for *Pandas.*

Buckingham was furious with Yingling. He approached her after the meeting and asked, "Have you any idea what you've just done?"

But Yingling hadn't killed *Pandas'* chances after all. Within weeks of that vote, the Dover School District mysteriously received a donation of sixty copies of the book. Buckingham and his allies on the board set about figuring out how to weave them, and ID, into the curriculum.

They presented their solution at the early-October 2004 meeting: put the copies of *Pandas* into the classroom and have them available for reference, and prepare the teachers to answer questions about ID as they arose. Dover's science teachers weren't happy. But hoping to see the end of the controversy and to finally get their textbooks, they reluctantly accepted this "compromise," says Spahr.

On October 18, 2004, the board approved, in a 6-to-3 vote, a resolution that amended the school district's science curriculum in the first officially mandated mention of intelligent design in U.S. public schools. The amendment says: "Students will be made aware of gaps/problems in Darwin's theory and of other theories of evolution including, but not limited to, intelligent design. Note: *Origins of Life* is not taught."[2]

At the end of that meeting two board members resigned in protest. One of them said that she had been repeatedly asked by other board members if she was "born again," and that she now understood that "holding a certain religious belief is of paramount importance" to the zealous majority on the board.

On November 19, the board announced through a press release that it would require teachers to read to all incoming biology students a four-paragraph statement disparaging evolution and pointing students toward ID. They did so against the advice of the science teachers, led by Spahr; of their own lawyer (who knew that the ACLU would likely take legal action); and of the Seattle-based Discovery Institute, the preeminent ID-promoting think tank. Discovery recommended that the board adopt a "teach the controversy" policy about evolution. They wanted to avoid a constitutional battle like this one, they said, at least until ID earned its stripes as an alternative scientific theory. They were determined that ID not be legally branded as creationism, and wary about what might happen here.

Spahr and the other science teachers were furious. They responded with a memo requesting the right to opt out and turn their classes over to administrators for the reading of the statement, their frustration reflected in their emphatic use of all caps: "This request," the memo said, "is based upon our considered opinion that reading the statement violates our responsibilities as professional educators as set forth in the Code of Professional Practice and Conduct for Educators[.] INTELLIGENT DESIGN IS NOT SCIENCE. INTELLIGENT DESIGN IS NOT BIOLOGY. INTELLIGENT DESIGN IS NOT AN ACCEPTED SCIENTIFIC THEORY."

No one in Dover was unaware of the school controversy. By Dover standards, the fall board meetings were enormous. They were also fractious, and raucous. The community had divided into warring camps, the national press was on to the story, and another alienated and hopeless board member, Noel Wenrich, had resigned. He said that Buckingham and his staunchest allies had become unreasonable and ferocious bullies, questioning the patriotism and faith of anyone who didn't agree with them.

Angie Yingling, just trying to do the right thing, became another board casualty. She explains that in October 2004, when the board originally voted to insert ID into the curriculum, she was cajoled into voting in favor of the change by members who said that not to vote yes would mean she was an atheist. She just couldn't stand the pressure, she said. But in December, when it became clear the board was blithely leading the district into a costly legal battle, she found the courage to change her mind and tried to get the rest of the board to do the same.

"We've got our point across to the local, state, and national levels," Yingling said at the time. "It's wrong, I think it's wrong, and you know it's wrong; it's against state and federal law, and you know it."

Finally, in December, as she too resigned, Yingling explained that she had been misled about what the curriculum changes meant. The board's religious agendas "are spiraling out of control," she said. And members of the board were acting like "religious zealots, preaching from the shadows."

As a tactic, however, quitting the board was of dubious value because the remaining board members simply choose replacements to fill vacancies. The resignations, far from making a point, actually encouraged the further concentration of pro-ID power. In late November, the board considered eighteen applicants to fill the vacated spots. Some of those applicants were highly educated and qualified professionals. But in the end, the seats went to four super-Christians whose primary qualifications were their clear support of the board's intelligent design policy. The board had already decided to ignore the advice of its teachers, its own local lawyer—who warned that if the board lost the case it could be responsible for a million dollars or more in legal fees—its dissenting members, and the majority of the school district community. Now, with a fully packed board and with the pro bono support of a big-city super-conservative law firm determined to take the issue to the Supreme Court, nothing could stop them.

"It's like being on the *Titanic*. Everyone seems to see the iceberg, but no one is steering away," Yingling said. How right she was.

By now, I've read the statement adopted by the board a thousand times. I can (and sometimes do) recite it in my sleep. I still find it riveting: as a writer, editor, and lover of English, and as an admirer of Darwin's theories, I find it almost painful to read. At the same time, its 166 words express so much about the history of this conflict:

> The Pennsylvania Academic Standards require students to learn about Darwin's Theory of Evolution and eventually to take a standardized test of which evolution is a part.
>
> Because Darwin's Theory is a theory, it continues to be tested as new evidence is discovered. The Theory is not a fact. Gaps in the Theory exist for which there is no evidence. A theory is defined as a well-tested explanation that unifies a broad range of observations. Intelligent Design is an explanation of the origin of life that differs from Darwin's view. The reference book, *Of Pandas and People,* is available for students who might be interested in gaining an understanding of what Intelligent Design actually involves.
>
> With respect to any theory, students are encouraged to keep an open mind. The school leaves the discussion of the *Origins of Life* to individual students and their families. As a Standards-driven district, class instruction focuses upon preparing students to achieve proficiency on Standards-based assessments.

Deconstructing this short and convoluted statement is largely the job set out for Judge John Jones III, who will preside over the Middle District Court of Pennsylvania destined to try this case. I can't wait to see him get started.

CHAPTER TWO

THE TRAIN TO DOVER

RICHARD THOMPSON: "The big bang theory is a
scientific theory. Is that correct?"
JOHN HAUGHT: "Yes."
THOMPSON: "Does it have religious implications?"
HAUGHT: "Yes. And I believe everything has religious implications."

 take the redeye into New York's JFK airport from my hometown, Oakland, California, arriving before the crack of dawn and making my way downtown to Penn Station, where I sit on Amtrak's Train 659 Keystone, scheduled to roll toward Harrisburg, Pennsylvania. It's 7:10 A.M. Tomorrow morning, in Dover, Pennsylvania, Judge John Jones III will call the court to session for the first day of *Kitzmiller* v. *Dover Area School District,* a trial that promises to be largely about God and whether or not science has anything to say about His existence.

Through the train's window, as we move away from the platform, I see New Yorkers, citizens of the world: Jews, Catholics, WASPS, Sikhs, Muslims, Shintoists, Buddhists, Rastafarians. Some wear their religion on their sleeves, others on their heads or around their necks, and others less overtly. But the great majority of Americans are believers, and most of the men and women crowding the platform—even those not wearing turbans or yarmulkes or crosses, habits, or saffron robes—most likely believe in some kind of God or other.

As the train hurtles across New Jersey I find myself marveling at the incredible variety of American gods. I can count half a dozen quite different ones worshiped by my own closest family members. One of my sisters is a Hindu, the other a Jew. My mother is a spiritualist, my father an evangelical Christian, my wife an agnostic. My eight-year-old son is a pantheist, though my eleven-year-old is a hardening skeptic. My mother-in-law is a Jew, but not a believer, while her husband recently converted from the Catholic to the Episcopal Church. As for me, I was raised a Christian Scientist, practiced Buddhism in my twenties, but now describe myself simply as a very curious journalist . . . and an evolutionist.

The train pulls into the Princeton Junction; Albert Einstein lived in Princeton for the last two decades of his life, and he must have disembarked here when he took the train home from New York. Squinting out the window into the bright morning light, I can imagine him, hair tousled and shoulders hunched, zigzagging his way across the platform, lost in thought, his worn briefcase hanging half open.

Einstein was at the Institute for Advanced Study in the 1950s when my father, Charles William Slack, was a graduate student studying experimental psychology at Princeton University. Dad used to watch "The Great Man," as he still calls him, from some distance when Einstein took his famous strolls to work. "I knew Einstein extremely well," my father says, "though I'm not so sure he knew me at all." Like most Princetonians, my father sought out any chance to rub shoulders with the millennium's greatest thinker.

In 1951, Dad, still a grad student, was invited to Einstein's house for a United Jewish Appeal fundraiser. On the wall of Einstein's den hung a picture of Mohandas Gandhi standing next to the Archbishop of Canterbury. Gandhi was wearing a loincloth and the Archbishop robes of gold. Under the photo, Einstein had handwritten the question, "Which is the Christian?"

Einstein, of course, was a Jew. But his God, it is said, was Baruch Spinoza's God, who, from the point of view of the Pennsylvanian creationists into whose realm I'm heading today, would probably be considered no God at all. Spinoza, the seventeenth-century Dutch Jewish philosopher, built a tightly argued case out of logical axioms and proofs that either there was no God or that *everything* was God. He chose the latter conclusion, unifying God and nature. To gain knowledge of nature, the physical world, was for Spinoza to move a little closer to the divine. But to unravel one of nature's essential mysteries, like the nature of space-time, the way Einstein had, was akin to curling up in God's lap.

In those days, a half century ago, my father probably would have described his own God in terms Einstein and Spinoza would have recognized, though Dad says he was far less "spiritually oriented" than the philosopher or the physicist. Spinoza's God fit well into the mid-century east-coast Ivy League worldview, not only because Spinoza was a martyred Jewish exile, like so many great European scientists who took refuge in America, but also because by 1950 science had come to represent the great moral force of modernity, especially in physics departments such as Princeton's; after all, $E = MC^2$ had saved the world from an evil fate, whereas the Catholic Church, and much of mainstream European Protestantism, had largely capitulated to fascism, or at least failed to rise up effectively against it.

And Spinoza's God was a thinking person's middle path between the no God of Bertrand Russell and the personal Christian God of Alfred North Whitehead; these two philosopher mathematicians also represented intellect, morality, and modernity. Whether Einstein's God was really a God god or not, by all accounts the Great Man talked about Him a lot. Enough, in any case, to lead the Dutch playwright Friedrich Dürrenmatt to say he suspected Einstein of being "a theologian in disguise."

The important thing to know about my father, when he was at Einstein's Princeton in the 1950s, is that above all else he believed in Science— not just that it would lead to a more interesting kind of job than, say, business or engineering, but that there was something nearly divine about it, something that, though it relied on skepticism to operate, inspired hope and even a kind of faith. Hope, that is, for progress, and faith in Truth and its attainability, and in the benefit it would bring to the future of mankind.

Science, which the Ivy League until that time had considered merely one of the liberal arts, was mushrooming in political clout, in economic pull, and in cultural prestige. The mainstream religious forces on Princeton's campus broadly embraced the emerging scientism of the day. It was not until the 1960s that overt antireligious sentiment broke out. But even in the 1950s, when everyone at Princeton was expected to show up at the university chapel on Sunday morning, the feeling was that the world of the future was secular, that religion may be deep and broad, but that the waters once flowing into it were flowing toward science now. So while science would just keep growing in both knowledge and significance, traditional religious belief would shrink over time and, eventually, probably stagnate and finally evaporate altogether.

Those were heady days for science. Especially physics, chemistry, and the new biology. But even experimental psychology, my father's field, although just recently emerging as a serious discipline, was making big promises: to quantify the mind, nail down perception, document the role of the observer (a job that even had a place—since Einstein and Heisenberg—in the new physics), and give people a new control over their own destinies. My father was one of its young stars. He was going to liberate the ultimate victims and perpetrators of urban injustice by giving juvenile delinquents the tools to become model citizens.

My train pulls gently out of the Princeton Junction, heading for Pennsylvania.

My father left Princeton for Harvard the same year Einstein died: 1955. Dad was only twenty-six years old, and had just become the youngest Harvard assistant professor on record. Pretty quickly, he'd fallen in with fellow psychologist and soon-to-be counterculture hero Timothy Leary and

19

his crowd. Dad's God may have been nature and truth up to that point, as Spinoza and Einstein said, but it seemed He also had a more focused expression in Leary's bathroom: in a light bulb burning over the john to be exact. And that drug-invoked deity was visible to any observer on that toilet who had taken LSD, which was not yet illegal and promised to help cure every psychological disorder and hang-up and to illuminate every philosophical conundrum. (Mind-body connection? Perception? Consciousness? Political uptightness? No problem.)

My father had great ambitions and promise, but by the time I was born six years later, in 1961, his fortunes had turned south. For one thing, that whole LSD scene engendered some habits that weren't conducive to career advancement. Two failed marriages, three university positions, and a move to Australia later, Dad hit what in twelve-step jargon is known as "the bottom." My father's bottom came, as he tells it, in the middle of a playing field in the middle of a rainy night in the middle of Melbourne, Australia. It was there that his unhappy life brought him to his knees and he began to pray. Apparently, yet another God was listening. The next day, his AA sponsor told him that twelve-step sobriety was second prize; first prize was—you guessed it—Jesus.

And so it was that in 1980 my Ivy League liberal intellectual dad became not only a tongues-speaking, born-again Christian but also a neo-creationist. At first, he kept his creationism in the closet; it came along with his church, without which he would be dead, he said, so he didn't question it. But although he could readily translate his religious conversion into psychological terms for family and friends—"group contentment reflex" was his theoretical expression for the joyful experience of God—a literal theory about world history was harder to convert. There was no way to mitigate the embarrassment of holding absurd and antiscientific beliefs. Saying "yes" to Jesus was, for my father, less difficult than saying "no" to carbon dating. But then Dad read Phillip Johnson's book *Darwin on Trial,* and his problem was solved, or at least deferred.

The famous Oxford evolutionist Richard Dawkins wrote, "Darwin made it possible to be an intellectually fulfilled atheist."[1] My father countered, "Johnson made it possible again to be a credible, intellectually ful-filled creationist."

Dad sent copies of *Darwin on Trial* to everyone in the family and, after giving us a few days to read them (I didn't actually read the book until years later) he stepped out of the creationist closet.

At the time, I was an editor at *Pacific Discovery,* the science and natu-ral history magazine published by the California Academy of Sciences in San Francisco. In addition to assigning and editing stories by scientists that were largely about evolution, I wrote a column called "Horizons" that covered advances in the natural sciences and tended to focus on evolutionary biol-ogy. When Dad told me that he'd joined a new church and accepted Jesus into his heart as his own personal savior, I was surprised. It was radical, even for my religiously eccentric family. But when he said he no longer believed in evolution, I thought he must be kidding.

Pacific Discovery had its editorial offices tucked behind the archives in the stacks of the California Academy of Sciences' library. The windows over-looked San Francisco's Golden Gate Park, and a pair of red-tailed hawks nested in a Douglas fir nearby. I kept binoculars on my desk and could bird watch between bouts of editing and writing. Whenever I think of those first weird days of defending Darwin's theories to my Dad, and receiving his e-mail diatribes against them, I think of those red tails shooting past my win-dow. They were so clearly, to me, the products of evolutionary adaptations. Their fitness as predators, their precision flight, mating rituals—all this fit seamlessly into the big evolution picture my work strove to fill in the details of. And behind me was a museum full of the fruits of and evidence for evo-lution.

At the time, I really had no idea what was at stake in the debate my Dad and I were having. There was no broader context for me than the familial one. Remember, in 1993 Bill Clinton had just been elected presi-dent. Though the signs were there, many of us had no idea that evangelical

Christianity was going to become the salient political force of the early twenty-first century and that intelligent design was going to be one of its most popular and empowering ideas. Certainly I had no idea that my father's very personal discovery of the Holy Spirit was also part of a major demographic trend.

The train's windowpane reflects my computer, and through that ghostly reflection I see a neat black wagon pulled along a nearby road by a sturdy brown horse. In the wagon ride two young Amish men wearing their telltale brimmed black hats. As a kid, I was fascinated by Amish integrity and self-discipline, the wary eye they cast on the innovations so lustily, faithfully embraced by the rest of America. Their extreme humility. Their dedication to nonviolence. Their innovative practicality.

So many worlds, so many Gods, I think, and the train slows: some so brutal, others so gentle and lovely. Are they all made up? Do we need them anyway? Can we survive another century with them? Could we get by for any time at all without them?

Amtrak Train 659 pulls into the old-fashioned Harrisburg station. I am tired and disembark slowly, reluctant to leave the comfort of the train. But it feels good to be free, on my own feet again, as I carry my bags into this unknown city. Now I must find my hotel, down by the Susquehanna River, on the edge of town. Tomorrow morning begins the trial that brought me here. And I hope to get some sleep tonight.

CHAPTER THREE

THE **THEORY IS**
NOT A FACT

WITOLD WALCZAC: "Does science consider issues of
meaning and purpose in the universe?"
KENNETH MILLER: "If I could solve the question of the meaning of
my life by doing an experiment in the laboratory, I assure you I
would rush off and do it right now. But these questions simply lie
outside the purview of science."

he Ronald Reagan Federal Building and U.S. Courthouse, the
structure that houses the Middle District Court of Pennsylvania, is one of those concrete-and-glass monstrosities
made in the late 1960s that is all power and authority. But it is the dreary
authority of the bureaucrat, not the inspired power of the architect—just
plain old Cold War ugly. The law, however, is not bound to beauty; it is
bound to authority and truth. So this building may be a perfectly apt place
for the law to ask the age-old question at the heart of *Kitzmiller,* Did someone actually design this stuff? And to that I would add, What the hell was
She or He thinking?

The Middle District Court of Pennsylvania has seen other controversial, crowd-drawing cases. One was the huge civil case in which neighbors of
the nearby Three Mile Island Nuclear Generating Station sued for recovery
of health damages they believed stemmed from exposure to radiation

released during the 1979 core meltdown there. Like *Kitzmiller,* the arguments over Three Mile Island relied heavily on scientific evidence, and a study of its limits.

Before that was the 1972 case of the Harrisburg Seven. Anti-Vietnam War activists Philip and Daniel Berrigan, both priests, and five others were accused of conspiring to blow up underground steam tunnels in Washington and of trying to kidnap Henry Kissinger. The jury dropped the major charges, eventually convicting only two defendants, Father Philip Berrigan and Sister Elizabeth McAlister, on the lesser charge of smuggling letters into the federal prison in Lewisburg, Pennsylvania.

As I enter Courtroom 2 on the ninth floor of the courthouse on this first day of *Kitzmiller,* I wonder if the older men working the metal detectors and X-ray machine at the entrance were present at those other trials, making sure no one brought their tape-recorder or camera or gun or flare launcher or andiron into the courtroom. These grave and hefty peace officers might well have been designed by the same architect as the building.

The courtroom is packed with participants. Looking out at the lawyers and plaintiffs and defendants and expert witnesses and the judge's clerk and the bailiffs and the press and the wide array of spectators, I experience a reporter's thrill at being present at the beginning of a Big Story. Soon I will come to recognize all of these people; nearly each one of them will stand for something, will represent a story to me. For now, though, they are just a confusing mass of bodies, some in suits or uniforms, others in sneakers and T-shirts, a woman wearing a muu-muu, a teenager in a bowler.

Wait, I do recognize ID proponent and biochemist Michael Behe, who, in his coke-bottle-thick glasses, tweed jacket, and worn Hush Puppies, is playing the role of the frumpy professor nerd to the nines. Behe is the author of *Darwin's Black Box,* the first purportedly scientific book from a major publisher to promote intelligent design.

And there, milling among some professorial-looking gentlemen, is the double-star system of Nick Matzke and Eugenie Scott, who've traveled the same three thousand miles I have from Oakland, California, where they work for the National Center for Science Education. The NCSE is the only national organization dedicated solely to keeping evolution in public school classrooms and creationism out.

Just then, Judge John Jones III enters from his chambers somewhere to the right of his bench, and the courtroom deputy says, "All rise." Lawyers for the pro-evolution plaintiffs and pro-ID defense stand at attention behind their respective tables, the plaintiffs on the right (from the gallery's point of view) and the defendants on the left. Local journalists stand in front of their seats in the jury box, where they enjoy a privileged view, second only to that of the judge himself. (There is no jury in this case. It is a "bench trial" decided by the judge alone.) The clerk stands behind the table on the left. Out-of-town journalists, like me, stand in the back two rows on the left side of the court, behind the supporters of the defense. Supporters of the plaintiffs have seated themselves on the right side of the gallery. Judge John Jones III takes a seat up on the bench and smiles, looking out over the courtroom; it is suddenly quiet enough to hear a gene drop.

Judge Jones is neither tall nor short. He is a trim and athletic fifty, and has a full head of salt-and-pepper hair. *New Yorker* reporter Margaret Talbot says he looks like a cross between Robert Mitchum and William Holden, and there definitely is something of the conservative 1950s-father-figure about him, which, frankly, makes me a little nervous. Jones is a life-long Republican, an appointee of George W. Bush, and he comes from a wealthy family in Pottsville, Pennsylvania, where his grandfather made a fortune engineering and building a chain of golf courses. The judge ran for Congress a decade ago and was supported in his bid by the conservative Senator Rick Santorum (*Time* magazine called Santorum one of the twenty-five most influential evangelicals in America), who'd recently come out in favor of "teaching all sides of the debate" about evolution.

("Teaching all sides," Eugenie Scott had told me, "is code for supporting the teaching of ID.")

I look hard at Judge John Jones for any overt signs of religious fanaticism: snake bites on his neck, maybe, or the bulge of a wooden crucifix under his robes, preternaturally bushy eyebrows, polyester bellbottoms? I don't know what I'm looking for, really, but I don't find it. He just looks like a well-fed, well-bred, conservative moderate.[1]

In a calm and friendly tone belying the jittery pensiveness in the courtroom, he opens the proceedings by saying, "Good morning to all." It is something Santa Claus would say, and it seems to put everyone at ease.

If Jones is the father figure, the lead counsel for the plaintiffs, Eric Rothschild, is the precocious kid. Rothschild is a compact five-foot-five-inch man with an appealing gap between his top front teeth and an egg-shaped balding head, which he tips forward and rubs when he is nervous. At thirty-eight, Rothschild still looks like a kid; he is a controlled, smart, handsome, and well-behaved child, however, one who plays the role of the grownup lawyer remarkably well.

Rothschild is a partner at Pepper Hamilton, a big Philadelphia-based law firm that is working along with the American Civil Liberties Union (ACLU) and Americans United for the Separation of Church and State (AU) for the plaintiffs in this case. It's a new job for Rothschild. He is far more accustomed to corporate cases (reinsurance is his forte), in which all that's at stake is a ton of money. This trial could have broader-reaching consequences of a much different kind.

"Are you prepared to open?" asks the judge.

"I am," says Rothschild. He approaches the podium calmly, pauses a few moments and then begins.

"Good morning, Your Honor. My co-counsel and I represent eleven parents who are challenging the Dover Area School District's change to its biology curriculum."

From the beginning, the school board was driven by religious concerns, Rothschild says, and though its members attempted to hide their evangelical purposes in the cloak of scientific jargon, intelligent design is nothing more than a modernized version of creation science, which the U.S. Supreme Court ruled unconstitutional nineteen years ago. The Establishment Clause of the First Amendment promises that "Congress shall make no law respecting an establishment of religion." Furthermore, Rothschild says, his team will prove that those who promote intelligent design are trying to supernaturalize the foundations of modern science "so that" he says, "science can be Christian and theistic."

Rothschild says that the book mentioned in the school board's statement, *Of Pandas and People,* is a creationist text that has been re-crafted to evade the constitutional barriers to teaching religion as science in the public schools. His team won't merely establish that ID is at bottom religious, however. They will also prove that the school board knew it and that they were driven by that very fact.

Now he pulls out the visual aids. On a courtroom projection screen, we see newspaper articles, notes from school board meetings, and even a clip from a local TV news broadcast all showing that board members used the word *creationism* in the early stages of their discussion about curriculum changes. This is an important point. The Supreme Court clearly considers creationism to be religion, and the board's open advocacy of it casts a shadow of unconstitutionality over their later decision to adopt intelligent design. At some point, says Rothschild, the school shifted to the language of intelligent design—but they did so on the advice of others, not because they had any special attachment to the theory itself.

In fact, argues Rothschild, "The board added creationism to the biology curriculum under its new name, intelligent design. They did everything you would do," he says, "if you wanted to incorporate a religious topic in science class but cared nothing for the scientific validity of the curriculum introduced."

The plaintiffs' case will have two strangely disproportionate prongs. One will address the immense questions that underlie the crisis in Dover, in this case, and across our nation: What is science? What is religion? What is scientific truth? What is a theory? Where are we from? Is there a continuous chain of life linking us to our ancient microbial ancestors? Can science say anything about the existence of God?

The other prong of the plaintiffs' argument deals with the smaller but legally critical questions: Are the Dover school board members lying when they deny having talked about creationism at their meetings? Did they want to get religion back into their school, or were they promoting ID merely as an alternative scientific theory?

As he winds up, Rothschild explains that at the end of the trial, he will request that the court find the Dover School Board's curriculum change unconstitutional and permanently enjoin the district from implementing it.

"Thank you, Your Honor," says Rothschild, looking Jones in the eye and appearing even to make a slight bow.

"Thank you, Mr. Rothschild," says the judge, who then invites attorney Patrick Gillen to take Rothschild's place and make the opening argument for the defense. If Modigliani had painted barristers, they would have resembled Gillen, whose elongate and slightly asymmetrical face reflects kindness and sensitivity but also a touch of disorientation.

There is nothing intimidating about Gillen. He is gracious and almost meek as he begins to outline the school board's defense. His voice is gentle, and it is sometimes too quiet to make out from the back of the gallery where I sit. I listen extra intently to his argument.

The school board members, Gillen says, were dedicated to the scientific curriculum, not to promoting their own religious views. Individually, some of them might be interested in creationism and might hold religious views, but those are distinct from their interest in seeing intelligent design taught as a scientifically valid alternative approach to biology. Presenting ID to students, as well as teaching evolution, encourages critical thinking, he argues.

"The board quite rightly concluded that its modest curriculum change would, in fact, enhance the biology curriculum and that the primary effect of their policy would be to advance science education, not religion," he says.

"Intelligent design theory is not creationism," continues Gillen. "It does not even require the action of a supernatural creator. . . . it is not religion or inherently religious. It's a theoretical argument advanced in terms of empirical evidence and technical knowledge proper to scientific and academic specialties."

Over the course of the trial, Gillen explains, the defense team will prove that ID is good science, even if it is still a minority view. Plenty of credentialed and respected scientists recognize the strong evidence for ID.

"Intelligent design theory is really science in its purest form," he says, "the refusal to foreclose possible explanations based on the claims of the dominant theory or the conventions of the day." It "proceed(s) from the same sort of perspective that led Newton to explore and ultimately explicate gravity. It shares the attitude of those who worked in the field of quantum mechanics, who posited the wave-particle duality, despite the fact that to some it smacked of the supernatural. It shares the determination of scientists who this very day will look at paranormal phenomena or phenomena that defy our current understanding, such as the mind."

Furthermore, says Gillen, there is a bona fide controversy over the validity of evolutionary theory, and exposing students to that controversy won't harm them. On the contrary, witnesses for the defense will show that introducing students to the arguments will only heighten their interest in biology and their critical skills.

"This case is about free inquiry and education, not about a religious agenda," Gillen says. "Your Honor, we look forward to presenting a defense in this case. Thank you." And he takes a seat.

Before getting started, the judge takes a moment to establish the golden rule for courtroom decorum. We will all be in close quarters for many weeks, and he asks all in attendance to avoid going in and out of the courtroom except when necessary and to "respect the witnesses on both sides as they testify and avoid any expressions that would disrupt the court in any way." Then he invites the plaintiffs to present their first witness.

Attorney Witold "Vic" Walczak approaches the podium. Walczak is the legal director of the Pennsylvania ACLU. And even though his neckties are the proper width, his suits fit well, and his shirts are just as bright and his shoes just as shiny as Rothschild's, his corporate counterpart, you can tell that he is no big-firm law partner. He's only forty-four, and very fit, but he doesn't have that freshly scrubbed glow of affluence. The tousled brown hair, bags under the eyes—he has the look of someone who's seen more than his share of suffering. All of this together spells "public interest."

Walczac begins the plaintiffs' case with biologist Kenneth Miller, the evolution team's star scientific witness. Miller, a Brown University professor of biology, is a celebrated biologist and a seasoned combatant in the creationism-evolution wars. It is Miller's textbook, *Biology*, which originally snagged board member Bill Buckingham's ire because it was "laced with Darwinism." And he is also a devout Catholic: "I believe that God is the author of all things seen and unseen," Miller tells the court, preempting any effort to portray the conflict as one between godless science and Divine Truth. Ironically, while the IDers and the board members will try during this trial to avoid any focus on their religious beliefs, because such attention only strengthens the plaintiffs' argument that religion, not science, is driving ID, proponents of evolution can talk about their belief in God all they want.

The fifty-seven-year-old Miller has a square, bearded jaw, thinning brown hair parted on the side, and blue eyes. He looks quintessentially New England Ivy League in his brass-buttoned blue blazer. He is a know-it-all, and occasionally swerves for moments at a time over the double-yellow line dividing charming and irritating. He is prone to saying "Yes, sir," and "No, sir," or "I don't know, sir," in a way that reminds me of the thinly veiled sanctimony of a boarding school student under interrogation by a gym teacher. (Is a microbiologist a scientist? he is asked later, during cross-examination. "Yes sir. Yes sir, a microbiologist *is* a scientist," Miller says.)

At times, Miller seems to be running the courtroom; he has the defense lawyers themselves on the defensive. For example, when Robert Muise, one of the three defense attorneys, tries to coax Miller into saying that proteins are essentially "machines" (because machines are designed and design is intentional and thus evidence of intelligence), Miller gets quite specific: "Proteins are compounds that are built out of polypeptides. And there are small and simple proteins like insulin, for example, that [have] only sixty or seventy amino acids, which is really . . . one coherent part. There are other more complex proteins. For example, the C^3 component . . ." and on and on. After his exceedingly thorough and arcane reply he adds, "Is that a complete answer to your question, sir?" Muise, in way over his head, can do nothing but swim back to shore by dropping the question and moving on.

Despite his occasional forays into superciliousness, however, Miller remains likable. No one seems to question his integrity, and his affection for biology and evolution are infectious.

As one of the most celebrated and visible opponents of intelligent design, and other more traditional forms of creationism, he says he spent so much time explaining how he could juggle belief in both evolution and Christianity that he wrote a book on the subject. "That way, I can just tell people, 'Read the book.'"

Finding Darwin's God: A Scientist's Search for Common Ground Between God and Evolution, is Miller's effort to explain what's so great and powerful about evolution from a scientific point of view, but also how the theory can be appreciated in the context of "the great Abrahamic faiths." *The New York Review of Books* called it a "startling disjunction of sensibility . . . a Jekyll-Hyde metamorphosis," suggesting that there was nothing rational or even sane about trying to force a wedding between Christianity and evolution. All the same, Miller says, he got lots of positive feedback from people who said the book helped them reconcile their religious faith and their regard for science. When geneticist Francis Collins mentioned Miller's book in an interview on National Public Radio a couple of years ago, it bounced up to between the twentieth and thirtieth best-selling books on Amazon. "It was only there for a couple of hours, but it was pretty exciting nonetheless," Miller says.

Today, though, his job is not to explain why evolution and religion are such compatible partners. He's here to embody that compatibility while explaining what evolution is, what science is, why science and evolution work so well, why there is so much agreement among scientists that they do work, and why there is no need for, indeed no room for, intelligent design in the public high school science classroom.

First, Miller must lay the foundation for the court's understanding of evolutionary biology. Every foundation must be built on something else, however, and the rock underlying evolution is science itself. So Walczak begins with the bedrock question of this case: "What is science?"

"You ask a good question," answers Miller dryly.

Science, he says, is the systematic attempt to "provide natural explanations for natural phenomena." There are certain immutable rules that limit the way scientists can work, as long as they claim to be doing science. Namely, explanations must be limited to things that can be observed, tested, and verified. "Everything in science is open to critical examination, replication, peer review, and discussion by other scientists. I could never publish a result saying I had made an observation on a particular protein," Miller says, "without also telling people what my methods were and how I made that observation."

And this is not *my* definition of science, says Miller. It is *the* definition. "I think science might be the closest thing we have on this planet to a universal culture, and these rules apply everywhere."

Next, Walczak asks five questions that provide a kind of framework for the whole portion of the trial that examines ID's scientific status, and compares it to that of evolutionary biology.

1. Is evolution a testable theory that is accepted by the scientific community? Walczak begins. Yes, replies Miller, evolution is an "eminently testable" theory that is "broadly embraced by the scientific community."

2. Is intelligent design a testable theory that is accepted by the scientific community? asks Walczak. No, says Miller, ID is not a testable theory in any sense, and so is not accepted by the scientific community.

3. Is intelligent design properly considered a scientific theory? asks Walczak. No, intelligent design is not science, and therefore it cannot be construed as a scientific theory, says Miller.

4. Is intelligent design a particular religious view? asks Walczak. Yes, sir, says Miller. Intelligent design is an inherently religious form of creationism known as "special creationism."

5. Does the statement read by the Dover School District promote students' understanding of evolution and science? asks Walczak, finally. No, says Miller, the statement falsely undermines the scientific status of the theory of evolution, and therefore it certainly does not promote student understanding or even critical thinking. It does a great disservice to science education in Dover and to the students of Dover.

The animated and thorough professor spends the rest of the day and half of the next explaining why he holds these truths to be self-evident. For those of us lucky enough to be there, it is a crash course in evolution, "the biology course you wish you could have taken," wrote the *New Yorker*'s Margaret Talbot later.

❦

Evolution has three core, defining elements, explains Professor Miller: life-forms change over time; they all descended from one or a few common ancestors; and natural selection produces these effects.

It's clear that life has changed in the 3.5 billion years or so since it first appeared on earth. This observation is vividly and broadly reflected in the fossil record: rocks of different vintage contain fossils of different kinds of plants and animals. The oldest fossils contain simple layered mounds of microbial slime known as stromatolites and not much else. For more than a billion years, these single-celled creatures dominated the water-covered earth. Then, about two billion years ago, multicelled creatures appeared. The fossils we've got of them are called "carbon films." They won't sell any *National Geographic* calendars; at best, they look like tiny ribbon- or leaf-shaped stains, but they are quite different from stromatolites, which is the point. About a billion years ago, the first fossils of what we generally consider to be animals appeared, and those are quite distinctive blobs and worm-shaped little guys.

Another half-a-billion years later, during the Cambrian Period, 543 to 490 million years ago, biologists say that evolutionary change was thrown into super-high gear. After two billion years of relative idle, crab-like creatures evolved, and trilobites and sponges, too. There were some jawless vertebrate fish, though they still looked more like worms than trout. How and why there was so much change during the Cambrian is still a hot topic among evolutionary biologists. Most of them love the "Cambrian Explosion," as they call this orgy of creativity; it represents evolution at its most generative, though it irks biologists, too, posing persistent puzzles about just why the pace of change has been so irregular through time.

In the half-billion years since the Cambrian there is super-abundant fossil evidence of those first well-established forms slowly, and sometimes not so slowly, being replaced by more modern ones. The great majority of types seen in the fossil record vanish at some point, while others survive and are replaced by a long chain of subtly different and more modern forms. You can still find stromatolites, much like the originals of three billion years ago, living off the coast of Australia.

The first primitive plants show up in the fossil record in the Ordovician Period, about 490 to 443 million years ago. And around 350 million years ago there were lots of types of land plants that would be pretty recognizable to us today, including creeping plants and forests.

About 200 million years ago, we start to see the emergence of dinosaurs, but most of these go abruptly missing in the Cretaceous period, only 150 million years later, and are replaced by a wide variety of smaller animals, including little mammals. The rest, as they say, is prehistory.

If you dip into the prehistoric world at any particular point, you find a different set of living things. That is the first core principle of evolution, Miller recaps: life changes.

The story of life is a great one, possibly *the* great story. But not the way I've told it here so far. What makes it much more compelling is the second core principle of evolution, which is known as common descent. A common ancestry unites all living things, Miller explains, so not only has life changed over time, but species transform gradually from one kind of creature into another. Probably the most poetic expression of this second principle is found in the conclusion of Charles Darwin's *On the Origin of Species:* "There is grandeur in this view of life," he wrote, "with its several powers, having been originally breathed into a few forms or into one; and that, whilst this planet has gone cycling on according to the fixed law of gravity, from so simple a beginning endless forms most beautiful and most wonderful have been, and are being, evolved."[2]

So evolution holds that (1) life forms change over time, and (2) they also all descended from one or a few common ancestors. Finally, Miller says, "evolution" also refers to Darwin's explanation of *how* life changed from "one or a few forms" to the "endless forms most beautiful and most wonderful" that we see today. Others had noted change over time, and a few had already even proposed common descent. But "What Darwin did for the first time," says a wide-eyed Miller, leaning now toward Walczak, "was to propose a plausible, workable, and ultimately *testable* mechanism for the processes that drove that change, and that is the mechanism of natural selection."

"And what," asks Walczak, "is natural selection?"

It had been common knowledge for centuries if not millennia that animal breeders and horticulturalists could influence the characteristics of, say, a kind of dog or flowering plant by repeatedly selecting and breeding individuals with desired traits. If you wanted to make a small dog, you'd pull out the smallest ones from a population and breed them, then pull out the smallest of their offspring and breed them with other small dogs, and so on. Whatever it was that made them small somehow persisted and even appeared to concentrate in subsequent generations. Darwin didn't know about genes, so he couldn't have known through what medium traits were passed along, but it was clear to him that traits somehow were preserved from one generation to the next.

Darwin's insight was that the same selection process happens in nature, but without a breeder, says Miller. Darwin recognized that far more offspring are born than can possibly survive. If all offspring survived and reproduced, the planet would quickly be overrun by the exponential growth of elephant populations alone. In the competitive struggle for existence, and given the random introduction of novel traits (we now know this comes in the form of genetic mutations), those individuals with traits most likely to convey survival and reproductive advantages would also be most likely to have offspring who would be more likely than others in the general population to pass along and amplify those same traits.

Survival, reproductive success, and the harsh challenges of an ever-changing world stand in for an intentional breeder, selecting and amplifying traits that give individuals even a tiny advantage. "Over time," Miller says, "the average characteristics of a population could change in one direction or another. And they could change quite dramatically."

Miller sits back in his chair. "And that is the essential idea of natural selection."

As one species changes in response to such pressures, new selection pressures will be placed on those species that relate to it, directly as predators or prey, say, or indirectly as habitat. Those that adapt well survive, those that don't, perish, creating swirling feedback loops of selective pressures within ecosystems. Those pressures keep plants and animals continually changing, competing, innovating, and adapting to new conditions: evolving.

So, again, *evolution* refers to the idea that (1) species change through time, (2) they are all descended from one or more common ancestors, and (3) natural selection produces that effect, Miller tells the court. There would seem to be nothing more to say on the subject, but these three core principles of evolution get progressively more controversial among the theory's opponents.

Intelligent design proponents almost unanimously reject the creative powers of what Miller is calling the third core principle of evolution, natural selection, but they don't necessarily reject the first two. Among the real scientists who are also proponents of ID, virtually all believe that life has changed and continues to change over time, but a few also acknowledge descent from common ancestry. Yes, they say, we descended along various lineages that could be traced back to the first forms. But no, they go on, natural selection just isn't up to the job of explaining how that change is driven.

This point is usually lost in accounts of this debate that caricature IDers. But the truth is, it is possible, even fairly common, to be an ID advocate and still believe in the first one or two parts of Miller's account of evolution. In fact, it would be a good litmus test for separating the serious ID scientists from the mere ideologues. That plants and animals change over time is clearly reflected in the fossil record and in observations of modern, quickly adapting organisms such as viruses. You'd have to have your head in the sand to deny this (and clearly, many creationists do). The evidence for common ancestry is also abundant. The arguments against it are hollow old ones closely associated with traditional creationism. Again, the fossil record speaks articulately on this point, as do the studies of systematic biology and modern genetics. Whether or not natural selection is powerful enough to drive the changes in life over the past 3.5 billion years is a much more interesting and substantial question, and it will, I suspect, be the focus of the ID attack on evolution as this case unfolds.

As Miller talks, I recognize my own bias here, pointed out by Phillip Johnson many years ago: even if natural selection proves insufficient to explain what drives evolutionary change, I would confidently assume that some other naturalistic explanation would one day come along to fill in the gap. Intelligent design advocates have a very different reflex. To them, the falsification of natural selection would leave a gap that only an intelligent designer could fill.

Over the years, ID-proponent and biochemist Michael Behe, who will testify later in this trial, has waffled on common descent. Sometimes he's acknowledged the evidence for it, says there is nothing in principle wrong with it, sometimes he seems to disapprove, and sometimes he just refuses to offer an opinion. Generally, though, like most of his ID colleagues, he avoids the subject, says it's not the point. Natural selection is the real target.

For natural selection to deserve the generative powers Darwin attributed to it, any biological structure—say, the eye—must have an unbroken chain, over time, of small adaptations leading up to that structure. Each and every one of those adaptations must convey some advantage to the individuals that inherit them. For natural selection to work, there cannot be a single link missing in that chain.

Darwin was excruciatingly aware of this. "Natural selection acts only by taking advantage of slight successive variations," he wrote. "She can never take a great leap, but must advance by short and sure though slow steps.

"If it could be demonstrated that any complex organ existed which could not possibly have been formed by numerous successive slight modifications, my theory would absolutely break down," Darwin wrote, posing a long-standing challenge to his opponents.[3]

The crux of the ID critique of evolution, and of natural selection in particular, is that there are things in the biological world that are complex in a way that would have required "great leaps" to explain. Walczak knows very well which examples the defenders of ID will rely on, and he wants Miller to set them up, before the other side gets a chance to, and then knock them down.

Which brings us to the ID movement's poster child: the bacterial flagellum. It is a spinning whip-like filament that projects through the membrane of certain bacteria and works like an outboard motor, moving the little guys from here to there. One of Behe's central arguments in *Darwin's Black Box* is that there is no unbroken chain of positive adaptations that could possibly explain the evolution of the flagellum. It is, Behe claims, exactly the kind of "complex organ" Darwin said would test—and, if it could not be explained in terms of small adaptive steps would disprove—his theory.

Miller agrees with Behe—and with Darwin. If it can be proven that the flagellum, or any other cellular component, could not have evolved by the continuous addition of positive or neutral adaptations, that would disprove natural selection.

Behe uses the analogy of a mousetrap: you can tell that a mousetrap didn't evolve by natural selection; if you remove even one of its main components, it wouldn't function as a mousetrap at all. All of its parts must be in place for it to convey any adaptive mouse-trapping advantage.

Miller vehemently disagrees about both the mousetrap and the flagellum. (This morning he arrived at court wearing a tie clip made out of a disassembled mousetrap, presumably to show that something could be selectable for one function and then end up being employed for an altogether different selectable advantage-conveying trait.)

Miller presents to the court what he argues is the likely step-by-step evolutionary pathway for the flagellum: before there were flagella, he says, some bacteria possessed a kind of syringe used to inject poison into neighboring cells. Known as the Type III Secretory System (TTSS), the syringe mechanism uses many of the same components as the flagellum to accomplish entirely different objectives. In essence, the syringe became the pump that powers the motor that drives the flagellum.

In his cross-examination, Pat Gillen just isn't up to the task of debating cellular biology with Miller. Unfortunately for the debate, he can only do his best to cast vague doubts and leave it at that.

Finally, we come to an important question of semantics: What is a theory? Is a theory always open to debate? Is the theory of evolution, as the statement read to the Dover High School students by school administrators claims, "not a fact"? Is it less than a fact? More?

As it turns out, the common understanding of the word *theory* and its scientific usage are two different animals. The school board's assertion that "The theory [of evolution] is not a fact," says Miller, while literally true, exploits a misunderstanding of the meaning of the word *theory* as it is used in science. And it is, he says, a misrepresentation that has long been exploited by creationists trying to cast doubts about evolution.

In conversation, people often say "theory" to refer to a hypothesis or "best guess," as in, "I have a theory about why so few ID advocates are actually biologists."

But its scientific meaning is quite different, Miller explains. A scientific theory is a "broad, useful, powerful generalization that explains and unites a broad range of facts," he says. So, in its scientific sense, a theory is a *higher* order of truth than a fact, not a lower one, as the Dover statement suggests. In its colloquial use, saying that something is just a theory is an insult. In its scientific use, calling something a theory is a high compliment.

Creationists have historically exploited this confusion of terms, taking scientists' use of the expression "evolutionary theory" to be an admission of uncertainty about the idea. There are a lot of evolutionary facts, but it is *evolutionary theory* that makes their relationship to each other and to the rest of the world coherent.

Intelligent design, however, is *not* a scientific theory, says Miller, because it doesn't make sense of any broad range of natural facts. Furthermore, to be useful, a bona fide scientific theory has to make testable predictions that lead to testable hypotheses so that people can go into the laboratory, can make those tests, and can confirm or refute the theory.

Evolution is a powerful, useful, and predictive explanation of a whole range of scientific facts, says Miller, so "'evolution is a theory' is true in the same way that the atomic theory of matter is just a theory, the Copernican Theory of the Solar System is just a theory, or the germ theory of disease is just a theory."

Evolution makes predictions, Miller says, and 150 years of research and data collection has borne those predictions out. The theory of evolution provides the foundation of modern genetics, biochemistry, neurobiology, physiology, and ecology. A century and a half of fossil collection, biosystematics (the study of organisms past and present and their evolutionary relationships), and biogeography (the study of the distribution of organisms around the globe) have all bolstered Darwin's claims by revealing ever more, and ever more powerful, evidence of common ancestry and the creative power of natural selection.

"Evolutionary theory helps to explain the emergence of new infectious diseases," says Miller, quoting from the National Academy of Sciences statement on evolution, "the development of antibiotic resistance in bacteria, the agricultural relationships among wild and domestic plants and animals, the composition of the earth's atmosphere, the molecular machinery of the cell, the similarities between human beings and other primates, and countless other features of the biological and physical world. As the great geneticist and evolutionist Theodosius Dobzhansky wrote in 1973, 'Nothing in biology makes sense except in light of evolution.'"[4]

Evolution, Miller concludes, "turns out to be a hard-working theory which is at the core of biological discovery and biological exploration."

❧

Evolution's scientist supporters have always embraced natural selection because it gives them a plausible and testable scientific explanation for what had been, until Darwin, attributed to supernatural acts of the Creator. Without a coherent nonsupernatural theory about what drives evolutionary change, it was arguably more rational to assume that it was the work of God. But when God's supernatural creative power was cited as an explanation for the diversity of life on earth, it cut off exploration right where biological research got really interesting, moving beyond *what* happened and into *how* it happened. By giving researchers a basic, law-driven mechanism to test and investigate, natural selection opened up a whole world to the biological sciences. Over the century and a half since Darwin's first publication, the scientific story emerging from that world has produced a detailed historical narrative that's at odds with the traditional, religious one previously holding the near monopoly.

Darwin's theory of natural selection was controversial the moment *On the Origin of Species* hit the street in 1859. Darwin was reluctant to publish, and when he did, he presented his work carefully and modestly, playing down— you might even say smuggling in—the profound philosophical and religious ramifications of his work. In a now-famous letter to a friend he said that to admit to such a radically naturalistic theory was "like confessing a murder."

41

The murder he was admitting to must have been that of the kind of creative, hands-on Christian God his wife, his colleagues, and most of the intellectuals of his day strongly believed in; the kind of God he himself had embraced as a younger man; the kind of God the proponents of the ID movement are today working so hard to resurrect.

Judge Jones ends the day by saying, "Class dismissed."

CHAPTER FOUR

ASSEMBLING GOLIATH

FRED CALLAHAN: "What am I supposed to tolerate? A small encroachment on my First Amendment rights? Well, I'm not going to."

he National Center for Science Education's Nick Matzke once told me, "People used to ask me, 'Why are you spending your life debating creationists? It's totally pointless.' Then, suddenly, this weakness I have becomes my greatest strength."

Nick Matzke was the biggest Internet geek in the world. At least that's what he says. Back in 2003 he was working on his geography master's thesis at UC Santa Barbara, but his passion already lay elsewhere. If you saw him late at night hammering away at his keyboard you might have thought he was playing the role of a medieval knight in a low-stakes game of "Dungeons and Dragons." In fact, he was on the front lines of the cyberbattle over evolution and creationism. Armed with flames, ratiocination, and a dual degree in biology and chemistry, he combed the Internet each night for the enemy's arguments against evolution and assertions of scientific evidence of intelligent design.

Only in his wildest fantasy could he have imagined that he would soon be sharing a stage with some of the most capable civil liberties and corporate lawyers around, not to mention evolutionary biology celebrities such as Kenneth Miller and UC Berkeley paleontologist Kevin Padian. Or that that stage would be surrounded by journalists, well wishers, ill wishers, and others who wanted a piece of him.

Like a butterfly emerging from its chrysalis, Matzke emerged from obsessive Internet geekdom to become a crusading evolution-education hero overnight. After completing his master's thesis in the summer of 2003, Matzke took a couple of months off and, "on a lark" he says, wrote a long and thorough review article (*Evolution in (Brownian) Space: A Model for the Origin of the Bacterial Flagellum*) for a pro-evolution Website he himself created.

The article, which disputed ID's claims about the irreducible complexity of the bacterial flagellum, impressed Eugenie (Genie) Scott, executive director of the National Center for Science Education (NCSE), a nonprofit based in Oakland, California, dedicated to defending the teaching of evolution in the public schools. She and her deputy director, Glenn Branch, were already aware of Matzke from his Internet work, so when a position opened up there for an information specialist in early 2004, they invited him to fill it. It was like being called to battle by the Empress of the Evolutionary Forces. Matzke leaped at the chance to convert his obsession into a profession.

One of Matzke's duties was to monitor the news for what NCSE calls "flare-ups" in school districts around the country. He remembers first seeing the Dover case on his computer on June 8, 2004. It was "interesting," he remembers, "worth watching, but hardly exceptional." At the time, he assumed that after the ACLU fired off a threat to sue, the school board would run for cover, as other school boards did in similar cases.

"Demagogic politicians issuing blustery uninformed anti-evolution rhetoric are a dime a dozen," Matzke says. "But school boards willing to risk losing a costly and time-consuming court battle are much less common."

So Matzke was caught by surprise on the morning of October 20, 2004. "I came into the office and Genie [Scott], who was already on the phone about the case, waved a copy of the *York Daily Record* at me," says Matzke. "The bold headline on the front page read 'Intelligent Design Voted In.'

"I whacked my forehead with the palm of my hand, shocked, like Homer Simpson does."

As it turned out, Scott was on the phone with Vic Walczak, legal director of the ACLU's Pennsylvania office, who had just called her to scheme about how best to respond to Dover. Both knew it was a going to be a bigger case than the ACLU alone could handle. And both knew it was a case that they could not afford to lose: if a judge ruled that it was legal to teach ID in Dover High's science classroom, school boards around the country would be following suit. It would create a legal maelstrom—just what the backers of ID were looking for, says Matzke.

On the phone that morning, Walczak said to Scott, "I suppose you've heard about Dover. We're gonna need some help."

"You've got it. Do you have a cooperating firm yet?" she asked.

"No, but we're looking. Any ideas?"

As they strategized, Scott remembered a young lawyer from Pennsylvania who'd joined NCSE's legal advisory committee in 2000 after a controversy over the teaching of evolution and creationism in Kansas.[1] The advisory committee was little more than an e-mail list of lawyers (science and civil liberties fans, mostly) who were willing to advise NCSE on legal matters or, occasionally, to represent the organization. But the young man Scott had in mind was extraordinarily bright, really concerned about these issues, and a partner at a big law firm headquartered in downtown Philadelphia. The resources a big firm would bring to the case would be key to its success, Scott and Walczak agreed.

So Scott called Eric Rothschild.

It was already afternoon on the east coast, but within two hours Scott got a call back from Rothschild: "Don't do anything until you hear from me!

I'm going to go to my pro bono committee tomorrow morning. I've waited fifteen years for this."

As he made clear with his performance on day one of *Kitzmiller,* Rothschild is no Walter Mitty; he makes a bundle as a partner specializing in reinsurance law at Pepper Hamilton, one of the biggest east coast firms. He is wild about sports, and is fiercely dedicated to the teams of his undergraduate alma mater, Duke. He is married and has two young kids. But he always had a feeling something more would come along. And this was it.

Rothschild walked down the hall and knocked on the office door of his friend and colleague Steve Harvey.

Harvey and Rothschild are an odd couple; Rothschild is a Democrat, Harvey a Republican. Rothschild is Jewish, Harvey Catholic. Rothschild is balding on top. Harvey's pate is covered with a thick shock of close-cropped prematurely gray hair. Rothschild is congenial. Harvey, well he is congenial, too, but he can also turn frighteningly intense.

Despite their superficial differences, they share a great deal. Both of them are funny as hell and love to have a good time. And both of them are intellectually curious, ethically driven, hard working, and smart as whips.

Harvey didn't take any convincing; he was ready to join the team. If they could get the pro bono committee at the firm to sign on, they'd be ready to go. If Harvey and Rothschild are anything, they are persuasive. The very next morning the committee gave them the go-ahead. (In First Amendment cases such as this one, if the plaintiffs bringing the suit prevail they are generally awarded "reasonable fees" to cover the cost of bringing the case. If they lose, they cover the costs themselves. From a financial point of view, a firm like Pepper Hamilton had little to gain from a case like this, and a lot to lose.)

Meanwhile, Vic Walczak and Genie Scott were assembling the rest of the plaintiffs' team. They'd been in touch with Americans United for the Separation of Church and State (AU), which had been monitoring the Dover situation for some time. Americans United, a public advocacy group focused solely on church-state issues that is based in Washington, D.C., didn't have to think long. The importance of the First Amendment rights at stake, the huge significance of any decision in the battle over religiously motivated attacks on evolution, and AU's abundance of experience in Establishment Clause litigation and its expertise in creationism matters, too, would contribute a lot to the case. Americans United assigned Yale-trained lawyer and AU Assistant Legal Director Richard Katskee to the case. Katskee, an experienced strategist and an expert in constitutional law generally, the First Amendment and the Establishment Clause in particular, would be the primary brief writer, and an essential—albeit less publicly visible than Rothschild, Walczak, or Harvey—member of the legal team.

The NCSE was named as a formal, pro bono consultant for the plaintiffs' attorneys on the science and science education aspects of the case. Genie Scott assigned Matzke to the case, though she would spend a lot of time in Harrisburg herself and would follow the trial closely.

In addition to writing the complaint and signing up plaintiffs for the suit, the legal team spent much of the early and mid-fall of 2005 selecting and courting expert witnesses. They'd asked Scott and Matzke to recommend an all-star pro-evolution, anti-ID team. No holds barred. Fantasy wish list.

Matzke and Scott knew that Michael Behe's "irreducible complexity" would be central to the pro-ID case; they needed someone who knew Behe and his arguments inside out. The best possible person for that job would be Brown University professor Kenneth Miller. They also needed someone who could trace the history of the ID movement and link it to creationism's earlier manifestations. Philosophy professor Barbara Forrest, coauthor of *Creationism's Trojan Horse*, a book on ID's historical roots, would be perfect. She had also done an analysis of the ID textbook, *Of Pandas and People*, which would be central to the case.

They would also need an authoritative paleontologist who could show how the fossil record validates Darwin's predictions and affirms common descent. They easily snagged their first choice: Kevin Padian, professor of integrative biology and a curator in the Museum of Paleontology at UC

Berkeley. He is admired by his colleagues, is a clear and confident speaker, and is the president of NCSE's board of directors.

A theologian should address the religious aspects of the design argument. Again they got first choice, John Haught, retired professor of theology at Georgetown University and the author of some of the most widely read and respected works in the field.

And someone would have to contradict the argument that teaching ID is good for students, so they suggested an education specialist, McGill University professor Brian Alters.

Finally, one of the ID team's biggest hitters would be the philosopher and mathematician William Dembski, whose work proposes to show that design can be discovered in nature by the application of certain mathematical analyses. Matzke and Scott suggested a philosopher of science who was familiar with Dembski's work and the broader debate: Michigan State University professor Robert Pennock, author of *Tower of Babel: The Evidence Against the New Creationism.*

Matzke and Scott had identified alternates for each of their A-Team candidates, in the likely case that some of them would be unable or unwilling to appear in court. But there was no need. Each and every one of the NCSE's first-string witnesses was eager to help and willing to push aside whatever else they had planned in order to be there.

Eight months before the court date, Matzke began educating the plaintiffs' lawyers on the ins and outs of the pro- and anti-ID arguments. He flew back and forth between NCSE's Oakland office and the center of action in Pennsylvania, where he participated in the deposition of Behe and in various strategy sessions. He went to D.C. to plan for the deposition of Scott Minnich, a microbiologist at the University of Idaho who would be testifying for the defense. He also bombarded the lawyers with long e-mail essays on such subjects as the definition of *theory* in science. And already, months before the trial began, Matzke began scheming with Rothschild about how to cross-examine Michael Behe, who, everyone agreed, would be the key to the defendants' argument that ID was real science.

Vic Walczak, the lead attorney for the ACLU, was born in Sweden, where his Polish mother and grandfather had fled as refugees after World War II. They had survived the extermination camp in Treblinka, but Walczak's grandmother was one of the million or so Warsaw Jews who did not make it out of that Godforsaken place. Walczak's grandfather had spent much of his life after the war testifying in Nazi war trials.

To call Germany's "final solution" a civil liberties violation is like calling the annihilation of Hiroshima an air strike. There is no word up to the task. And yet, it can't be denied that the gradual erosion of the liberties of Germans, Italians, and others in Europe, and the acceptance of it among those not directly targeted for persecution, made possible the twentieth century's worst nightmare. Walczak takes that fact to heart, and the defense of American civil liberties runs in his blood.

In the early 1980s, Walczak studied philosophy at Colgate University in central New York. As one of the few fluent Polish speakers in the area, he got involved in the Polish Solidarity movement by helping refugees adjust to life here in the United States. After graduating in 1983, he went to Poland, where marshal law had been declared to quell the popular uprising led by shipyard worker, union activist, and president-to-be Lech Walesa. In Poland, Walczak was beaten, arrested, and strip searched, and his phone was bugged. "I learned firsthand about civil liberties violations, and what it's like to live in a place without civil liberties.

"In Poland at that time," he says, "people didn't have enough to eat, and had trouble getting basic material goods. But if you asked them what the one thing they'd want was, they all said it was civil liberties; the right to elect their officials, to criticize the government, and not to live in fear of oppression. It was a wonderful training ground for me. I knew then that I wanted to go to law school in order to do this kind of work."

Walczak got his law degree from Boston College in 1986, and then went to work for the Legal Aid Bureau in Maryland advocating for the rights of prisoners. He joined the ACLU in 1992 and served for twelve years as the Pittsburgh Chapter's executive director. In 2004 he became the legal director for the state of Pennsylvania.

With a dedicated and funded law firm opposing them and a judge apparently willing to open his court to all aspects of the case, Walczak and Scott could see that this was going to be a "battle royale," as they called it. Neither side would hold anything back. Both sides were ready, happy even, to go all the way to the Supreme Court if they had to, and if they could.

"If we lose," Walczak tells me, "we'll see intelligent design proposed in public school classrooms all across the country. There's no doubt in my mind. If they lose, it could put a damper on ID and its effort to put creation-ism into schools everywhere."

Old Doverians do not like the ACLU. "A lot of them consider it pretty much the anti-Christ," says Joel Lieb, the longhaired, mustachioed plaintiff whose family has been in the area since before the Revolutionary War.

For decades, going far back before the emergence of ID, the ACLU has been caricatured as an anti-religious by-product of Darwinism. In fact, the ACLU was really put on the national map by defending John Scopes in what was popularly called the "Monkey Trial" back in 1925.[2] If there were something called ACLUism, conservative, religious Dovarians would rank it along with Darwinism, Freudianism, and Marxism as one of the most loathsome agents of modern moral corruption.

Dover Area School Board president Alan Bonsell told Cyndi Sneath, a plaintiff, that he feared the ACLU more than he feared the Taliban.

But Walczak says that this attitude doesn't bother him. He sees people converted to the ACLU all the time. "The most common thing I hear from new clients is, 'Gosh I never thought I'd be calling *you guys* for help,'" says Walczak. "It's not until their own ox gets gored by the government that they really need us, and really need the Constitution."

❦

Pepper Hamilton's resources made a big difference to the plaintiff team's momentum. The most obvious boon is the lawyers, Rothschild and Harvey. But the firm also has loaned two legal assistants to the case full time. And I mean *full* time. Fresh out of college, Katherine Henson and Hedya Aryani knew they'd be making good money as paralegals at Pepper Hamilton, but they also thought they'd be suffering through cases having to do with labor law and reinsurance. (I ask if reinsurance law is more exciting than plain old insurance law; in tandem, both say "No!") But instead, they found themselves invited to aid the gladiators at the trial of the century. They jumped into the Coliseum with both feet.

They worked for a year on the case, preparing briefs and witness files, and, says Aryani, "keeping track of absolutely everything." There were the preliminary pleadings, deposition outlines, deposition exhibits, deposition transcripts, interrogatories, document requests, motions, memos of law, direct exam outlines, direct exam trial exhibits, cross-exam outlines, cross-exam exhibits, trial transcripts, expert reports, expert demonstratives, and the finding of fact/conclusions of law. In all, there were about nine hundred trial exhibits, which took up around twenty two-and-a-half- or three-inch binders. The entire set was reproduced five times so that the judge, his clerk, Thomas More Law Center, Pepper's Harrisburg office, and the plaintiff team could each have a set. Aryani says that there were over a hundred boxes of documents pertaining to the plaintiffs in their case room.

"If anyone wanted anything at any moment, we had to be able to put our fingers on it immediately."

To cheer themselves up at four in the morning after double shots of Starbucks espresso and hours spent kicking and cursing at various copy machines, "the Angels," as the paralegals were nicknamed for their ability to make miracles happen, made puppets out of Internet photos of Walczak, Rothschild, and Harvey. They cut out pictures of their bosses and taped them to the tops of pens and had them repeating characteristic commands over and over: "Revamp that compendium of documents!" was one of Harvey's regular lines.

During the trial itself, "our day begins at midnight," says Henson, and during their waking hours they do only two things, "present, or prepare to present."

The plaintiffs' team is huge. In addition to Pepper's Rothschild and Harvey, four other firm lawyers—Joseph Farber, Benjamin Mather, Thomas Schmidt, and Alfred Wilcox—all pitch in, too. Then there are Walczak from the ACLU and Katskee from Americans United. Add in the two paralegals, technology specialist Matthew McElvenny (the guy who runs exhibits on the digital projector for the plaintiffs' team), the NCSE's Matzke, and his boss Genie Scott—that's a lot of names to keep track of, let alone big egos to keep from bumping against other. But if there are any hard feelings or power struggles on the plaintiffs' legal team, no one lets it show.

I ask Walczak how they decided which lawyer was going to examine each of the witnesses. "Eric [Rothschild] just declared early on that he was doing Behe," says Walczak. "Some of it was thematic—I did our science experts—and some was convenience. For instance, Steve [Harvey] initially had all the plaintiffs. We ended up making last-minute adjustments, either to help out a colleague who may have been overloaded, or to give someone who had too little going on an opportunity to participate. But it was all very amiable. This was an amazing collaborative effort."

To save his firm a little money, Rothschild decided against renting rooms at the Hilton in downtown Harrisburg, which would have cost several hundred dollars a night. Instead he leased three suites in a place about a mile up the Susquehanna from the courthouse. Buddies Rothschild and Harvey bunk in one suite, which they call "the swamp"; paralegals Henson and Aryani took another, nicknamed "Tiffany's"; and Walczak and Matzke took the third, known as "the Penthouse."

Court days start early. Rothschild and Walczak get up and jog along the Susquehanna at 5:30 in the morning, while Matzke, the night-owl Internet geek, sleeps as late as he can afford to. Katskee, the Yale-trained Americans United lawyer, hadn't planned to spend as much time in Harrisburg, so he stays at the Hilton and misses out on some of the late-night camaraderie and hijinks.

After stopping off at the local newsstand–cigar store–porn shop to see what the headlines are from the previous day's performance, the whole team convenes at Pepper Hamilton's Harrisburg office at about 7:30 A.M. More than once, Matzke the geek and his roomie, Walczak the public interest lawyer, drive into town belting out Bruce Springsteen's "Part Man, Part Monkey," the only love song I know of that's about the Scopes trial.

Rothschild and Harvey usually drive together, and their musical tastes tend more toward 1980s rocker Pat Benatar and rapper Kanye West, says Henson, the intern Angel who is often asked to take the wheel while the lawyers go over their briefs.

During their part of the trial, the plaintiffs' lawyers will meet their witnesses for the day at the Pepper offices, making sure they have all their ducks in a row. Then, at 8:30, they take the short walk to the courthouse. By nine they're settled in the courtroom trenches and ready for the day's battle.

The nine plaintiff families come from a cross-section of Dover society. For the most part, they'd been strangers to each other up till the case began to take shape. Tammy Kitzmiller and Cyndi Sneath are neighbors, but had only a passing acquaintance. There is one thing all plaintiffs have in common, though: a child who either is or will eventually be taking ninth-grade biology at Dover High.

Beth Eveland and Cyndi Sneath were the first to express serious interest in joining the case, but their children are still young and have several years to go before they will be read the four-paragraph statement by Dover administrators. But when Sneath mentioned her neighbor, Tammy Kitzmiller, and said that Kitzmiller's daughter was going into ninth grade after that summer, Rothschild knew she would make a solid lead plaintiff.

The Pepper lawyers met individually with some of the candidates, and had phone conversations with all of them. "We reassured them that they could count on us," says Harvey, that they "could call us any time day or night with questions or concerns and that we would be there for them." Both lawyers gave the plaintiffs their home and cell phone numbers.

Kitzmiller and Sneath say that once they met the legal team, they knew they were in for the ride. "The lawyers were so capable, so accessible, so reassuring; they inspired complete confidence," says Kitzmiller.

It was a big commitment, the Pepper lawyers told them, but it was an important case; important not only to the Dover community but to the whole country.

The night before they filed the complaint, on December 14, 2004, all eleven parents gathered for a group meeting at Pepper's Harrisburg office. By that time all had officially signed on, but it was the first time they were together in the same place. And it was the first time many of them had even met. Rothschild says he can't remember what was said that night, but he does remember being struck by what a thoughtful group it was and how full of conviction they were, individually and collectively.

The next day the plaintiffs and their lawyers held a press conference in the rotunda at the State Capitol in downtown Harrisburg. When Cyndi Sneath walked out onto the Capitol's interior balcony and looked down into the rotunda she saw "a sea of suits and cameras and reporters." She felt faint, she says: "This was not my world."

There were protesters, too. One climbed onto the stage that had been set up for the event with a sign that said: "Evolution is a Lie."

Steve Harvey ran over to the protester and told him, in no uncertain terms, to get down. "I thought Steve was going to physically remove the guy," says Sneath. "You know how intense Steve is. Anyway, I felt like I was going to throw up. I realized then that we were getting into something very big and very different."

"It was scary standing there," says Kitzmiller, "but I knew that what we were doing was right."

Kitzmiller read a very simple, one-page statement that concluded, "The School Board has no business instructing children about religious matters. Those decisions belong to parents."

The lawyers gave statements, too, and answered questions, and that was that. They were on their way.

Kitzmiller, a divorced mom with two daughters, is wholesome, calm, and pretty. She has blond-brown hair and wears an anklet, a ring on her toe, and another one in her belly button. She is forty years old and works as an office manager at a nearby landscaping company. In 2005, seventeen-year-old daughter Megan is a senior at Dover High, an honor student, and is planning to go to Arcadia University, in Philadelphia, next year. The family of three lives with its huge dog, Dakota. He's just a puppy, but he is blind in one eye, 115 pounds, and thrilled to be alive. Beyond a couple of big, old crabapple trees in Kitzmiller's back yard stretches farmland, and beyond that, too far to make out clearly, a giant white box stands on the horizon— a food distribution warehouse, surrounded by small, newly developed homes. The development is distant, but it appears to be marching across the fields toward Kitzmiller's house.

When Tammy and her ex-husband moved to Dover in 1993, shortly before they were separated and then divorced, it was for the open space and the excellent schools. "Ironic," is all she'll say now about their attraction to the place.

Tammy's parents were religious, but she stopped going to church as a teenager, as soon as her father gave her a choice. "It was just going in one ear and out the other. It didn't really mean anything to me. I never believed any of it," she says now. "Even at a young age it didn't hold any water for me." She's not antireligious, she says, pausing for a moment, but, she continues, "I've seen what people do in the name of Christianity: the hatred, the violence."

Because Rothschild, Harvey, and the others were determined not to frame this case as a battle between religion and science, they were nervous about Kitzmiller's own lack of faith and afraid it might come up under cross-examination. The fact that she is a divorced mom was problematic, too, she says. "That's still not all that common or accepted in these parts," where, she says, "oldtimers are generally arch-conservatives and the newcomers are mostly just your basic conservative Republicans.

"For all Eric and Steve knew, my husband might end up on the stand as a witness for the defense," says Kitzmiller.

But because Kitzmiller's younger daughter, Jessica, was actually heading into ninth grade at the time, and because Kitzmiller has a kind of Erin Brockovich quality about her, the lawyers decided to run with her.[3]

In truth, says Kitzmiller, she cares less about the introduction of religion into the schools than about the corruption of science. "For me, the real issue is bad science and good science. It is obvious that the school board is trying to get creationism into the school, but I am more worried about undermining the good teaching of evolution."

Kitzmiller is gracious and calm under fire. Early on, in the weeks before the trial, she got threatening hate mail predicting that she would be punished, equating her with the famous founder of American Atheists, Madalyn Murray O'Hair, once known as "the most hated woman in America." O'Hair and her two grown children were kidnapped and murdered in 1995.

"One letter said that I should watch out for a bullet," says Kitzmiller. "Another said I should watch my kids."

❧

Bryan and Christy Rehm were natural candidates for the plaintiffs' list, too. The handsome young couple runs a Bible study camp together in the summer. Both are high school teachers; Bryan teaches physics and Christy teaches English. They have four children, three of whom are old enough to be in the Dover Area schools. The fourth is still a toddler. Bryan, a tall and burly man with a goatee and lots of wavy brown hair, has a sense of purpose about him. He takes his responsibilities seriously. Not only is he suing the school board, he is also campaigning for the upcoming November elections in the hope of joining that very same organization.

Bryan Rehm recalls a meeting with school board member Alan Bonsell, who told him that evolution wasn't compatible with his religious beliefs. Bonsell didn't think Rehm would care, because he was "just a physics teacher," says Rehm. But he did care. He cared a lot. The integrity of science means a lot to him.

Bryan Rehm left Dover High for a job in a neighboring school district. He wanted to be able to teach science without having to fend off creationists and worry about all the political ramifications of doing so, says Christy.

The battle in Dover had turned ugly, and it was too much to live and work under fire all the time, he says. "You used to be able to go out to any restaurant, sit down, not worry about who was next to you. You could walk down the street and say 'Hi' to everybody and get a nice pleasant return. Now people stare. You'll go out and regularly be called inappropriate things centering around the concept of atheist. . . . It goes beyond atheist to adding other words onto it that I don't care to repeat," says Rehm.

Christy Rehm teaches high school English, also in a neighboring school district, and her clan has been in Dover for generations. She is poised and well spoken, calm on the stand, even under cross-examination, and without a trace of arrogance or rancor. In addition to their full-time teaching jobs, four kids, and Bryan's run for the school board, both are also in graduate school.

Christy worried about her own students when she heard Dover curriculum committee chair Bill Buckingham say at a school board meeting that this country was founded on Christian principles, not Muslim ones or those from any other religions, and how it was not necessary to teach about any religions but Christianity.

She teaches students from all kinds of religious backgrounds. How could she tell some that their religion has no place in school, while other students' religion does?

As believers, the Rehms said, they reserved the right to oversee their own children's spiritual education. They don't want that left to high school teachers or school administrators.

Cyndi Sneath turns out to be the alpha-plaintiff. At thirty-seven years old, she is a solid but graceful woman with a blond shag haircut. She has an abundance of moxie, and the respect of everyone on the team. She stays on top of all aspects of the controversy and the trial, and is completely candid about her feelings and opinions. She is also fiercely and unapologetically protective of her kids, and she doesn't take bull from anyone.

Her seven-year-old son, Griffin, is a science buff. When I visit their house he shows me a textbook about sharks. And Sneath, who owns and runs AAA Appliance Services, Inc. with her husband, doesn't want anything interfering with Griffin's science education. "I'm not an educator. I have no big degrees. I depend on the school district to provide the fundamentals," she says. "And I consider evolution to be a fundamental of science."

"At the end of the day," Sneath says, "the word *designer* is a synonym for *Creator*, and you know, that takes a leap of faith for me. And I think it's my privilege to guide [my kids] in matters of faith, not a science teacher, not an administrator, and not the Dover Area School Board."

Joel Lieb, an underemployed art and animation teacher at a nearby junior college, has a long beard and mustache. Steve Harvey says he looks like an old hippie, but I'd say more like an old hillbilly. I mean that in a good way. He is authentic Old Dover material. At least he was Old Dover until he ended up on the wrong side in the *Kitzmiller* case. He and his partner, Deborah Fenimore, also a plaintiff, have an eighth-grade son, Ian, who will be going to Dover High next year. "Intelligent design is not science," Lieb says, and "every second that [Ian is] either in the class listening to it or out in the hallway objecting to it is a second he's not getting an education. These kids need education.

"It's driven a wedge where there hadn't been a wedge before," continues Lieb. "People are afraid to talk to people for fear. They're afraid to talk to me because I'm on the wrong side of the fence."

Steve Stough is a fifty-year-old life sciences teacher and coach, and a conservative, crew-cutted, religious Republican. Stough's son, Jake, is a friend of Zach Strausbaugh, the student who painted the mural that was burned. And his daughter, Ashley, is a ninth-grader at Dover High.

Beth Eveland, a legal assistant, has two young children. And though she acknowledges that neither one stands to be introduced to ID in Dover High any time soon, she says she fears the "trickle down" effect of the policy; if ID is embraced by the district there is nothing to keep it from trickling down to the elementary school.

Julie Smith, a medical technologist who lives in Dover with her husband and two children, Katherine, sixteen, and Michael, nineteen, recounts the day her daughter came home from school and said, "Mom, evolution is a lie. What kind of Christian are you, anyway?" Katherine and her friends had been talking about the ID-evolution debate at school, and her friends had told her that as a Christian she could not accept evolution.

Finally, the last plaintiffs in the case are Barrie and Fred Callahan. Fred is husband to the ebullient Sally Struthers–like former board member, Barrie, and the nattily dressed, reserved, but well-spoken president of Colony Papers, a paper products company in York. He takes an intellectual approach to the debate. He stood up at one school board meeting and asked board curriculum committee leader Buckingham if he thought Dover High teachers were prepared to address in science class the question of theodicy: the knotty theological problem of how to reconcile the concept of a kind, loving, and just God with the injustice and brutality so common in the world. There's an awful lot of ill in this world, he said. Is it possible that the intelligent designer is a force for evil? Discussion in class may well run to that possibility, he warned. How would you have a science teacher handle that?

The many months of preparation for the trial and the common experience of hunkering down, embattled in their community, brought this diverse group together. By the time the trial is under way in September, they have bonded like soldiers under fire.

Dover is a dry town, but just fifty feet beyond the township line is a great old bar called The Racehorse Tavern. Stough says it is the plaintiffs' "own little isolation ward." Attorney-client privilege keeps them from saying much about the trial to anyone beyond their group, so they will meet at the Racehorse and discuss the case, sometimes until the wee hours of the morning.

"I hate the word, but it was a 'bonding' point for us," says the macho Stough. "I was happy that there was even one other person who felt as I did," he continues, "and low and behold, there were ten others!"

In the summer of 2005, just a month before the trial, three of the families took a road trip together to the Outer Banks of North Carolina. The Sneaths, the Rehms, and the Kitzmillers sent a photo back to their legal team showing their families assembled beneath a homemade, mobile-home-sized flying saucer, a roadside attraction near Buxton, North Carolina. The photo is a testament to camp, with a rubber alien mask looking down on them from a window of the flying saucer. They believed, they wrote in a note to their legal team, that they'd finally found evidence of the intelligent designer after all.

CHAPTER FIVE

THOMAS MORE
AND ID LITE

GORDY SLACK: "You want to change the definition of science
to include the supernatural?"
RICHARD THOMPSON: "Yes, we need a total paradigm shift in science."

ichard Thompson, chief counsel for the defense, has a startling, almost Tourettes-like tic of thrusting his fist to his mouth and biting his index finger lengthwise, between the first and second knuckles, as if trying to keep himself from saying too much. But as quickly as it goes in, the finger comes out again and his words begin to flow. He cannot help himself. He must tell the truth. As he sees it.

Thompson makes a strong impression in his elegant dark suits. He is short and powerfully built, white-haired but bald on top, and endowed with an impressive Roman nose and preternaturally white teeth. He has the defiant, almost menacing energy of an armed man on a moral mission.

If *Kitzmiller* is, as some describe it, a twenty-first-century version of the Scopes Monkey Trial, history has cast Thompson in the role of William Jennings Bryan. And he appears to love it. Bryan was the lawyer, orator, statesman, and progressive evangelical Christian who, eighty years ago,

61

argued against teaching evolution in high school in the original Scopes trial in Dayton, Tennessee. Although he won the case, Bryan is better remembered for his pummeling on the stand by Clarence Darrow—perhaps the second-most famous lawyer of the day and an advocate for evolution and modernity.

(If Thompson is playing the role of William Jennings Bryan in this trial, then the ACLU's Walczak may be its Clarence Darrow, the witty, agnostic, deeply principled lawyer who represented the teacher John Scopes in that battle of giants eighty years ago. Like Darrow, Walczak is a world-weary defender of unpopular causes, directed by a strong moral compass and driven by a specific conviction in the importance of preserving the separation of church and state.)

For decades, the Scopes trial was also considered the beginning of what people thought would be the end for American creationism. But three-quarters of a century (and libraries full of evolution-supporting evidence) later, the same impulses and ideologies fueling Scopes have found expression in ID. Who could have guessed?

Well, Thompson could have, he says. "Questions about the role of design in creation have been asked for thousands of years. They haven't been put to rest at all. They're just getting stronger."

Thompson is holding forth on the courthouse steps in the drizzling rain after a long day of testimony. Reporters crowd around him as he lays out his strategy for the case: he and his associates will argue that no theory should be judged by its historical roots, even if they are religious. Even if they are creationist! (Not, he hastens to add, that ID's roots necessarily are.) Nor should a theory be judged by the personal ideologies of those who hold it; plenty of Darwinists are atheists, but that doesn't disqualify evolutionary biology as an ideology. (Not, he says, that Darwinism isn't an ideology.) He will argue that there is a bona fide scientific controversy between evolution and ID, and it is played out in scientific debates, academic books, and scientific articles around the world. Experts on the ID side will take the stand in weeks to come, he promises, and everyone will see that they are real scientists doing real research. So schools that want to include the debate in their curriculum deserve the right to. Denying them that right is a form of both scientific and religious discrimination and a violation of their right to free speech. "ID is seeking a place in the classroom because of its merits, but it's being kept out because it is harmonious with the Christian faith," Thompson says.

He explains his willingness to leave his wife and three sons back in Ann Arbor, Michigan, and commute five hundred miles to Harrisburg for this case: "There are two Americas today, one that's still very religiously based and another that has no foundation, where everything is relative, where everything goes." The moral relativism that dominates the second America, Thompson says, is an ideology enabled by Darwinism.

"All scientific theories have religious implications," he says, "including Darwinism," whose religious implication is atheism. And moral relativism, atheism, and the idolatry of science are all symptoms of our "floundering society," says Thompson. He wants to put society back on track, and the track, he believes, is there for us, laid down by God. "We do this, all of the attorneys I'm working with do, because of our religious commitment."

"Do you believe that we and other primates descended from common ancestors?" a British filmmaker calls out over the din. Thompson bites his finger and then says, "Do I think I evolved from an ape? No, I don't believe my ancestor was a monkey."

Thompson is stealing William Jennings Bryan's lines.

Thompson is the founder, president, and chief counsel of the Thomas More Law Center, a nonprofit in Ann Arbor, Michigan, that describes itself on its Website as "The Sword and Shield for People of Faith." The Law Center is representing the Dover school board pro bono in this case, just as the ACLU represented John Scopes against Dayton, Tennessee. The Law Center, with only three full-time attorneys on this case (and sometimes only one in the courtroom at a time), is playing David to the plaintiffs' legal team's Goliath, says Thompson. But David isn't exactly the right image. The

Law Center is funded by the Domino's Pizza millionaire Thomas Monaghan, who is, like Thompson, an ultra-conservative Catholic. Senator Rick Santorum sits on the Law Center's governing board.

When I tell Thompson later that he looks a little bit like William Jennings Bryan—it's not entirely untrue—he will laugh disarmingly, delighted. "Frederick March, the actor in the movie of *Inherit the Wind*, or the real William Jennings Bryan?"

The real Bryan had been secretary of state under Woodrow Wilson and had run for president, on a populist platform, three times. He was renowned for the power of his oratory, his ethical convictions, and his religious zealotry. Later in life, he focused the double barrels of his rhetorical shotgun on evolution (what he called "the monkey as he tries to enter the schoolroom") and the corrupt Republican Party ("the elephant as he tries to enter the treasury").

Thompson, however, was made famous as the Oakland County, Michigan, state prosecutor who sank his teeth into assisted-suicide advocate Jack Kevorkian and wouldn't let go until elected out of office for the favor. Thompson is also known for pushing through mandatory life sentences in Michigan for certain drug crimes and for successfully prosecuting more drug offenders under that law than anyone else. And though they would have been on opposite sides of the political aisle, Thompson shares with Bryan the conviction that Darwinism is the world's most dangerous idea and that it poses a deadly threat to modern society. Like Bryan, Thompson sees himself as a champion of traditional values under attack by the forces of cultural relativism and scientific materialism.

And, like Bryan, Thompson says he is ready and willing—"anxious" is the word he uses—to take this case against the ACLU up through the appellate system to the Supreme Court, which, he predicts, may well be suited to vote in his favor by the time the case gets to its door a few years from now. What Thompson may be missing in political nuance and scientific sophistication—he says he never took biology because "I didn't want to cut frogs apart"—he seems to be compensating for with faithful and manic determination. His is a faith-based legal practice.

But the hypocrisy he perceives in this case really gets his goat. For one thing, "In the Scopes trial in 1925 the ACLU was saying that there should be no orthodoxy in matters of education," he says. "They were suing the state of Tennessee because it was trying to maintain a uniform opinion among teachers on this subject.[1] Now, in Dover, the ACLU is arguing in favor of enforcing orthodoxy, Darwinian evolution, and it's the Thomas More Law Center that's saying school systems shouldn't try to maintain a uniform orthodox opinion on controversial scientific issues."

One prominent minister calls the Thomas More Law Center "the Christian answer to the ACLU." It has fought legal battles against abortion, the rights of homosexuals, and the court-mandated removal of a giant hilltop cross on Mt. Soledad in San Diego, California. Its legal work is not all *against* things, though; the Law Center also works for once again permitting American children to pray in the public schools, for the display of the Ten Commandments and nativity scenes in public places, and for the "constitutional right to fly the American flag or express faith in God." And the Law Center also defended a pro-life group's right to post a Web-based hit-list of the names and locations of doctors who performed abortions.[2]

In a later interview, Thompson will bristle at the notion that ID is and always will be *by definition* excluded from science. "What is science, and what is not science, is merely a convention. It can be challenged and changed at will by scientists themselves. And scientists are the products of their culture, too," he says.

Doesn't he find it a little odd that a champion of enduring truth and fundamental moral values such as he should take such a relativist stance on science? Thompson shrugs off the question.

"Look, scientists don't sit there and ask, 'Am I doing science or not?' No scientist is going to say, 'This is empirical truth about the wrong subject so I'm not going to study it.' No, they look at whatever the empirical data is, and draw conclusions from it."

"You want to change the definition of science to include the supernatural?" I ask.

"Yes," he says, "we need a total paradigm shift in science."[3]

"Intelligent design might be an underdog theory now," says Thompson, "but that shouldn't make it illegal to teach." The big bang theory was once both unpopular and thought to have been religiously motivated, he says. Belgian priest Georges Lemaître first proposed and defended it in the 1920s as both scientifically accurate and consistent with the Biblical account of the universe having a specific moment of creation.

"Einstein thought the big bang was wrong because it didn't fit his metaphysics," says Thompson. "But he was the one who was wrong. Should it have been illegal to discuss the big bang in schools just because it was consistent with Christianity?"

No, I think, it shouldn't have been illegal. But if the big bang had turned out to be big bologna, then we'd now be saying that they were right to keep it out of high school physics classes. The point being that inclusion of a new hypothesis, or an old outlier one like ID, should be based on its scientific strength, which only other scientists and, eventually, history can measure accurately. So far scientists haven't been too kind to ID, but the history of science has barely begun. I hope.

Science and the history of science are not Thompson's forte. He is himself moved, as are most Americans who disdain evolution, more by the implications of the theory than by the science itself.

Asked why this battle matters so much to him, Thompson will pause for a moment, putting his hands together as if in prayer. Then he begins, "If you are nothing but an accident of nature," he says, "then nothing you do is dependent on objective truth. You can set your own rules. There is no life after death. There are no set moral codes. If you go to bed and if you die it's okay, you're just another piece of matter bouncing around and you'll change into something else. That's why, even if a hundred million scientists say we are unplanned, that we're just purposeless beings in this universe, the general population won't buy it. And neither will I."

❀

Standing out on the steps of the courthouse in the drizzling rain, just a few yards away from Thompson, is Casey Luskin, a lawyer and program officer for Discovery Institute, the Seattle-based think tank that is the premier promoter of ID. Luskin looks like a dejected child trying to keep a stiff upper lip. He's been on the job for only three weeks. This is his first assignment, and it is a huge one. "Talk about trial by fire," he says.

Finally, intelligent design will have its day in court, a chance to air its arguments before millions of Americans in a rigorous, witnessed, head-to-head battle with evolution. But Luskin's first assignment is fraught with dangers. If he weren't such a hopeful person—in fact, such a faithful person—he might even say this assignment was doomed.

From the beginning, this case has evaded Luskin's bosses' control. Discovery, the brains of the ID movement, could only stand by and watch while Thompson confidently steered the case straight toward the thicket of First Amendment issues Discovery had worked so hard developing a strategy to avoid. At least that's the way Discovery tells it.

Luskin is intensely earnest and seems to be working hard at loving his enemies, though in this case it's hard to know just who his real enemies are. They were supposed to be the Darwinists on the case, the legal team for the plaintiffs and their witnesses. But at the moment, he looks more threatened by Thompson, who is now holding forth about how the separation of church and state is a myth, about the conspiracy of scientists and atheists trying to banish God from public space.

No, this case is just not cooperating with Discovery's grand plan. Back in 2004, when Discovery employees first read in the newspapers about the Dover school board's decision to introduce *Pandas* into its high school curriculum, they attempted some damage control. They called Bill Buckingham, then the chairman of the Dover board's curriculum committee, and told him it was a bad idea. Much better than mandating the teaching of ID, Discovery said, would be to recommend teaching *more* evolution in schools, but teaching both the strengths and weaknesses of evolutionary theory. This is the now-famous "teach the controversy" approach (a term borrowed, ironically, from Gerald Graff, a liberal English professor at the University of Illinois at Chicago). Intelligent design, Discovery says, is too young a science to be mandated in the schools. There is insufficient ID curriculum; mandating it would violate individual teachers' academic freedom, and many of those teachers don't agree with or even understand ID, and so shouldn't be forced to teach it.

John G. West, a senior fellow at Discovery and associate director of Discovery's ID wing, the Center for Science and Culture, says that he got the feeling from this early conversation that Buckingham had heard Discovery's message and taken it to heart. Nope.

In October 2004 West learned, again from the newspaper, that Dover was ignoring his advice. The school board had passed an amendment to the curriculum and planned to mandate the reading of a statement questioning the scientific validity of evolution, announcing the existence of competing theories, and making *Pandas* available to students. West and others at Discovery got in touch with board members. It soon became clear, West says, that many of them didn't even know what ID was. They had their own reasons for wanting to teach it in the school, says West. And those reasons were pretty obviously religious ones. When West told Buckingham that they were making a mistake and courting a lawsuit, he says, Buckingham replied that lawyers had assured them that what they were doing was constitutional. Ironically, that assurance came from the Thomas More Law Center, which was relying on material distributed by Discovery Institute.[4]

In December, when Discovery found out that the Thomas More Law Center was representing the Dover board, they called Thompson and tried to change his mind. Unable to do so, they tried damage control again and went public with their objections, issuing a press release urging Dover to repeal its policy. It was ill advised, they said, and they predicted that in all likelihood it would be deemed unconstitutional.

Even though Discovery disagreed with Thompson's approach, it did offer the expert testimony: William Dembski, a mathematician and philosopher and the guru of "specified complexity,"[5] Center for Science and Culture director Stephen Meyer, and University of Memphis rhetorician John Angus Campbell.

Their hope, I suspect, was that even if the Dover policy were to be struck down by the judge because the school board was religiously motivated, strong scientific testimony would still defend and promote the validity of ID itself, independent of the Dover school board's intentions. The world would be watching, as it had been at the Scopes trial, and even if Dover lost the case, as the ACLU had lost Scopes, it could still boost the public perception of ID and its status as an alternative to evolutionary theory.

But when Thompson refused to let Dembski, Meyer, and Campbell testify under the guidance of Discovery's own legal council, Discovery pulled them, leaving Thompson with only two scientist witnesses to promote the scientific credibility of ID: Michael Behe and Scott Minnich.

This all went down after the closure period, so there was no time for Thompson to get new scientific witnesses; not that there would be many qualified scientists out there with any appetite for that job.

Thompson felt betrayed by what he saw as Discovery Institute's pullout, its tactical practicality, its reluctance to throw itself faithfully into the Holy War against evolution.

"We had committed to defending the school board," Thompson later recalls, "which had chosen its curriculum plan based partly on advice it got from Discovery. We had a moral obligation to defend them, but Discovery Institute was thinking strategically, in terms of promoting their own broader policies, not in terms of defending the board members."[6]

Thompson suggests that Discovery was following a tactical pattern it had established earlier in Ohio, where a school board was encouraged to promote ID and then, when controversy arose, backed down to a "teach the controversy" compromise. He says that Discovery may have pulled their witnesses from *Kitzmiller* because the Dover school board wasn't cooperating with that tactic.

There is another possible explanation for Discovery's withdrawal. All of the expert witnesses submitted reports prior to the trial, and they were deposed by the attorneys for the opposing side. So were some of the school board members who would be witnesses for the defense. So each team had a pretty good idea what scientific or philosophical arguments the experts from the other side would make, as well as how well the board members' stories would hold up under examination. Barbara Forrest speculates that Discovery, reading the reports from the plaintiffs' expert witnesses (including herself) and the board members, sensed a crash coming and parachuted out.

Seeing them out there on the courthouse steps, I realize that the differences between Luskin and the Discovery Institute and Thompson and the Thomas More Law Center, let alone the differences between either group and the Dover school board itself, represent another kind of fault line, one predicted by philosopher Robert Pennock in his book *Tower of Babel*.

The "big tent" policy, for which Dad's pal Phillip Johnson mostly gets credit, is, on the one hand, largely responsible for ID's meteoric rise to national prominence; inviting everyone from young-earth creationists to New Age crystal-gazers under the "big tent" of ID by putting off discussions of doctrinal differences, gave the movement its critical mass. It allows educated scientists such as Behe and the folks from Discovery to join forces with Bible-thumping Christians who couldn't care less about irreducible complexity or the fossil record, New Age spiritualists, Raelians (who believe in intelligent design by "our human creators from space"), and anyone else who thinks that the world was designed and that science may have something to say about that possibility. (The only faithful group not welcome under the big tent, as far as I know, is theistic evolutionists. Apparently, you have to be both pro-ID and anti-Darwin; a revealing membership requirement.)

While "big tent" gets much credit for ID's broad base, on the other hand it is those very same glossed-over doctrinal matters that motivate each of the tribes gathered under the tent. When push comes to shove, says Pennock, the Bible thumpers aren't going to give up teaching about Noah's Ark so that pointy-headed guys from the University of Chicago can teach about the strengths and weaknesses of evolutionary theory. Of course young-earthers believe the world was intelligently designed, but that's not the end of it; they also believe it was made by God in six days six thousand years ago and that Jesus saved us from the sins of a literal Adam and Eve. So, says Pennock, while the big tent might get ID into courts and schools, once there, those loaded doctrinal differences may rip big holes in the canvas and may even bring the whole tent down.

I wonder whether what's happening here in Harrisburg may foreshadow the fate of that faulty alliance. Certainly some differences on the ID side are pretty stark in this case, even just on these courthouse steps. If the plaintiffs' story is right, it seems that teaching alternative theories of biology in Dover is more about giving Jesus his due, and showing why he would have been an American, than about anything more theoretical or scientific. The defendants' testimony may prove otherwise, but from what I've seen and read so far, they don't seem to care much about the ability of natural selection to explain the rise of species or the evolution of the bacterial flagellum.

Their chief counsel, Thompson, sympathizes with the school board's religious and patriotic concerns. He may be more educated and sophisticated than they are, but they are all on the same page of *Pandas* when it comes to teaching religion in school: they think it should be legal.

The scientists at Discovery have a different set of concerns. Though many are evangelicals and Biblical literalists, those I have talked to would rather let evolution stay in the science classroom than see the story of Adam and Eve replace it there.

I back through the throng of reporters and cameramen, away from the orating Thompson, and walk the few yards across the courthouse steps over to Luskin. The physical antithesis of Richard Thompson, at twenty-eight he's solitary, short, dark-haired, and thick-eyebrowed, looks like a teenager, and compensates for his youthful appearance by quickly letting people know that he is both a lawyer and a geologist.

I ask him what he thinks about the trial, and he seems eager and happy for the attention and the chance to talk. Before launching into his critique of the plaintiffs' position, Luskin reminds me that Discovery does not and never did stand behind the Dover school board's policy.

Fashioning ID into something legally teachable has been one of Discovery's highest priorities, he says, but they recognize that it has to be done carefully and gradually. The last thing Discovery wants right now is to rush into and lose the first legal test of ID's scientific status. Whereas the grandstanding Thompson may like the idea that this is the Scopes trial II, Discovery hates the analogy. They have worked hard to reform the image of God-friendly science from the primitive, anti-intellectual creationism embraced in Tennessee to a more sophisticated, buttoned-down, and mainstream one. There are several problems with this case from Discovery's point of view, but the fact that the Dover school board is made up of more than its share of ordinary folk who just love God and country, and don't give a hoot about science, is a big one.

The Seattle-based think tank has been remarkably successful at promoting the public perception that ID is a valid scientific theory and an alternative to evolution. In the months before this trial, ID has been everywhere from the lips of President George W. Bush, who said on national TV about ID and evolution that "both sides ought to be properly taught," to the pen of Cardinal Schönborn, close adviser to Pope Benedict, who suggested in July 2005 that maybe the new Pope was taking a second look at the Vatican's embrace of evolution. In one week that summer ID was on the covers of *Time, The New Republic, The American Spectator,* and *The Onion!* That same week, the *New York Times* published a four-part series on science and religion, largely focusing on ID and including major coverage of Discovery Institute. Fifty books and a several DVDs promoting ID theory have been produced by Discovery fellows. It may be one of the great promotional and public relations accomplishments of the twenty-first century.

Nonetheless, the pollsters and analysts at Discovery don't think ID is yet ready to be pushed in the schools. Too many teachers still don't understand it, and it is still too closely associated with Biblical creationism, they say. There's too great a danger of backlash. Much, much better, says Luskin, to promote academic freedom and let teachers carry ID into the classroom on their own later, rather than forcing them to take it there now.

Luskin's bosses back in Seattle must be wringing their hands like nervous parents. They are used to calling the shots, but the complex and delicate rhetorical, PR, and legal machine they've designed over the past several years has been turned over to Richard Thompson, a self-righteous, ideologically driven, scientifically and philosophically naïve lawyer with a chip on his shoulder the size of Plymouth Rock. And if Thompson uses their finely tuned, poll-driven, tactical arguments as blunt instruments to attack evolution here in the Harrisburg court, they may lose years of work and Discovery's biggest achievement.

CHAPTER SIX

ID HEAVY AND THE WEDGE

RICHARD THOMPSON: "Your belief is that this Wedge strategy,
which you have outlined in detail during your direct examination,
is there to create a theocratic state?"
BARBARA FORREST: "I think if the goals of the Wedge strategy were
fulfilled, that is what we would have."

iscovery Institute was formed in 1990 by conservative political theorist and writer Bruce Chapman, techno-guru George
Gilder, and philosopher Stephen Meyer as a think tank dedicated to promoting innovative but politically conservative approaches
to issues such as transportation, technology, and bioethics. For its first
five years Discovery sought a defining mission; it finally found one in the
mid-1990s in the work of Phillip Johnson. First through his writing and
then in person, Johnson helped the founders identify a common theme in
their work that could, they thought, be the seed of something important.
And fundable. That seed was antimaterialism; the mind-over-matter,
information-first, theistic metaphysics that underlies the ID worldview.
Very compelling to all of them, naturally, was the impact that staging an
intellectual battle royal between matter and mind would have on an

American culture that they believed to be rotting from the core. (The "mind" here refers to the "mind" of the intelligent designer and translates roughly to the idea that the IDer must have had an idea, blueprint, or design of the world before He made a material version of that idea in the world we know. Stephen Meyer later told me that the Center for Science and Culture was "essentially a mind-over-matter think tank.")

In 1996, Discovery got a three-year $750,000 grant from Howard Ahmanson, the evangelical, creationist, super-conservative southern California banking billionaire. That grant, along with another from the MacLellan Foundation—which, according to its Website, supports "organizations committed to the infallibility of the Scripture, to Jesus Christ as Lord and Savior, and to the fulfillment of the Great Commission: 'Therefore go and make disciples of all nations, baptizing them in the name of the Father and of the Son and of the Holy Spirit,'"—led to the birth of the Discovery Institute's Center for the Renewal of Science and Culture (CRSC).

Chapman, who'd served in Ronald Reagan's administration as director of the Census Bureau and had been a Seattle City Council member as well as a fellow at the conservative Hudson Institution, remained Discovery's president. Meyer, a Cambridge-trained philosopher of science and former professor at Whitworth, a Christian college in Spokane, was made CRSC's director.

The omnipresent Phillip Johnson, naturally, was also key in the formation of the CRSC, and his fingerprints are all over it. The Center's founding document could have been excerpted from one of Johnson's early books. It calls for challenging neo-Darwinian theory, cultivating and promoting ID, studying the influence of materialism on modern culture, and encouraging schools to teach the controversies within evolutionary biology as well as the theory's strengths.

In the decade since, the baby has far outgrown its father, and the CRSC—which, at some point dropped the R (for Renewal) from its name in order, one would assume, to make less explicit its commitment to restoring a premodern worldview, becoming simply the Center for Science and

Culture (CSC)—put Discovery on the national map. In fact, it put Discovery all over the national map. Today, the CSC is hands-down Discovery's number-one project.

The Center for Science and Culture funds forty fellows (one is a woman), and it has an annual operating fund of about $1.3 million. There is not a lot of bench science going on among Discovery's fellows—I asked Meyer for a list of ID scientists doing real biology and he's still not gotten back to me with any names beyond Scott Minnich and Michael Behe. For the most part, Discovery fellows are theorists, philosophers, mathematicians, and engineers who are, in Meyer's words, "laying the theoretical groundwork" for the intelligent design movement. Whether they have paved the way for a scientific revolution or not, they have unquestionably brought about a revolution in public perception; they have made ID a household acronym, and have given an eccentric theory an aura, in some circles anyway, of intellectual and scientific credibility.

A now-famous fundraising memo, leaked by a copy-store clerk who posted it to the Web in 1999, says a lot about the CSC that underlies its button-down establishment image. Here is the beginning of "The Wedge" document, as it is called:

> The proposition that human beings are created in the image of God is one of the bedrock principles on which Western civilization was built. Its influence can be detected in most, if not all, of the West's greatest achievements, including representative democracy, human rights, free enterprise, and progress in the arts and sciences.
>
> Yet a little over a century ago, this cardinal idea came under wholesale attack by intellectuals drawing on the discoveries of modern science. Debunking the traditional conceptions of both God and man, thinkers such as Charles Darwin, Karl Marx, and Sigmund Freud portrayed humans not as moral and spiritual beings, but as animals or machines who inhabited a universe ruled by purely impersonal forces and whose behavior and very thoughts were dictated by the unbending forces of biology, chemistry, and environment. This materialistic conception of reality eventually infected virtually every area of our culture, from politics and economics to literature and art.

The cultural consequences of this triumph of materialism were devastating. Materialists denied the existence of objective moral standards, claiming that environment dictates our behavior and beliefs. Such moral relativism was uncritically adopted by much of the social sciences, and it still undergirds much of modern economics, political science, psychology and sociology.

It's called "The Wedge" after the CSC's strategy for bringing down the "giant tree" of "materialistic science" by forcing into it a " 'wedge' that, while relatively small, can split the trunk when applied at its weakest points." At the thin edge of the wedge, the document goes on to say, were Johnson's and Behe's early critiques of Darwinism. The Center for Science and Culture has broadened it with "a positive scientific alternative to materialistic scientific theories . . . intelligent design (ID) . . . which promises to reverse the stifling dominance of the materialist worldview, and to replace it with a science consonant with Christian and theistic convictions."

The strategy breaks into three phases the task of felling the oak tree of Western modernism. First, the research phase, during which the Center supports the work of pro-ID scientists and philosophers and writers and gets them to publish their work about the "pressure points . . . most likely to crack the materialist edifice."

Second, the "publicity and opinion-making" phase, during which CSC will "prepare the popular reception of our ideas" by seeking to "cultivate and convince influential individuals in print and broadcast media, as well as think tank leaders, scientists and academics, congressional staff, talk show hosts, college and seminary presidents and faculty, future talent and potential academic allies."

In addition, the CSC will "also seek to build up a popular base of support among our natural constituency, namely, Christians. . . . We intend to encourage and equip believers with new scientific evidence's [sic] that support the faith, as well as to 'popularize' our ideas in the broader culture."

Finally, phase three of "The Wedge" is called "Cultural Confrontation and Renewal." "Once our research and writing have had time to mature," it reads, "and the public is prepared for the reception of design theory, we will move toward direct confrontation with the advocates of materialist science. . . . We will also pursue possible legal assistance in response to resistance to the integration of design theory into public school science curricula. The attention, publicity, and influence of design theory should draw scientific materialists into open debate with design theorists, and we will be ready. With an added emphasis to the social sciences and humanities, we will begin to address the specific social consequences of materialism and the Darwinist theory that supports it in the sciences."

Whatever you think of ID, you have to admire the impressive degree to which CSC has made good on its fundraising promises. Phases one and two were mostly completed on schedule, by 2003. As predicted, Darwinists were drawn out into "open debate with design theorists." And from a rhetorical if not evidentiary point of view, the design theorists were ready, and they succeeded in putting one of science's most powerful theories and constituencies on the defensive.

The part about giving legal assistance to those trying to integrate design theory into public school science curricula on the surface sounds like *Kitzmiller*. But from Discovery's point of view, it was just too soon. Thompson, though, is trying to bring the legal fight on. In fact, Thomas More Law Center attorneys had been visiting school boards around the country looking for one willing to take on an ID case.

Discovery Institute plays down the importance of the Wedge document, saying it was designed to raise money, not to express the core mission of the Institute or even to be a policy directive. That's hard to believe, though, given how closely the Wedge conforms to the actual game plan adopted by CSC.

Philosopher Barbara Forrest, who will soon testify for the plaintiffs, calls "The Wedge" "the best, most concise statement of what the movement is about in its entirety." The graphic design of the original Wedge document features a pyramid (the wedge, I suppose) thrusting up between Michelangelo's Sistine Chapel image of Adam and God reaching for one another. It stains the movement with a kind of revolutionary, secret-brotherhood-of-Illuminati conspiracy tint that Discovery just hasn't been able to wash out.

Luskin is new at Discovery, but his credentials make him a natural for the job. A lawyer with a science background, he's both Jewish by heritage and Christian by choice. In college Luskin cofounded an ID group called the IDEA (Intelligent Design and Evolution Awareness) Club. He formed the first chapter after seeing Phillip Johnson talk in 1999 when he was studying geology at UC San Diego. The club now has twenty-five chapters.

Luskin says that while his religion is very important to him, science is, too. And for him, the two don't mix. That's why people such as William Dembski have gone to such great lengths to make the study of intelligent design rigorous and evidence-based, he says. "We're not asking to be exempt from the rules of science, we just want science to be able to look objectively at the evidence for and against design."

Discovery tries, to its credit I think, to separate the intellectual, philosophical, and scientific aspects of its study from the religious ones. To do so without offending the religious sensibilities of its funders is a sharp line to walk sometimes. This approach is seen by ID's opponents as cynical, an effort to hide the true *raison d'être* for the work.

That's an especially frustrating accusation for Luskin. "We are criticized for being religious," he says, "which no one should have to apologize for. And on the other hand, we're criticized for being careful to keep our religion out of this work. People say we're hiding it. From our critics' point of view, we can't win when it comes to our religious views."

Out on the courthouse steps in the rain after the trial's first day, I ask Luskin if resorting to supernatural explanations isn't a violation of what has been one of the main tenets of science since the Enlightenment.

"I'm not a philosopher of science, or a historian—and anyway I hear there is no consensus among them on the question of methodological naturalism. But I do have a background in science, and there is nothing about ID that *requires* the IDer to be supernatural."

"You mean the intelligent designer could be natural?" I ask.

"That's possible," he says.

"What would a natural designer be like?" I ask. Luskin refers to Michael Behe, who has said maybe it's the God of Christianity, or an angel, or Plato's demi-urge, or some mystical New Age force, or space aliens from Alpha Centauri, or time travelers, or some so far completely unknown intelligent being.

"But there is no way that ID or any science can say anything about the designer, natural or supernatural, other than that there is evidence of his intelligence," says Luskin.

Now *this* is getting interesting! I, who do not buy ID, want to argue that it is illogical for Luskin to claim that science can't say anything substantial about the designer, despite the assertion that "He" could be part of nature. Whereas Luskin, who believes in an intelligent designer, and in science's ability to detect His handiwork, argues that nothing can be said about Him. Even if the designer is outside this universe as we now know it, and is not bound by our natural laws, there's still no justification I can see for claiming that a rigorous application of science could never say anything substantial about the intelligent designer. No one knows what tools science will have at its disposal in future millennia or what its limits will be, but if there is a designer it seems disingenuous to insist that ID could never give up the goods on the Big Guy, whomever or whatever He is.

When I press Luskin on this, he acknowledges "it's not literally impossible that ID might one day be able to tell us something about the nature of the designer. But for now," he says, "there's no evidence that it will be able to. You don't see on the flagellum stamped anywhere, 'I was made by a natural designer, I was made by Yahweh, I was made by Yoda, or I was made by a spiritual or cosmic force.' All you see is the informational signature that indicates a designer. I don't see how you'd ever be able to say, from that informational signature,[1] anything about the nature of the designer."

Well, if the designer is natural, certainly we might be able to learn its identity and a thing or two about Him. Those scientists who today deal with absent intelligent designers of the only kind we know much about—people—draw conclusions about them all the time. Physical anthropologists, for example, can tell a lot about the designer and the designer's culture and way of life from a simple shard of pottery. Or at least they say they can.

Luskin's argument might reflect Discovery's political strategy and a widespread theological assumption, but there's nothing scientific about it.

While Discovery wants to establish, with the authority of science, that a designer must exist (or that it looks like there's a pretty good chance that the designer does exist), speculating about the designer's nature would put them in trouble with two kinds of law: the U.S. Constitution (because the first hypothesis might be that the designer was their own God, and saying so would make them a religious organization) and Divine law. Unless they're sure the IDer is their God, looking into it risks an idolatrous violation of the First Commandment: You Shall Have No Other Gods Before Me.

Centuries ago, when someone found a shard of ancient pottery, they might have thought, "Wow there must have been people living here a long time ago, too bad we'll never be able to know anything about them." But today, anthropologists conclude all kinds of things about the intelligent designers who made the pottery: how long ago they lived, what they ate, what kinds of technologies they employed, and maybe even what kinds of things they cared about. If IDers are detecting evidence of design in the world, then it seems rash for them to say they'll never be able to draw any conclusions from that evidence.

"We don't know, and we don't really care to know, what science can tell us about the designer," would seem the prudent response. But that's a lot different than holding that nothing could ever be said.

"I'll grant you the possibility that some day, if evidence leads that way, it's conceivable that we could learn something about the designer," Luskin says. "But that's kind of beside the point. That's not what ID is about. That's not what it's looking for."

As our discussion heats up, a few people wander over to join Luskin and me. One of them is Giulio Meotti, a tall, curly haired, carefully dressed young reporter for the Italian paper *Il Foglio*. He is nodding thoughtfully as

Luskin and I debate, but I have no idea whose side of the argument Meotti is on or if he can even follow what we're saying.

I tell Luskin it is disingenuous to say that IDers just don't care about the nature of the designer. All studies of intelligent design, from psychology to anthropology to forensics and even to NASA's SETI (Search for Extraterrestrial Life) program, are interested in finding intelligence because they want to know *about* the designer not just *that* the designer exists.

Now Luskin is getting hot under the collar. When he furrows his brow, as he is doing now, his eyebrows come together like two big black magnets in the center of his forehead. He didn't say IDers didn't *care* about the nature of the designer, he tells me. He himself cares a great deal, and he is proud to say that he believes the designer is the Christian God and that it is possible to learn a lot about him—just not through science. He learns about God in other ways, through his personal relationship with Him or through his religious practice.

I tell him that's like stem-cell researchers saying that developing embryonic stem-cell technologies won't promote human cloning because the scientists agree that they don't want to do that anyway. It doesn't follow. If you're going to be logical and scientific about finding evidence of God in the natural world, then you've just got to be open to the possibility that you might learn more than your religion says you ought to know.

The theological resistance to the idea that the intelligent designer could be studied and known through science is shared by creationists, Biblical literalists, Christian evolutionists, agnostics, and atheists, too. It is a basic tenet of the Judeo-Christian faiths (and a truism to atheists) that God isn't in our material world, unless, for the theists, He sends His Son here or drops in to commit miracles—which I must say I don't really understand because those seem like very big and hard-to-explain exceptions. (If science could work fast enough, could it study God, for instance, while He was here doing a miracle?)

I'm sure Discovery realizes, too, that the promise of getting the vitals of the designer wouldn't do much to sell ID to the public either. Frankly, it's scary. What if they discovered that the intelligent designer was a Hindu, or a libertarian, or how about an alien TV producer using us as a pilot for a kind of *Truman Show*—like series? Much better then, from a political and theological point of view, to just say you think you've established that there is a Creator and all you know, and all you "can" know, about Him is that He is intelligent.

And then, you can always go on to say that you've got this book, say the Bible, and though you can't prove via science that it goes together with your scientifically established intelligent designer, without evidence (or the possibility of finding it) to the contrary, it might be safe and reasonable to assume that connection.

This, as we will later see, is political dynamite wrapped up in plain brown paper.

I think Luskin and I like each other. Anyway, I like him and like that he let me at least feel that I won our argument and that even though he got kind of riled up, he never resorted to telling me that if I didn't get my act together, I would spend eternity in Hell. I say goodbye to Luskin and join the gaggle of reporters still clustered around Thompson.

A question pops into my head.

"Counselor," I ask Thompson, "if the limits of science aren't hard and fast, do you think it's possible that science could one day discover that the stories found in the Bible are true?"

Thompson thinks for a moment and then says, "Sure."

"And if that happened, would it be okay to teach Genesis in high school biology class?"

He pauses a little longer this time. "I guess," he says. "Yes. Theoretically."

I wish I'd looked over at Luskin just then. I bet I would have seen one very dense unibrow, and one very expressive cringe, the kind an earnest, science-leaning evangelical lawyer makes when he sees a delicately constructed and elaborate house of cards being knocked to the ground.

Apparently the Italian reporter, Giulio Meotti, and I are gluttons for pun-ishment. After the impromptu press conference, we stand around in the rain and chat a little longer. He's perceptive and very smart; in that amazing and annoying European way, he knows more about American politics than I do.

Turns out he understood everything Luskin and I were saying. He finds my *Truman Show* idea funny; Ed Harris, in a beret and round glasses, over-sees everything from his swiveling Aeron chair behind the moon. It's actu-ally a strangely appealing thought, and it makes sense of a lot of things I wonder about: why I'm me, for instance? What are the chances of that? And why I'm at the center of the drama so much of the time; and why the moon sometimes looks so unnaturally big; and why my wife stays with me even though she could do much better; and how a limited casting budget would explain why I see people I know all over the place. "If it's the *Slack Show*," I say, "that would also explain why my father found Christ and I found Dar-win; to pump up the dramatic tension."

"The *Slack Show?*" says Meotti. "No, no, no, no. It's the *Meotti Show!*" We're laughing now. I walk him to the Crowne Plaza Hotel, which is on the way to the Comfort Inn, my own crusty trusty hotel with iffy wireless.

I don't know what makes me think of it, but I suddenly remember a time, several years before, when I prayed as if I believed in God. Leo, my two-and-a-half-year-old son, was lying in a bed in the ICU at Children's Hospital in Oakland: tubes in his nose, needles in his arms, heart monitors on his little chest. The helmet he'd been wearing for the past couple of weeks hung over the back of a chair. For weeks he'd been racked by uncon-trollable seizures and now, due to an allergic reaction to one of his medica-tions, his pancreas was digesting itself in one of the most painful diseases in the human repertoire. For an hour, I stood over him watching him breath, trying to burn his perfect face into my memory.

Is he going to die? my seven-year-old, Jonah, had asked the doctor a few hours before. He might, was all she would say.

I was beyond desperate, long ago drained of tears. That night I said a prayer, the only one I ever delivered as if someone might really be listening.

It was consoling, I suppose, though not enough to let me sleep.

84

CHAPTER SEVEN

DOWN BY LAW

PHILLIP JOHNSON: "People of differing theological views should learn who's close to them, form alliances, and put aside divisive issues until later. After we have settled the issue of a creator, we'll have a wonderful time arguing about the age of the earth."

atthew Chapman rented this black Taurus in Manhattan just a couple of days ago but it is already festooned with crushed coffee cups and maps and books and receipts. We are driving south toward Dover, and as we pass through the Harrisburg city limits on State Highway 83, Giulio Meotti sits quietly, folded into the back seat like a praying mantis, his small reporter's notebook in his pincers. Someone has to sit back there, and Giulio is twenty years younger than I am and thirty years younger than Matthew, and besides, it's Matthew's car. As usual, Giulio is stylishly dressed in a tie, wool slacks, a cashmere sweater, and shiny-black lace-up shoes.

Matthew is Manhattan chic, wearing black jeans, a T-shirt, and a black leather blazer, and telling us about his fifteen-year-old daughter, Anna Bella Charles Darwin Teixeira Chapman. She is spoiled, he supposes, takes their high life, which he works "like hell" as a screenwriter to sustain, for granted.

She goes to an elite Manhattan girls' school. Very "white glove" he says. But she is so curious, so beautiful, so funny, and so intoxicatingly delightful that being spoiled hardly matters. "She is the meaning of my life," he says.

"The meaning *off* my *live*," Giulio repeats, sotto voce, from the back seat. Giulio's English is good, but he sometimes repeats phrases this way as if trying to commit them to memory.

Meaning. Meaning of my life. What is the meaning of *my* life? I sympathize with Matthew; my two sons are the apples of my eye. But the meaning of my life? My mind fumbles this question each time it tries to catch it. The great twentieth-century philosopher Ludwig Wittgenstein said that the urge to ask the question about life's meaning is a mistake we're led to make more by an accident of grammar (because it makes sense to ask about the meaning of a word, we think it makes sense to ask about the meaning of a life) than by the promise, or even the possibility, of a satisfactory answer. But if there is a Darwinian answer to the question of life's meaning—and Matthew is not only a Darwinian, he is a Darwin, Charles Darwin's great-great-grandson—it is fitting that he should find it in his daughter, the inheritor of half his genes.

Matthew, Giulio, and I met only two days ago. Matthew is on assignment from *Harper's* and I'm writing a pair of stories for *Salon.com,* an online magazine based in San Francisco. Giulio's paper is a neoconservative Italian daily called *Il Foglio*. In the last several days, by the time we are driving to Dover together, he has already filed four fifteen-thousand-word reports. That's beyond prolific, and intimidating. After our conversation yesterday, when we laughed so hard about the *Truman Show*, I'm surprised when Giulio tells me that his editors at *Il Foglio* are pro-ID, and that he does not disagree with their orientation.

We've turned off of Highway 83 and are now on the smaller, meandering State Highway 93. It has rained a little, but is clearing, and the bucolic landscape we're rolling through is alive and lovely. It is late September so the cornfields are brown, but the leaves in the trees are beginning to color and everything seems to be glowing a little.

"Don't your editors believe in evolution?" I ask Giulio.

"Yes, they believe it," he says. "They know evolution is right. Of course! They know ID is *stupido,* not good science. But these Born Again people are amazing; they are free, they care, and they pray every day. In Italy, this could never happen. You are l-u-c-k-y," Giulio says. "Believe me, America is lucky."

The issue for Giulio—as for Phillip Johnson and for the Discovery characters who wrote the Wedge Document, and for Richard Thompson—is cultural relativism. Giulio, who is "Catholic, of course," he says, but not himself religious, sees the erosion of strong, enduring values as posing the greatest danger to Italian culture, and Western Civilization as a whole. The antidote: widespread belief in God. Belief in the absolute burns off relativism and concentrates strong moral convictions, Giulio says.

But this is absurd, I argue. Religious truths are much more relative than scientific ones. They change all the time. Sometimes it's okay to stone adulterers and sometimes it's not. Sometimes it's "turn the other cheek" and sometimes it's "an eye for an eye." Sometimes polygamy is legal and encouraged, sometimes it's one of the worst sins around. And that's all within one religion, Christianity. If you look across religions, it varies even more. What's enduring about that?

Well, the creationists in Dover are definitely moral absolutists, Giulio says, whereas Italy is a country where "no one really believes anything." The Born Again conviction is "beautiful." Moreover, he says, the creationists are antimaterialists. By that he doesn't mean that they don't like to acquire stuff—Giulio does like to acquire stuff, he says—but that they don't believe that the whole calzone of the universe is explicable as, or reducible to, configurations of matter alone. That kind of philosophical materialism, the signature of science-oriented leftist icons from Richard Dawkins to Karl Marx and Sigmund Freud, is equally anathema, apparently, to both intellectual Italian neocons like Giulio and anti-intellectual American creationists.

And Charles Darwin, the father of evolutionary theory, is the High Priest and Chief Enabler of modern materialism, or so says Giulio.

He and his neoconservative editors, and the Bush administration, and the whole ID crowd share the conviction that the restoration of moral absolutes is a do-or-die proposition. "Neo-Darwinian culture is just the mask for atheism," says Giulio, "it's the door for relativism, euthanasia, embryo manipulation, and genetic engineering to enter. That will lead us to Aldous Huxley's Hell."[1]

"Born Again culture has saved the United States from cultural desolation, moral relativism, and empty politics—the European destiny," he says. "I don't believe in intelligent design theory as science, but it doesn't matter. The crucial point is that science alone shouldn't be able to decide the meaning of education or tell people what to think about the origin of life."

❧

Locally, Highway 93 is called East Canal Street, a country road dotted with silos, picturesque farmhouses, and newer, less charming ranch-style houses. By my counting, the ratio of American flags to churches is about three to one, but there are lots and lots of both. As we enter the tiny town of Dover, East Canal Street narrows and turns into West Canal, and we pass the Bingo Hall ("500-dollar jackpots every Monday night!"), the Tiny Blessings Daycare Center, and Classic Arms, a little gun shop. We're looking for the high school, where we hope to see for ourselves the frontline trench du jour in America's cultural war.

A cameraman and a reporter had the same idea and are roving the sidewalk across the street from the school. Another man, maybe their producer, is scurrying after a tall, lanky kid who's taking long quick strides away from the group. We drive onto the high school parking lot, climb out of the Taurus, and wave down a red Camaro rolling slowly by the school's entrance. The woman inside is Cathy Unger, mom of two Dover High students, a freshman and a senior. She looks young enough to be in high school herself, and Matthew tells her so. She smiles shyly and agrees to give us a minute.

"What do you think about evolution?" Matthew asks.

"Not much," she says, poking at the bobble-headed football player on her dashboard.

"How about intelligent design? Do you think it should be taught here in the high school?"

Giulio has appeared on the far side of her car and is looking in the passenger window with his little pad.

"Honestly, I don't know much about either one," she says. "But I don't think we come from apes. And I don't see why that's the only thing teachers should be allowed to tell my children."

"If humans didn't evolve, where did we come from?" I ask.

"There's only one way the world could be made, and that's by God," she says. "I don't need everyone to believe that, but that's what I believe."

"And you know you're not supposed to be on school property," she says, ending the interview by putting up her windows and driving away.

We have broken the ice, and the three of us call after her gratefully, "Thanks." "Bye." "Ciao." She throws back a dismissive little wave.

As the Camaro rumbles off, a gaggle of about twenty girls in running shorts comes around the corner of the high school. The three of us head instinctively toward them like sharks. They veer away from us, equally instinctively, like an alarmed school of fish, and begin heading back toward the athletic field.

We catch up to their coach, who reaffirms that we're not supposed to be hunting for interviews on school grounds, that we are trespassing, and that the police could be called. Could we maybe talk to some of the girls across the street where it is legal, I ask? Tentatively, the coach, who won't tell us her name, agrees and asks one of the girls, Natalie, if she wants to talk to us. Natalie says okay, and we meet them twenty minutes later at KT Pizza, the local high school hangout.

Natalie is a serious girl with blond hair just long enough for a ponytail, blue eyes, and freckles. As we introduce ourselves, she looks from one of us to the next as if we're from various foreign worlds. She's not heard of *Harper's* nor *Salon.com,* let alone *Il Foglio*. Soon enough, though, she relaxes and starts to tell us about herself. She is a freshman, and in addition to running cross-country she is also a cheerleader. She stopped going to church with her family a couple of years ago, though she still sometimes accompanies friends.

"Believe it or not," she says, leaning toward us, "kids I know don't really care much whether we're read a statement about design or whatever during biology class. What's the difference?" she laughs. "Nobody's really listening anyway."

More important, she says, leaning back in her chair, "the news is giving the world the wrong idea of Dover," and here she throws a conspiratorial glance at her coach, who's sitting next to her. "It's not a backward, Bible-thumping place," she says. "At least it isn't *just* that. There's lots of different kinds of students here; not just Christians. We've got Mennonites, Muslims, Catholics. And there are lots and lots of other things happening here besides the school board's evolution thing," she says.

"What, for instance?" Giulio asks, breaking his silence.

"Like the high school sports program. Our cross-country team is really excellent. And the school has one of the best marching bands in the area."

We say goodbye to Natalie and push deeper into the pizza parlor asking kids what they think of the controversy. There is a wide range of religious conviction and metaphysical interpretation, but when it comes down to it, nobody we talk to either cares much about evolution or thinks the plaintiffs' lawsuit is worth all the trouble it's stirred up here.

"I don't see why it's a big deal," says Stephen Hampton, sixteen, who wants to be an airplane pilot. "I think it's all kind of dumb. Evolution can't be proven and God can't be proven, so they should teach both. Personally, I don't think we were ever monkeys; people were created by God. But other people think it was Darwin's evolution. So they should teach both."

So this is the front line of America's culture war: pimply kids who don't have the foggiest idea, or care much, if at all, what natural selection or "irreducible complexity" are, let alone which one suggests a better explanation for the diversity of life on earth.

Disheartened by the apathy, Giulio, Matthew, and I order some pepperoni slices and decide to drive west a few more miles to the Dover Volunteer Fire Department stationhouse, where, I'd been told, Kent Hovind will be speaking tonight. Hovind, or Dr. Dino, as his devotees call him, is a notorious young-earth creationist lecturer who also created and runs

Dinosaur Adventure Land, a creationist theme park in Pensacola, Florida, "a place where dinosaurs and the Bible meet." I'd heard about Hovind; his crude attacks on evolution are an embarrassment even to many other young-earth creationists.

So I am disappointed when at the front of the firehouse assembly stands, instead of Hovind, a nineteen-inch TV sitting on a cart with a VCR. Next to the setup is Pastor Jim Grove, a short, bearded, wiry, sixty-five-year-old preacher whom I'd seen handing out fliers at the Federal Court-house in Harrisburg earlier in the week. Grove, wearing a tight blue polyester suit, introduces the Hovind video to the 150 in attendance (at least six of whom were reporters) by recounting the "legal travesty" in Harris-burg, where scientists are "brainwashing" the court.

"First was Dr. Fluffdoodle," Grove says, referring to Kenneth Miller, the author of *Biology,* who had earlier held the courtroom in thrall with his explanation of evolution. He calls Robert Pennock, the Michigan State philosopher and the author of *Tower of Babel: The Evidence Against the New Cre-ationism,* "Dr. Flapping Lips." And of John Haught, a recently retired pro-fessor of theology at Georgetown University, and the author of thirteen books, including *God After Darwin* and *Science and Religion in Search of Cos-mic Purpose,* Grove says, "well, he's no theologian, I'll tell you that right now, *because he doesn't have the body of Christ!*" "Amens" rise up from the spir-ited crowd.

Pastor Grove is famous in these parts for an anti-abortion float he rides in York's annual Halloween parade. His float, which he calls "Dr. Butcher's Chop Shop of Choice Cuts," features mutilated body parts and fake bloody fetuses in various stages of development. Town leaders banned the float from the parade one year so he brought a First Amendment suit against the town and won. Now his gruesome floats are an annual tradition and have a kind of cult following on both sides of the debate.

"The more degrees these scientists get, the further it seems they get from God," Grove tells the firehouse full of people.

He presses "play" and Kent Hovind's video starts: "I believe evolution is one of the dumbest and most dangerous religions in the world," says

Hovind. The universe was made in six days, he asserts, and evolution "simply does not make sense. . . . Have you ever seen order come out of a big bang? No. It's just stupid." Hovind's argument has two main thrusts: Anyone who has half a brain (and if that half brain hasn't been "washed" by a university or a high school teaching it evolution) can see that Darwin's theory of natural selection is just ridiculous. You can't make something complex and beautiful and alive out of something simple and ugly and dead. Second, the Bible is true. "I believe every word," he says, "even the cover."

Dr. Dino is not making apologies or bridging divides between believers and nonbelievers. "There is a war going on in our culture," he says. "One side says that God made man, and the other side says that man made God. Darwinism leads someplace," he continues, "and that place is atheism.

"Trying to reconcile evolution and the Bible is like trying to ride two horses galloping in opposite directions at the same time. It's dangerous. Don't do it." (This part of the argument could be coming from Richard Dawkins, the Oxford University evolutionary biologist and the world's most famous out-of-the-closet atheist.)

The video goes on and on explaining how Noah's Ark has been found in Turkey, how the plants and animals appeared in their final form six thousand years ago, and how Darwinism is responsible for Nazism and the Holocaust, the Khmer Rouge, and Stalin's pogroms, how evolution is no more than an elaborate but still transparent ruse perpetrated by corrupt, stupid, and cynical biologists.

From across the table, Matthew throws me a sad smile as if to say, perhaps we *have* found the front lines of the culture war after all. Who but cultural warriors would come out through the rain on a Thursday night to sit in uncomfortable folding chairs for hours just to throw dung at Matthew's great-great-grandfather? The parishioners laugh aloud nearly every time Hovind says, about some scientific assertion, "Now that's just stupid!"

I look around for Giulio and he is gone. Has he run away? For me Hovind's performance is just painful anthropology—Hovind's view is as exotic a perspective as might come from a member of a New Guinea cargo cult—but Giulio came here with a great deal of hope riding on the integrity of American fundamentalists. "Born-Again culture has saved the U.S. from the European destiny," he'd argued earnestly in the car. "Italy is sinking in cultural desolation, moral relativism, and political emptiness. America is still alive."

Apparently a commitment to traditional values is one thing, and a self-righteous celebration of ignorance like Hovind's performance is another. And after squirming in his chair for over an hour, Giulio has fled into the moist night air for a good old filter-free European cigarette.

So when the lights come up and the discussion begins, Giulio is absent. The audience loved the video, that much is clear from the applause and the amens that follow it.

"That *Kitzmiller* trial: the ACLU, the American *Communist Liberation Union,* is doing this to us," someone yells. "They get a million dollars from the government every time they bring a suit like this. They're chasing God out of this country. But it's God's country and we're going to keep Him here."

"They're Satan," someone else cries out.

One mild-mannered and well-groomed fellow in a button-down oxford shirt stands out in the middle of the crowd. He has note cards spread out before him, and when Pastor Grove points to him, he clears his throat and then comes to evolution's defense, saying that it underlies advances in modern medicine from antibiotics to the study of new diseases such as West Nile virus and avian flu. If you take advantage of those advances it seems hypocritical to deny and insult their heritage, he says. Catcalls come from parishioners as he tries to talk; "Brainwashed," someone yells, and the young man's defense of Darwin is interrupted by Pastor Grove, who quickly brings the evening to an end. On the way out, though, I introduce myself to the young man and get his card. Dr. Burt C. Humburg is his name and he is an internist at the Penn State Medical Center in Hershey, about thirty-five miles northeast of Dover. He tells me he grew up in a fundamentalist community like this, scared to death of what an eternity in hell would be like.

"It's fear; all fear," he says. "The thing is, there actually are a lot of things in the world to be afraid of. But Hell isn't one of them."

By the time we get back into the car I am despondent. "If we believe absurdities we shall commit atrocities," said Voltaire. And it seemed that despite Dr. Humburg's efforts to administer antivenin in response to the absurdities spread by Hovind's tape, the parishioners were determined to ignore him. What atrocities will follow if the most powerful nation in the history of the world embraces the absurdities we've seen tonight?

In an essay titled "Welcome to Doomsday," PBS commentator Bill Moyers points to a *Newsweek* poll that shows 36 percent of respondents believing in the Book of Revelation as "true prophecy." Another, more recent Pew poll, found that one out of five Americans believes that Jesus will return, bringing the Rapture with Him, in their own lifetimes. When He does, the saved will ascend to the right hand of God and watch in comfort as the rest of us suffer the plagues of boils, sores, locusts, and frogs for the years of tribulation that follow. For those in the know, this is a most welcome thing, a cause for jubilation. It marks the completion of the world, not the end of it.

Those who believe in the Revelation don't believe the world itself can be saved, Moyers points out. For them, the world is destined to go up in smoke. Bring it on.

If such a significant percentage of Americans, and many in high places, believe that the end of the world is a good thing, and that it's coming soon, what are the chances we will take steps necessary to curb global warming, for example, or address the Middle East conflagration that many believe signals the return of the savior? As a foundation for political policy in the perilous twenty-first century, the Revelation is several orders of magnitude scarier than frogs or boils.

No authority other than the Bible, or some far-out interpretation of it, needs be cited to hold or spread this view. It has nothing to do with the kind of evidence that is the bottom line of any good public policy—foreign, economic, or environmental. Popular disregard, even disdain, for demonstrable truth is the most dangerous thing that can happen to a democracy. And it is happening here. Not only here tonight in Dover, but in Washington, too, where the Bush Administration's contempt for science and evidence-based policy is everywhere evident, including its inhibition of stem-cell research; its censoring of Clean Air Act, climate change, and other environmental reports; and its depleting of NASA's science budget to pursue vanity projects such as sending humans to Mars. If beliefs trump facts, politicians can launch wars that have no basis, imprison suspects without explicit justification, and quell efforts to explore solutions to long-term environmental problems. If belief trumps fact, in these days of very dangerous truths, we're screwed.

Bars are illegal in Dover, and it cheers us all up a little when the car is finally purring toward York, where we can get a drink. Eyal Press, a writer for *The Nation,* has been staying in York, and he knows a place there called the Harp and Fiddle, an Irish pub that serves fish and chips and Irish rock.

The talk is lively, but it's fair to say, I think, that we are all demoralized. Eyal Press is a populist who writes eloquently and with dignity about the disenfranchised and overlooked parts of America; his articles always go beyond knee-jerk observations to the experience of real Americans. Press had hoped to gain some insight tonight about the character behind the caricature of the evangelical anti-evolutionist. I was looking for something similar, a way to dramatize the humanity of a group that most *Salon.com, Nation,* and *Harper's* readers are too happy to dismiss as mindless bigots.

The problem was, as far as we could tell, the anti-evolution crowd at the firehouse was about as bigoted and as mindless as they come. If they represent the evangelical movement that put President Bush in power, and if their numbers are as big and their influence is rising as fast as we hear, what hope is there that America can find its way through the ever-thornier thicket of ethical, political, environmental, and technological problems we face?

What does ID have to do with all this? Kent Hovind wasn't promoting ID, he was arguing for old-time creationism. But the arguments are

95

related, and Pastor Grove knows that, which is why he's been hanging around the Harrisburg courthouse. What is similar about Hovind's primitive creationism and ID is that both are insisting that their views of the world are so obviously true that they deserve whatever stripes our society grants to the truest of things.

The truth, what we today call scientific fact, has the only incontrovertible status around. Some argue that religious truths may be more valuable than scientific ones, but everyone agrees that it sounds absurd to say that they are more true. Science, which has given us God-like control of many aspects of our lives (after all, we can destroy whole cities on the far side of the world, disassemble atoms, and reverse the growth of cancers), is a tremendously authoritative power. When push comes to shove, Americans turn to science. Dr. Hovind's antics, and ID, are both efforts, whether genuine or cynical, to shift some of this scientific authority back to religion.

Religious people have always said their religion is true, but these guys are saying it is really, really true. True like aerodynamics, which makes flight possible, true like quantum theory, which makes CD players possible, or true like germ theory, which makes low infant mortality possible. Religion, and specifically the religious right wing of the Republican party, is looking at all the authority science has and thinking, Gimme some of that!

But it's not fair, Matthew points out; the Republicans already have both houses of Congress and the presidency. Now they want science, too?

Yes they do. It's funny, but it's also true. Think what they could do with it, what they could justify with that kind of authority. A popular acceptance of ID would convert the president's occasional claims that God told him to go to war or to do this or that from a presumed metaphor (or schizophrenic episode) to a scientifically validated form of interdimensional president-to-God consultation.

We debate all this till the Harp and Fiddle shuts down around us, and then we head back to Harrisburg. Perhaps it's only the pints of Guinness, but I am feeling better. Much better. As rain spatters the windshield we are quiet, each, I imagine, going over the day in his own mind, each making his own interpretation and preparing his story for tomorrow. I feel at home again. It seems right that I am part of the unlikely trio hurtling through space in this rented Taurus, that I am heading back to the cheap Harrisburg Comfort Inn, that I am trying to get a grip on what happened to my father, and that I am struggling to understand the religious rightward lurch America has made in the last half-dozen years. Suddenly, things again seem a little more . . . coherent. Not intelligently designed, mind you, but understandable and astounding at the same time. Where does this feeling come from, I wonder? It's *not* a religious feeling, I reassure myself. It's like finding myself a character in a book with a seductive plot and a quirky but trustworthy narrator, with characters who work—a book that, whether it turns out to be heroic, comic, or tragic, is definitely meaningful.

CHAPTER EIGHT

SEARCH AND REPLACE

RICHARD THOMPSON: "When did you become a
card-carrying member of the ACLU?"
BARBARA FORREST: "1979, I believe."

'm hungover from the Harp and Fiddle, but I don't want to miss
a word of today's testimony, so I stop for a double espresso on my
way to court.

The expert witness today is philosopher Barbara Forrest. I've read her
book about ID, in which she argues that Discovery Institute ultimately aims
to establish a theocratic state. Casey Luskin and other ID proponents there
would scoff at the allegation and call it paranoid. But I have a persistent and
growing feeling that Forrest is right, that "scientifically" establishing the existence of a creative designer—God—would give the government license to
enact the kinds of laws and policies that define a theocracy. A president
could cite God's word as justification for going to war, say, or for outlawing certain medical practices or avenues of scientific research.

Does my horror at this scenario mean ID is wrong? No, but it means
that in my lucid moments I sure as hell hope so.

Forrest is a small, neat, fit Southern woman who wears her brown hair in a bob. A philosopher at Southeastern Louisiana University, Forrest joins NCSE's Eugenie Scott as one of the very few professional pro-Darwin women officers in the battle over teaching evolution. There is another woman on the ID side, a Discovery Institute fellow named Nancy Pearcey. She's a friend of ID's founder, Phillip Johnson, and wrote the foreword to his book *The Right Questions* in 2002. Pearcey was an avowedly young-earth creationist before signing on to ID; for all I know she still is. Otherwise, for professionals at least, this battlefield is full of brothers fighting over the existence and nature of the Father.

Not only is Forrest not a man, she is also not religious, which I find refreshing since almost everyone on both sides of this trial so far seems to be competing for the title of true Christian. She will tell me that although she is reluctant to label herself, clearly the label she would choose if forced would be "humanist." She is a member of the New Orleans Secular Humanist Association, the ACLU, Americans United for the Separation of Church and State, and the National Center for Science Education. She wrote her dissertation at Tulane University about the philosophy of Sidney Hook, who, along with his teacher John Dewey, was a proponent of "pragmatic naturalism," a philosophy that Forrest believes is "very compatible" with methodological naturalism, which, in turn, is "just a fancy term for the scientific method." Methodological naturalism is used every day by every human being who has to solve a problem or answer a question. It's completely noncontroversial, and it "coincides with just about any philosophical position that one might take on the nature of reality. It does not logically entail philosophical naturalism."[1]

Before she even rises to the stand, Forrest is a controversial figure here, a special threat to the pro-ID defense. She is the coauthor, with biologist Paul Gross, of a book called *Creationism's Trojan Horse: The Wedge of Intelligent Design*. The book is a harsh critique of the ID movement's Wedge strategy and an effort to show how its leaders are driven more by religious zeal and cultural conservatism than by any scientific insight or theory. In the three-and-a-half years she has spent researching ID, she has gone over everything she can find by or about the movement and its leaders. *Creationism's Trojan Horse* constructs an argument against ID's scientific authenticity using ID proponents' own words and concludes that ID is nothing more than a retread of creation science.[2]

But as Forrest is sworn in, Discovery and the defense team know something about her that I don't yet know. And it frightens them. They have read her expert report, and they know that there is a bomb in there that could blow a sizable hole in their case. So they are going to try as hard as they can to have her and her report dismissed on the grounds that she is not really an expert on anything pertinent to the case and that her membership in the aforementioned organizations makes her a biased nonexpert to boot. In a desperate plea to the court to exclude her testimony, the defense team describes her as a "web-surfing, 'cyber-stalker' of the Discovery Institute and its supporters and allies."[3]

After failing in that effort, Richard Thompson and one of his co-counsels take turns trying to discredit her. At one point, Thompson harkens to the McCarthy era by asking Forrest how long she has been "a card-carrying member of the ACLU." Yikes.

The defense paints Forrest as a biased advocate for the secular humanists movement. To establish her godless credentials, Thompson has her read from the statement of principles of the New Orleans Secular Humanist Association: "We reject efforts to denigrate human intelligence, to seek to explain the world in supernatural terms, and to look outside nature for salvation," she reads.

"Do you subscribe to that principle that you just read?" Thompson asks.

"Yes," says Forrest.

Then he has her read from the mission statement of the Council for Secular Humanism and then from a pamphlet called "What Is Secular Humanism?"

> Secular humanism is a term which has come into use in the last 30 years to describe a world view with the following elements and

principles: The first one is a conviction that dogmas, ideologies and traditions, whether religious, political or social, must be weighed and tested by each individual and not simply accepted on faith. Commitment to the use of critical reason, factual evidence, and scientific methods of inquiry rather than faith and mysticism, in seeking solutions to human problems and answers to important human questions. A primary concern with fulfillment, growth, and creativity for both the individual and humankind in general. The constant search for objective truth with the understanding that new knowledge and experience constantly alter our imperfect perception of it. A concern for this life and a commitment to making it meaningful through better understanding of ourselves, our history, our intellectual and artistic achievements, and the outlooks of those who differ from us. A search for viable individual, social, and political principles of ethical conduct, judging them on their ability to enhance human well-being and individual responsibility. A conviction that with reason, an open marketplace of ideas, good will, and tolerance, progress can be made in building a better world for ourselves and our children.

Thompson goes on, "And you don't believe in the supernatural, do you?"

"I do not," says Forrest.

"And you don't believe in the immortality of the soul?"

"I do not," says Forrest.

She says that the theory of evolution is something virtually all secular humanists embrace because of their respect for the practice of science.

"Do you believe that nature is all there is?" asks the counselor.

"That is my own personal understanding of the cosmos, yes, sir," she replies. "I cannot prove that that's all there is, but that is my considered view."

Thompson vigorously attacks the methodology employed in Forrest's study of ID, asserting that she has selectively chosen to quote design proponents only when they are conveying religious opinions about their scientific work, not when they are giving scientific opinions about it.

Forrest the humanist is not a scientist—as the defense points out over and over again. They say it when they are trying to get the judge to exclude

101

her testimony. They say it once she is on the stand. In one instance, she is asked if it is true that her lack of science means that she is not in a position to evaluate the scientific claims of ID. She says that would be true except that ID proponents aren't making any scientific claims. Their claims are all in the realm of philosophy and religion, she says, and those are areas in which she does have expertise. And unlike the design proponents, she says, she does not pretend that what she does is science.

The court seems to come to a standstill for a moment to absorb her dry, Southern delivery, which, for all its modesty, only sharpens the deadly rhetorical point.

Forrest recounts the father of ID's own story of how he came to intelligent design and why it matters to him. In his writings, Phillip Johnson tells of a year-long sabbatical to England in 1987, after his religious awakening provoked a kind of mid-life crisis of purpose. He passed by a bookstore that displayed both Richard Dawkins's *The Blind Watchmaker* and Michael Denton's *Evolution: A Theory in Crisis*. He bought and read both volumes and realized, he says, that Dawkins was wrong and Denton was right, that natural selection was insufficient as an explanation for the diversity of life, including human life. So, he wrote, he went looking for another one.

An article by John Perry in the December 2003 issue of *World Magazine* quotes Johnson: "I looked for the best place to start the search [for a better explanation than natural selection] and I found it in the prologue to the Gospel of John."[4]

The Book of John reads "In the beginning was the Word, and the Word was with God, and the Word was God. . . . And the Word was made flesh, and dwelt among us, (and we beheld his glory, the glory as of the only begotten of the Father,) full of grace and truth."

"And I ask this question," Johnson went on, "does scientific evidence tend to support this conclusion, or the contrary conclusion of the materialists, that in the beginning were the particles?"

This interest in the New Testament's Gospel of John—also known as the Evangelistic Gospel—is key to understanding the evangelical IDers. If the world started with "the word" that means that information predated matter and has a more fundamental status. Without information, without a design, without the word, the IDers argue, there could be no universe, certainly there could be no life.

Forrest goes on to quote Johnson from the same article saying that once the ID movement can cast doubt on natural selection, raising the possibility that the approach suggested in the Bible is more scientific, "we haven't proved the Bible's claims about creation, but we've removed a powerful obstacle in the way of such belief. And all I really want to do with the scientific evidence is to clear away the obstacle that it presents to a belief that the creator is the God of the Bible. . . . It's a great error Christian leaders and intellectual leaders have made to think the origin of life is just one of those things scientists and professors argue about. The fundamental question is whether God is real or imaginary.

"What's at stake," Johnson went on to argue, "isn't just the first chapter of Genesis, but the whole Bible from beginning to end, and whether or not nature really is all there is.

"Once God is culturally determined to be imaginary, then God's morality loses its foundation and withers away. It may stay standing for a historical moment without a foundation until the winds of change blow hard enough to knock it over, like a cartoon character staying suspended for an instant after he runs off the cliff. We are at the end of that period now."

Eric Rothschild asks Forrest, "Fair to say that this is the whole shooting match for Mr. Johnson? He's challenging evolution because of God's morality and the truth of the Bible?"

"Yes," says Forrest, "he regards evolution as a threat to the Bible in its entirety and as a threat to the moral fabric of American culture."

Forrest quotes Johnson again, this time from a book review that he posted on the Access Research Network, a pro-ID Website, in 1996: "My colleagues and I speak of theistic realism, or sometimes mere creation, as the defining concept of our movement. This means that we affirm that God is objectively real as creator, and that the reality of God is tangibly recorded in evidence accessible to science, particularly in biology."[5]

Forrest goes on to quote mathematician and theologian William Dembski, a Discovery senior fellow, who wrote in an article in *Touchstone* magazine called "Signs of Intelligence, A Primer on the Discernment of Intelligent Design," "The world is a mirror representing the divine life. The mechanical philosophy [read materialism] was ever blind to this fact. Intelligent design, on the other hand, readily embraces the sacramental nature of physical reality. Indeed, intelligent design is just the Logos theology of John's Gospel restated in the idiom of information theory."[6]

It has a nice ring to it, "the Logos theology of John's Gospel." Logos theology was the effort by the early church to make sense of Jesus Christ's materiality, his blood and guts, in terms of the "word" or "reason" of God. Intelligent design is a modern effort to make sense of the whole world's material aspect in terms of the reason, or word, or intelligence of God.

All this evidence that ID's top theorists are driven by religious ambitions is interesting enough, but it is not enough just to show that IDers have religious concerns that motivate their work. The plaintiffs must also show that ID is not science. When Thompson points this out, Forrest replies that Brown University biologist Kenneth Miller and others have already done a perfectly good job of showing that ID does not fit the basic definition of science, and anyway, she says, science is not her field.

Though Forrest doesn't claim to be a scientist, she is a tenacious researcher, and she goes on to quote IDers themselves bemoaning the lack of a foundation for a biological theory in ID.

In the *Touchstone* article about Johnson, the author, ID theorist and Discovery fellow Paul Nelson, wrote, "Easily, the biggest challenge facing the ID community is to develop a full-fledged theory of biological design. We don't have such a theory right now, and that's a real problem. Without a theory, it's very hard to know where to direct your research focus. Right now, we've got a bag of powerful intuitions and a handful of notions such as irreducible complexity and specified complexity, but as yet, no general theory of biological design."

A bag of intuitions and a handful of notions? That's pretty candid. And pretty far from a convincing description of a cutting-edge scientific competitor to the cornerstone theory of modern biology.

*

But the bomb Forrest has to drop is neither philosophical nor scientific. It has nothing to do with the supernatural or methodological materialism. It is historical. And it is evolutionary; it traces the change over time not of a biological organism, but of an editorial one that nonetheless left quite a clear fossil record.

The textbook the Dover school board wants inserted into its high school curriculum, *Of Pandas and People,* turns out to have a colorful lineage traceable all the way back to 1983, when the first draft of the book, then provisionally called *Creation Biology,* was coauthored by Dean H. Kenyon, a San Francisco State University biologist, and writer Percival Davis. (Davis, who has a master's degree in zoology, is also the author of a 1983 book called *The Case for Creation.* About his authorship of *Pandas,* Davis told the *Wall Street Journal,* "Of course my motives were religious. There's no question about it.")

Just as the third draft of *Pandas* was in preparation, in the summer of 1987, the Supreme Court was hearing what was to be another landmark creationism case. The Louisiana legislature had tried to mandate the teaching of "creation science" as an alternative to evolution whenever evolutionary biology was going to be taught to high school students. The court decided against Louisiana, ruling that creation science was a thinly veiled version of creationism and that teaching it would promote a particular religious view, and hence violate the Establishment Clause of the First Amendment. *Edwards* v. *Aguillard,* as the case was called, was an important decision that marked the legal defeat of creation science. Or rather, it signaled not its end, but its evolution into a new species.

Kenyon, coauthor of *Pandas,* was enlisted as an expert for Louisiana in that case. He was to be the state's chief scientific witness defending the

105

credibility of creation science, and he prepared an affidavit for the court that tried to do just that.[7] Forrest testifies that he made the same basic arguments in his *Edwards* affidavit that ID is making today in *Kitzmiller*: that it is distinct from its creationist antecedents, not religious, and is the only scientifically valid alternative to evolution. Because they are the only plausible theories, he'd argued in *Edwards,* the evidence for each should be taught whenever one of them is.

Kenyon was well aware of the impact the *Edwards* defeat for creation science would have both on getting creation science into public schools and on selling his new textbook, *Of Pandas and People*. So, too, was his sponsor in creating the book, the Texas-based Christian nonprofit called the Foundation for Thought and Ethics.[8]

The Supreme Court ruling in *Edwards,* while making it unconstitutional to teach creation science or any other kind of creationism, did leave open a small window by suggesting that "Teaching a variety of scientific theories about the origins of humankind to school children might be validly done with the clear secular intent of enhancing the effectiveness of science instruction." The question the defeated creationists faced after *Edwards* then was whether to give up and retreat to home schooling and private schools, or to try to squeeze through that little window.

Late one night, as Forrest was preparing for the Dover trial, she combed through reams of pages relating to *Pandas*. The material had been subpoenaed from the Foundation for Thought and Ethics on a hunch that it might provide some insight into the evolution of the book.[9] Then, suddenly, Eureka! she found it, a smoking gun that was both undeniable proof of her thesis in *Creationism's Trojan Horse* and the key to presenting her argument to Judge Jones. She was looking at four different editions of *Of Pandas and People,* one from 1983 (titled *Creation Biology*), one from 1986 (*Biology and Creation*), and two from 1987. Three of them were written in explicitly creationist language. Beginning in the 1986 draft, the book defined creation this way: "Creation means that the various forms of life began abruptly through the agency of an intelligent creator with their distinctive features already intact. Fish with fins and scales, birds with feathers, beaks, and wings, etc." This is a classic creation science description of what is called "abrupt appearance."

But the second 1987 draft had a crucial difference. It was written after the *Edwards* decision outlawing creation science in the public schools.[10] And in that second version, virtually all of the explicitly creationist terminology had been swapped out for new language: that of intelligent design.

Forrest read aloud to the court the definition of intelligent design from the post-*Edwards* 1987 version of *Pandas:* "Intelligent design means that the various forms of life began abruptly through an intelligent agency with their distinctive features already intact. Fish with fins and scales, birds with feathers, beaks, and wings, etc."

Once I get beyond the contortions of imagination required to envision fish with fins and scales popping into being fully intact, I realize the importance of this revelation to the case. I'm not alone; the jury box full of reporters is suddenly scribbling furiously in their notebooks.

The defense is arguing that ID had no relationship to creation science, and yet here, in different drafts of the very textbook the Dover board was hoping to use, ID and creationism were given identical descriptions. What better evidence could there be that ID was a direct descendent from something that the Supreme Court had already defined as creationism?

Because *Of Pandas and People* is closely associated with Discovery Institute and not just the Dover school board, the indictment will stick to the whole ID movement. It will be very hard for Discovery to distance itself from *Pandas;* a senior fellow, William Dembski, is the scientific editor at the Foundation for Thought and Ethics, and long-time Discovery fellow Dean Kenyon is one of the book's authors.

Forrest's argument continues: not only did the authors of *Pandas* change one of the primary definitions in the book by substituting *intelligent designer* for *creator,* they apparently went through the whole thing with an early-generation word processor and replaced every instance of the word *creator* in its various grammatical forms with *intelligent designer.* To illustrate the scope of the conversion, Forrest asked computer wiz Nick Matzke at NCSE to go through an ASCII file of the book and count the number of times *creation* and its cognates appear and how many times *design* and its related forms do. The graph was unequivocal: in the early, pre-*Edwards* versions of the manuscript there were between 150 and 200 occurrences of *creation*. In 1987, after *Edwards,* that number dropped to ten or fewer. Correspondingly, *design*, which had only 50 to 100 uses in the versions of the book written before 1987, suddenly jumped to nearly 300 uses. Those were the early days of word processing, and some careless editor or author must have tried to do a search-and-replace without taking sufficient care. They tried to replace *creationists* with *design proponents* and ended up creating an infertile hybrid instead: *cdesign proponentsists.* [11]

Forrest had long alleged that once the Supreme Court made its decision in *Edwards,* creation science as a subject for promotion in the public schools had either to adapt (shrink to fit through the little window left open by the Supreme Court) or perish. The dimensions of that window were exactly the environmental pressures that brought us the latest subspecies of creation science, according to Forrest. That subspecies is intelligent design.

It is remarkable how quickly forms can change under such intense selective pressure. But however much and quickly they do, they always carry their genetic history with them. This is as true, apparently, for ID as it is for a finch.

CHAPTER NINE

THE VARIETIES OF MATERIALISTIC EXPERIENCE

ROBERT PENNCK: "Scientists think all the time about the meaning of their work, about the purpose of life, about the purpose of their own lives. I certainly do. But these questions, as important as they are, are not scientific questions."

his morning, September 28, the day of philosopher Robert Pennock's testimony, I wake up worried. And I am worried still as I walk along the broad and beautiful Susquehanna River toward downtown Harrisburg. I have a whole reservoir of fears ready to spill over the sluice on days like today: the safety and health of my two young sons; my career; my aging parents; my money problems; my marriage, which, after fifteen years, has hit a turbulent patch. With just a bit more precipitation, out pour the broader worries about political and environmental crises, about the rise of greed and the decline of kindness, about the money madness infecting virtually everyone I know. Terrorism. The military quagmire in Iraq. Genocide in the Congo and Rwanda, Darfur, and the Sudan. Melting polar ice caps. West Nile Virus, Avian Flu, Ebola.

I march north up the riverside path and try to focus on what is before me. Everything is fine, I tell myself, looking at the broad and beautiful

Susquehanna, trying to draw on its steady confidence. And then I remember that the Three Mile Island nuclear power plant is a short way downstream, and I shudder to think about the revival of the nuclear industry, not to mention the energy crisis and the wars that may ensue without alternatives to fossil fuels. Not to mention the horrifying polarization of American politics, the seemingly endless domination of right-wing religious fanatics over the Republican Party—or the very real possibility that American schools might be permitted to teach creationism again under the guise of intelligent design.

My worries are grounded in fact, but this sudden surge of anxieties, churned up by the trial, seems more of an existential crisis.

It kills me that the universe—what I could call God, if I believed—doesn't care. As far as nature is concerned, an infected hangnail on my little finger, the end of my marriage, the death of my children, or the end of civilization are all just fine, no better or worse than any other outcomes. If only the universe cared, how much easier that would be.

If I could believe in a caring God, in moods like this I might well choose to. The idea that someone who knows what He or She is doing is in charge and is working hard to make things better, would be very consoling. If I could "let go and let God" as they say in AA, that would be great. Instead, when I let go, I just have to wait for the other shoe to drop. Even if God doesn't exist, I might well function better in the cool shade of religious illusion than I do under the uncaring sun of the truth. But it doesn't matter, I haven't believed for a long, long time. And I can't fake it. Not even when I confront the fact of my son Leo's return from the brink of death and the remission of his epilepsy—a recovery every believer I know would count as a miracle.

I make it into the courtroom and onto my pew-like bench just as Eric Rothschild, the short, bespectacled chief counsel for the plaintiffs, begins to examine his next witness. Robert Pennock is a philosopher of science from Michigan State University. He is wearing a dark business-like suit that contrasts with his professorial bearing and his curly reddish blond hair and goatee. His eyes are friendly and intelligent, but tired, too.

Pennock is the author of one book about the intelligent design movement and the editor of another. The first, *Tower of Babel: The Evidence Against the New Creationism* (1999), is, as it sounds, an argument aimed directly at the scientific validity of ID. The second, *Intelligent Design Creationism and Its Critics: Philosophical, Theological, and Scientific Perspectives* (2001), is a collection of essays by people on all sides of the ID debate.

Now, on the stand, Pennock is explaining that he was first drawn into the ID debate when he was still at the University of Texas back in the early 1990s. In a philosophy of science course he taught the evolution-creationism controversy as a way to "explore the nature of science and its relationship to politics and culture and religion." A former ace student of his brought him a copy of *Of Pandas and People,* and said that her local school board was trying to work it into the science curriculum as a supplementary text.

She wanted Pennock's opinion of *Pandas,* which had only recently been published. Coincidentally, Pennock had just heard Phillip Johnson give a talk on ID and had recognized a significant rhetorical shift from the standard creationist argument. For one thing, the avuncular UC Berkeley professor did everything he could to belie the stereotype of the Bible-thumping creationist: he described himself as a skeptic, whose arguments were based on reason and evidence, not doctrine. He was making the same old creationist arguments, Pennock says, but by adjusting the message a little here and there, by bringing in the academic language of postmodern deconstructionists, and by eliminating mention of the Bible and God, he was able to sidestep the scientific arguments and make the debate sound philosophical. Pennock had a feeling that the appearance in Texas school boards of *Pandas* and the appearance on the lecture circuit of Johnson meant that a new creationism had emerged from the ashes of past legal defeats and was on the march. How right he was.

Texas was an early hotbed of ID activity. The state was home to the Foundation for Thought and Ethics, the publisher of *Pandas,* as well as many of the early ID enthusiasts, several of whom were at Pennock's university in Austin. Professor Pennock will say wryly of his presence at the genesis of the modern ID movement, "I was just at the wrong place at the wrong time."

As plaintiffs' attorney Rothschild sees it, Pennock's job as a friendly witness is to fortify the contention that ID is nothing more than dressed-up creationism, that it is not science at all, and does not deserve a place in the science classroom. In addition, the philosopher is also charged with introducing what will turn out to be a central concept in the trial, and a very controversial one. Science, he will testify, absolutely relies on what is called "materialism," a concept that all IDers reject, and the fundamentalists among them demonize.

When I came of age in the 1970s the word *materialism* was thrown around a lot and mostly was used to describe mindless consumerism. That kind of materialism is such a dominant mind-set today that it barely needs a name—virtually everyone in America is that kind of materialist. But that's a completely different kind of materialism than Pennock is referring to. When philosophers like Pennock use the M-word, or the roughly synonymous N-word, *naturalism,* they are referring to the idea that ours is a material world and that to the degree that it can be explained at all, it can be described in terms of its material properties alone.

Intelligent design advocates use the words *naturalism* and *materialism* pretty much synonymously, but philosophers prefer *naturalism* these days, Pennock says, because *materialism* implies that everything is really limited to matter itself and it doesn't indicate the role of energy and other natural forces. *Naturalism,* however, suggests that you are talking about matter and energy and anything else that the natural sciences can empirically discover and describe. Clearly, matter is part of nature, but there are other features of the natural world that science can measure, too.

(Despite the philosopher's preference for *naturalism,* I prefer *materialism*—partly because the IDers use it and partly because it has a more radical sound to it, which I like. The materialists are to philosophy what the behaviorists were to psychology: the hard-line reductionists. "If it ain't matter, it don't matter," reads the credo under the skull and crossbones on their leather jackets.

Anyway, what's most important about materialism in this context is not what it includes, but what it excludes: that is, everything supernatural—no gods, spirits, or other entities that don't obey the laws of nature. And, this is no arbitrary practice, says Pennock. In the history of science, excluding the supernatural turns out to be key.

Why is materialism so important for doing good science? He will get to that. But first, Pennock describes what he claims is a central distinction in this debate: between what philosophers call "*methodological* materialism" and what they call "*philosophical* materialism." You can think of the former, methodological materialism (MM), as being the special theory, applicable only to doing scientific research; it's a particular approach to examining the natural world. The latter, philosophical materialism (PM), is the general theory, applicable to everything. It is a philosophy about the nature of the world. All scientists must embrace MM if they intend to do science, Pennock says. But only a small minority embraces PM, and it's an extracurricular decision to do so.

Pennock says that there have been whiffs of both MM and full-fledged PM for a couple of thousand years. The earliest in Western philosophy were from the pre-Socratic Greek atomists, going back to 600 B.C. In 400 B.C. Hippocrates displayed a materialist bias by insisting that epilepsy should no longer be considered a kind of sacred or demonic possession but rather a condition brought on by natural causes, like any other. His insistence on sticking to empirical fact was an early flash of materialism, Pennock says, and it gave early medical science a steroidal shot in the arm. But it was not until the seventeenth century that people such as Sir Isaac Newton really got the hang of categorically excluding the supernatural from their research. When they did, though, the kind of science that had been running and flapping its wings for a long time took off and began to soar. Alchemy became chemistry. Astrology became astronomy. Newtonian physics was born.

Like Kenneth Miller, Pennock loves his work. And he's good at talking about it. The judge, however, seems to be fading at just the points that I perk up. The history of philosophy may not be Judge Jones's cup of tea. But the professor persists.

Before Newton, Pennock testifies, gravity was sometimes described by scientific authorities of the day as "spooky action at a distance," and was considered an occult force. But Newton insisted on studying it as a natural property of matter and looked for regularity in its apparent "spookiness." He had, as it turned out, well-founded faith—along with his faith in the Bible—that gravity obeyed reliable, comprehendible, and universal laws of nature. Due to his work, gravity was removed from the realm of the mystical and became a part of nature.

A hundred years later, Ben Franklin did the same thing for lightning. Before Franklin, bolts from the sky were believed to be expressions of God's displeasure; He would hit things with them to show how pissed off He was. When Franklin experimented with lightning, assuming it would be found to follow natural laws, he discovered not only that it behaved predictably and according to law but also that we could, by installing lightning rods, keep it from burning down our houses. Next thing we knew, we had MP3 players and cell phones, MRIs and antibiotics, insulin pumps and liposuction, Google searches, a growing economy, and democratic revolutions.

Okay, maybe the connections between acting as if matter were everything and the fruits of modernity aren't quite that direct, but it's hard to think of any idea that was more influential in its material and intellectual consequences than the exclusion of the supernatural from scientific accounts.

What makes materialism work so well in science? asks Rothschild. Is it because the world really is only matter and energy? Well, no, not necessarily, responds Pennock. This is where the distinction between MM and PM comes in. The fact that you employ MM so effectively when doing science says nothing about whether you are a PMist or not.

*Method*ological materialism is something like *method* acting: while you're on the stage, you *act as if* your uncle Claudius really killed the king. The theory is that if you act as if it's real, it will help you do a better job. In real life, maybe your uncle killed the king and most likely he didn't, but that's none of the audience's business; all they care about is that you act like he really did during the play. While you're in character, for the sake of your performance, it's best not even to think about whether your real uncle is a murderer.

Similarly, the MM at the foundation of science requires that scientists, as long as they are on the stage of science, *act as if* matter is all there is, and as if they reject out of hand any efforts at explanation that are not materialistic.

When scientists are doing science, only naturalistic causes can be invoked to explain things, Pennock says. Supernatural explanations are simply not kosher. Of course, scientists can use them to explain whatever they want beyond their science—why their uncle killed the king, for instance—but they aren't allowed to come out of character as long as they want to be taken seriously as scientists or, as Pennock puts it (professional philosopher that he is, and sounding a little like a quacking duck), as long as they are acting "qua scientist" and not "qua theologian" or "qua philosopher."

It is common, very common indeed, for individual scientists to be rigorous MMs on the one hand, while completely rejecting PM on the other. It is the philosophical versus methodological distinction that enables biologists such as Brown biology professor Kenneth Miller to reject citations to God's or any other intelligent designer's creativity while doing scientific work, but still to hold as a core belief that "God is the author of all things seen and unseen."

"God's weariness of New York Yankees owner George Steinbrenner might be a very satisfying explanation of why the Boston Red Sox were able to come back and win the 2004 World Series," says Miller, "but it's not a scientific explanation."

If you defy the naturalistic limits and invoke supernatural causes, such as gods and designers, in your supposedly scientific explanations, your colleagues won't necessarily think you're mad, but they will insist that you've stopped doing science. And while they might be happy to take your advice about how to keep a marriage afloat, they won't publish your scientific papers.

115

Why, Rothschild asks Pennock once again, is this methodological requirement important for science?

It doesn't just *help* science, explains Pennock. It *is* science. What scientists do is pose hypotheses that can potentially be tested—through experiment and observation—without reference to any but naturalistic explanations. If a question is about the supernatural, and thus not testable through experiment and observation, then it's not a scientific question. Conversely, if an answer to a scientific question relies on the supernatural, then it's not a scientific answer.

"Why is this methodological rule important for science?" asks Rothschild one last time, rubbing his head with his hand.

"What methodological naturalism [read materialism] does is say we can't cheat," Pennock answers. "We can't just call for quick assistance to some supernatural power. . . . You've undermined that notion of empirical evidence if you start to introduce the supernatural."

Methodological materialism keeps scientists honest, Pennock says, but "honesty" is defined as excluding anything that science doesn't already acknowledge as natural or material.

Pennock says that science *is* a study of the natural world limited to naturalistic explanations. Intelligent design, he says, employs supernatural explanations for at least some natural phenomenon. Thus ID is not science. On the right side of the courtroom, where the plaintiffs and their supporters are sitting, heads are nodding, "Yes." It's as simple as that: science is about nature, not about God, who, whether you believe in Him or not, is supernatural, in other words, beyond nature.

But on the left side of the courtroom, where the pro-ID defendants and their supporters are sitting, heads are wagging "No." Allowing scientists, let alone philosophers, to decide where science can look and where it can't gives them far too much arbitrary power. Of course the intelligent designer will remain undetected, and thus supernatural, if seeking evidence of Him is by definition unscientific.

Lawyers for the plaintiffs, most of whom are religious, want it to be clear that they are not pitting science against religion in this case. And it is to this end that Pennock's PM-MM distinction really comes in handy. It is a way to defuse the ID side's argument that Darwinism leads to PM, which leads to atheism. Johnson and Dembski and others who promote that equation are failing to make the key distinction between materialism of the methodological sort (science) and materialism of the philosophical kind.

Of course there are Darwinist philosophical materialists, who believe that the reason methodological materialism works so well is that the world is really essentially and entirely material. These hardcore, Harley-driving, helmet-free materialists will insist that a scientific explanation for the Red Sox comeback is possible, that all those human ambitions and plans and steroids could be broken down into their material components and analyzed thoroughly enough to explain how the Red Sox won. But even the hardliners would admit that such a scientific explanation would not be practical in this world; there's just too much information and analysis that would have to go into, say, looking at the physical substrates of a single thought, let alone a whole game plan differently interpreted by eighteen different players and numerous coaches and so on, and that's just the mental side of a physical game. But the point is, the PMs would insist that there was some naturalistic explanation at the bottom of it all, even if it were too complex ever to get at.

The MMs, on the other hand, need only be careful to limit themselves to the kinds of claims made in the name of science. In fact, the claim that all things that have not yet been shown amenable to naturalistic explanation does not itself conform to the limits of methodological materialism. It does not follow from the fact that we have been able to learn a lot from the natural world by adopting a naturalistic approach that that same approach will take us all the way. Some have faith that it will, but that is faith in science, not science.

Probably the leader of that faithful pack, the most famous materialist philosopher alive, is Tufts professor Daniel Dennett, who confidently says that humans are wet machines, arrangements of atoms and nothing more. Even things as ephemeral as minds, he says, will one day be understood in terms of the workings of brains, which are made up of tiny robots called cells. Dennett is famous, too, because he is an out-of-the-closet atheist, as is his counterpart in the biological world, Oxford geneticist Richard Dawkins, another notorious materialist. Their kind of materialism indeed seems pretty cozy with atheism, and they are happy to admit it. If nothing is real except matter and energy, and if everything can be explained in terms of various arrangements of atoms and forces, that doesn't leave room for much of a supernatural God.

❧

The philosophical materialists see the theory of evolution as the coup de grace in an ongoing imperial expansion of rationality across the natural world. Dennett writes, "The theory of evolution demolishes the best reason anyone has ever suggested for believing in a divine creator. This does not demonstrate that there is no divine creator, or course, but only shows that if there is one, He needn't have bothered to create anything, since natural selection would have taken care of all that."[1]

Oxford don Richard Dawkins says that even most scientists who are believers (IDers excepted, of course) do not claim evidence for that belief. "The most they will claim is that there is no evidence against," Dawkins says, "which is pathetically weak. There is no evidence against all sorts of things, but we don't waste our time believing in them."[2]

When ID proponents refer to ideologically driven materialistic atheistic scientists, then, they may justifiably be talking about folks like Dennett and Dawkins, both of whom are nearly full-time promoters of evolution and crusading critics of all kinds of creationism. And in the cases of Dawkins and Dennett, the IDers have a point—there is surely a big dose of supra-scientific ideology moving their arguments along. But the IDers make a mistake when they label all evolutionists and scientists who embrace MM as ideologically driven "materialists" and from that conclude that they are also atheists. Most MMs are not PMs, or so Pennock's argument goes, just like most actors who play Hamlet don't have uncles who killed their fathers.

According to Pennock, the belief among creationists that science assumes and promotes PM, aka atheism, amounts to what philosophers call a "category mistake." By putting up a firewall between the two kinds of materialism, the plaintiffs hope to make the world safe for both the materialistic rigors of science—particularly evolutionary biology—and God. Brown University biologist Kenneth Miller embraces this line of reasoning, as did his now-deceased friend, the Harvard evolutionary biologist Stephen J. Gould. Gould, in his 1999 book *Rocks of Ages,* wrote about the "non-overlapping magisteria" of science and religion, claiming that while science addresses the "what" and "how" questions about the world, religion addresses the "why" questions about the meaning of life.[3]

Pennock is making points for the plaintiffs thick and fast. He's introduced the key distinction between MM and PM and argued that science must embrace MM while rejecting or remaining noncommittal on PM. Now he makes another key argument: that ID is not science because its supernatural claims are not falsifiable. If a claim can't potentially be proven false, then it isn't a scientific claim at all, says Pennock.

If qualities of the natural world can be attributed to a supernatural force, then anything goes. Creationists can claim, for instance, that the earth *appears* to be 4.5 billion years old but is really only six thousand years old because God intentionally made it appear older than it is to confuse us. Could God have designed the flagellum to appear irreducibly complex just to trick us into thinking He exists when He actually doesn't?

Intelligent design is a purely negative argument, Pennock continues. It bends over backwards not to make claims about, for example, the age of the earth or the literal reality of the Biblical story of Noah, or even the common ancestry of modern organisms. Why? Because if it took a stance on these things, as creation science did in the 1980s, it could be proven wrong.

Furthermore, Pennock presses on, growing more enthusiastic (even as his audience flags), ID poses a false dichotomy, claiming that either natural selection accounts for biological diversity or design does. Then it tries to punch enough holes in natural selection to sink it, leaving ID floating on its own. But, Pennock notes, an argument against natural selection isn't an argument for ID any more than it's an argument for the Flying Spaghetti Monster.

(Bobby Henderson, a graduate student at Oregon State University, created a satirical religion in 2005 called Pastafarianism, the Church of the Flying Spaghetti Monster, to parody intelligent design. Henderson, who claims to have "millions, if not thousands" of worshipers, threatened to sue the Kansas school board if it didn't begin teaching that "God exists and He is made of pasta.")

If Pennock is right—if PM and MM are entirely different species— then the world is safe for both religion and science, even evolutionary biology. Certainly that is the contention of the plaintiffs' team, which is trying very hard *not* to portray this as a battle between the two dominant, authoritative worldviews of the day—a battle, I can't help thinking, over the meaning of everything.

I suspect the MM-PM distinction appeals so powerfully to science-minded theists not because it describes an actual dividing line in the world but because it works as a kind of clutch to be pushed in when shifting between the two competing worldviews that so many of us hold simultaneously, despite the awkwardness of their relationship. Not that we think, "Okay I'm shifting from the materialist paradigm to the theist paradigm," when we stop working and start praying. We just clutch-and-shift a hundred times a day, as naturally as we do while driving. Except that we're not shifting up or down between gears, but over between worldviews. We are mightily reluctant to give up either view of the world, and we're willing to make some dubious philosophical moves to make it possible not to.

Several years ago I coedited a collection of interviews, conducted by philosopher Philip Clayton and myself, with top scientists who were also religious.[4] What I drew from my dozens of interviews, some with Nobel laureates, was that plenty of great scientists believe in a personal God, they virtually all try hard to keep that belief out of their research, and when they talk about the relationship between their science and their religion they can be quite moving. But they don't make a whole lot of logical sense, at least not a lot more than your average undergraduate stoner.

In any case, both sides of this debate agree that much turns on the validity or invalidity of this distinction; the theistic evolutionists (including most of the plaintiffs and the scientists on the evolution side) say it keeps God and religion safe from the underlying God-free zone that empowers their work. For their part, the intelligent designers say the distinction between MM and PM is merely a rhetorical move on the part of conflict-avoidant but deluded evolutionists, especially religious evolutionists, made in an effort to keep their cake (their faith in the scientific method) and eat it (continue to pray as if it mattered and engage in other supernaturally oriented activities and beliefs), too.

What is needed for science to progress, say the IDers, is the overthrow of the whole materialistic paradigm. Pennock quotes from William Dembski's book *Intelligent Design: The Bridge Between Science and Theology:* "The scientific picture of the world championed since the Enlightenment is not just wrong, but massively wrong. Indeed entire fields of inquiry, including especially the human sciences, will need to be rethought from the ground up in terms of intelligent design."[5]

Then Pennock quotes from an article by Dembski, "What Every Theologian Should Know About Creation, Evolution and Design": "So long as methodological naturalism sets the ground rules for how the game of science is to be played, IDT [intelligent design theory] has no chance in Hades."[6]

In other words, even Dembski is admitting that ID is not science, at least not as it is now conducted. He and his ID colleagues are saying that ID would fit in fine with a new kind of science, one that was not bound by the limits of methodological materialism.

"What would it mean for science if intelligent design's project of over-turning methodological naturalism was successful?" Eric Rothschild asks Pennock.

Essentially, Pennock responds, it would return us to the pre-Enlightenment era. It would be a number of steps backward.

After the break, in his cross-examination, Gillen takes some shots. First, he tries to get Pennock to acknowledge that even if an evolutionary theorist such as Dawkins draws metaphysical conclusions (in this case atheism) from his work, that doesn't mean that the research he does is itself metaphysical or unscientific.

Pennock replies that what determines the scientific status of a proposed explanation for the diversity of life is not whether it gives rise to religious or ideological faith or speculation. Dawkins can't make evolution nonscience by discussing its religious, or atheistic, implications any more than Johnson can change ID's scientific status by drawing religious conclusions from it. The difference between the two is that while Dawkins is doing a metaphysical riff on the science of evolution, Johnson is attempting a scientific riff on the metaphysics of ID. They can riff all they want, in whatever ways they want, and it doesn't change the scientific status of either ID or evolutionary biology.

But people arguing against ID, Gillen points out, often cite the predominance of Christians in the ID movement as evidence that ID is a religious movement and not a scientific one. That doesn't logically follow, he says, and he's right. But legally, it matters a lot. If ID is driven by a religious view of the world and is a closeted close relative of earlier forms of creationism, forms already deemed not scientific but religious, and thus in violation of the First Amendment when taught in public schools, then the defense's goose is cooked.

To be fair, though, the science and the ideology that may spring from it should be evaluated independently, says Gillen. Okay, Pennock says, and when you evaluate evolution you find a science. With atheism you find an ideology. Christianity is a religion. And when you evaluate ID, Pennock says, you get a religious metaphysics that is struggling to make scientific claims. But, he goes on, the reason ID makes those claims is in order to promote a religious view of the world. So ID begins with a religious insight and is pursued for religious reasons and it draws religious conclusions. Those things alone, however, in themselves don't make ID nonscience. What makes ID nonscience, says Pennock, is the missing science part: the falsifiable hypotheses, reproducible research, and peer-review publications.

When Pennock's testimony is through, Pat Gillen, the sensitive Modiglianiesque defense attorney, looks dejected. Maybe it is dawning on him that what he thought was an unequivocally righteous battle is actually something more complex. Or maybe it's just the end of a long day.

I have been trying for years, decades, to find a way closer to my father, trying to bring his world and mine together. Lying in bed the night of Pennock's testimony, I realize that there may be no navigable way. We may simply live in different worlds that share no bridge.

CHAPTER TEN

THE
FLAGELLAR FANDANGO

ERIC ROTHCHILD: "And just my hand? I can grab things with it. I can point.
Is that a purposeful arrangement of parts?"
MICHAEL BAHE: "Is it a purposeful arrangement of parts? Yes, I think it is."

cience writers such as me, by and large, are the soap opera walk-ons of the science world. There are exceptions, but for the most part, we aren't real scientists at all—we only rarely even get to play them on TV. We just write about them for magazines.

Mostly we're science nerds and groupies all too keenly attuned to our sources' tastes and proclivities. If scientists dislike something, then science writers will probably like it even less, vilify it, even, just to let the real scientists know that we can hang. If a physicist scoffs at cold fusion, the science writer at her side is likely to chuckle knowingly, even though he may not know a klystron from a hole in the ground.

The scientists I know—and so even more the science writers—see IDers not only as the intellectual opposition but as Barbarians massing at the gates. They don't just disrespect them, they despise them.

A few months ago I interviewed Joan Roughgarden, a renowned Stanford ecologist, and something of an iconoclast in the world of evolutionary biology. I respect and admire her work (read: I would be her groupie if she'd have me) and the courage she shows bucking the trends of science, and I thought our interview was going well. But when I told her that I was writing a book about ID in order to understand what drove its proponents, her attitude and demeanor swung around 180 degrees. "This isn't ethically neutral, you know," she said. "These people aren't just trying to present a flawed scientific perspective; they are trying to classify people like me as evil." Roughgarden, whose first name used to be Jonathan, is a transsexual. "They want to define me as inhuman. This is deadly serious," she said.

Yes, it is serious. All the more reason to understand it as well as possible. Whatever happens at this trial, this argument will go on for a long time to come. Its roots reach not only into the American evangelical movement but also down into the foundations of Western culture and philosophy. Is the world driven purely by matter and the laws of nature, or are those things mere embodiments of another, immaterial, intelligent aspect of the universe? It's not a crazy question, and, though my colleagues will chastise me for saying so, I don't think it is absurd to imagine that science might some day have something to say about it.

How will this battle be fought? If both sides can, without blunting their convictions and commitments, persist honestly, fairly, and respectfully, that will in itself be a kind of moral victory for decency. It will be an accomplishment no matter which model or worldview prevails, or even if a peace accord is reached and the world remains, cleaved in half, in an awkward détente for another half a millennium. It occurs to me that such a respectful and honest exchange may be exactly what we are seeing here in Harrisburg. And frankly, I am heartened. We have found a way to examine these issues fairly, thoroughly, and without brutality. There is hope.

Three weeks into the trial, after nine full days of plaintiffs' witnesses, this is the day that ID proponents have been waiting for. Finally, the intelligent design team will have its chance to show the court, and to convince

America and the world, that they are more than just a fringe bunch of fanatics on a moral crusade. Even if the school board loses the case, if today's witness, Lehigh University professor Michael Behe, gives a strong show, it could put intelligent design into orbit.

To win this case, the pro-ID defense team representing the school board is going to have to show two things: that intelligent design is not religion, *and* that it is credible science. So far, it isn't looking good. The plaintiffs' pro-evolution attorneys have had a firm grasp of the wheel until now, since they have been presenting only their own witnesses. And they have marshaled a strong collection of arguments:

Robert Pennock argued that ID is not science. But more important, he explained the difference between methodological and philosophical materialism, and he assured us that the practice of the former does not entail a commitment to the latter. In other words, naturalistic science (also known today as "just plain science,") is not the same as atheism.

Barbara Forrest made a tight and dramatic case that ID has its historical roots firmly planted in American religious creationism.

Kevin Padian, the UC Berkeley paleontologist, critiqued assertions in the ID textbook *Pandas* that there is no good fossil evidence for evolution. He showed well-documented examples from the fossil record of complex features, such as the arrangement of the inner ear bones, arising in a step-by-step fashion. The problem with teaching ID, Padian said, is that it "makes people stupid. . . . It confuses them unnecessarily about things that are well understood in science, about which there is no controversy."

And, back in the beginning, Kenneth Miller dismissed ID's arguments for irreducible complexity, explaining what distinguishes science from non-science and why ID is the latter.

I thought the plaintiffs had made an impressive case, but lead counsel for the defense, Richard Thompson, disagreed. Several days ago, he'd assured me that "Michael Behe will refute everything Miller said." He seemed confident. Now we'll see, I thought.

Michael Behe (pronounced "be he") is a biochemistry professor at Lehigh University, in Bethlehem (yes, Bethlehem!) Pennsylvania, and the author of the seminal ID book, *Darwin's Black Box*. Behe is the face of intelligent design; he is for the ID movement, and for Thompson's defense, what Miller is to evolution and the plaintiffs'.

Both Miller and Behe are religious Catholics, which puts an interesting twist on their testimony. In Miller's case, his Catholicism helps dispel the mythical equation Science = Atheism. In Behe's case, it dispels the myth ID = Evangelical Christianity. But of greater value to the ID movement are Behe's scientific credentials: he's a bona fide biologist.

In the ranks of Ph.D. scientists in the ID crowd, the ratio of biologists to engineers, mathematicians, and philosophers is very low. The IDers say that's because it's hard to get very far in biology if you are an ID proponent. And, they add, by the time you've got a degree in biology you've been so thoroughly indoctrinated by the Darwin-Materialist-Marxist-University-anti-Industrial-Complex that you actually think you *believe* in natural selection. Of course, biologists have a different explanation: they've been taught to look at the data, which are unequivocal; review them critically; and draw an unbiased conclusion from them: that is, evolution occurs and is driven by natural selection and other natural forces. But whatever the explanation for their rarity, intelligent designers prize the few biologists who are firmly on their side.

Behe is likeable, reasonable, friendly, and accessible; a died-in-the-wool nerd with his great big glasses, bald head, scruffy graying beard, and tweed jacket. He is civil, modestly intellectual, and academic to the core. I saw him in 1997 on a televised *Firing Line* debate in which he, William F. Buckley Jr., Phillip Johnson, and David Berlinski debated Barry Lynn, from Americans United for the Separation of Church and State; Eugenie Scott; pro-evolution philosopher Michael Ruse; and Kenneth Miller—and Behe came across in the field of shrill, arrogant, or angry combatants as a humble and authentic guy. I think he was even wearing a plaid flannel shirt. On national TV!

Behe got his biochemistry degree from the University of Pennsylvania and has been teaching college for twenty-three years. He's been part of the ID movement from its genesis. He was at a 1993 brainstorming

meeting in Pajaro Dunes, California, with Phillip Johnson, William Dembski, Paul Nelson, Dean Kenyon, and Stephen Meyer that led to the formation of Discovery Institute's Center for the Renewal of Science and Culture.
Behe has been a fellow there since the beginning. His book *Darwin's Black
Box*, published in 1996, has sold more than four hundred thousand copies,
he says, and has been translated into ten languages. It played the scientific
counterpoint to Phillip Johnson's *Darwin on Trial*. It was in that book that
Behe coined the phrase *irreducible complexity*, and it was with that coinage
that ID first bought a modicum of scientific credibility.

Today, Behe will be examined on the stand by Robert Muise. Behe
looks relaxed and happy to be here. He is a witness, but in a way he is an
exhibit, too. He is "Exhibit ID-S"—S for Scientist. Muise spends an hour
examining his academic credentials, the talks he's given, and conferences
he's participated in, and in generally establishing Behe as a real-life biochemist with plenty of scientific publications to his name. The he leads Behe
into what may be his most important contribution to the defense.

Taking full advantage of Behe's now-evident authenticity, Muise runs
him through a string of pointed questions so that the court, and the world,
can hear a real scientist answer them thusly:

"Do you have any religious commitment to intelligent design?"

"No."

"Do you have any private religious convictions that require you to
advocate in favor of intelligent design?"

"No, I do not."

"Is your interest in intelligent design based on what the scientific evidence shows?"

"Yes."

"Do you consider yourself to be a young-earth creationist?"

"No, I'm not."

"Do you consider yourself to be an old-earth creationist?"

"No."

"Do you consider yourself a creationist in terms of special creation?"

"No."

There, in the first blip of what, in the end, would seem an eternal three days on the stand, Behe's done the biggest part of his job. He's shown the skeptical world that a bona fide professor who studies the biochemical substrates of life for a credible university believes in ID because he thinks it reflects reality.

Next, Behe tries to reclaim the definition of irreducible complexity from the plaintiffs' witnesses. Irreducible complexity is Behe's big idea, the main theme of *Darwin's Black Box,* and the anchoring scientific argument for ID.

Although his opponents often describe ID, and the argument for irreducible complexity specifically, as negative arguments, Behe says that is a mischaracterization. Intelligent design, though it has a negative aspect, is fundamentally a positive argument for the recognition of design. It is not, despite all we have heard, an argument against evolution. At least, not against three-fifths of the theory.

Behe cites the late, great Harvard evolutionary theorist Ernst Mayr, who died in 2005 at the age of one hundred, as parsing the theory of evolution into five distinct parts: (1) change over time, (2) common descent, (3) multiplication of species (as time passes we get more species rather than fewer, and species divide and branch out), (4) gradualism (change occurs steadily over time), and (5) natural selection.[1] Behe says that personally he has no big problem with the first three of Mayr's five Darwinian parts. It is natural selection, and to a degree gradualism, that he finds problematic.

He explains that he too once embraced natural selection—until the 1980s, when he read Michael Denton's proto-ID book *Evolution: A Theory in Crisis*[2] and began to question the power of natural selection to explain the elaborate machines composing the molecular worlds he found within each cell. Like other biochemists, he recognized that these structures were a lot like machines; and, like other biochemists, he often called them machines. But unlike his colleagues, at some point Behe decided that they actually were *literally* machines. He could tell, he says, because like human-made machines, they display "a purposeful arrangement of parts." And like all of the human-made machines that populate our lives, he concluded, they must have been designed.

Reporters are scribbling like mad. Finally a real scientist defending ID. Now this is a story.

Behe says that a century and a half ago, without microscopes powerful enough to detect these intricate tiny structures, Darwin couldn't have dreamed how complex the components of cells were. In his day, cells were thought to be the basic building blocks of life. Now, says Behe, we can see that each one contains a city-like network of systems that direct and sustain it. For the cell to function at all, an astounding number of intricate parts need to be in exactly the right places doing exactly the right things. This is Behe's positive argument for ID: molecular "machines" are real machines, we can tell by looking at them and their purposeful arrangement of parts. And machines are designed. Machines don't just happen. Someone has to *create* machines.

The more Behe studied some of these parts, the more convinced he became that such intricate machines could not feasibly be the products of natural selection. For one thing, the job is just too big; there hasn't been enough time, even assuming the earth is four-and-a-half billion years old— as Behe does, real scientist that he is. But his more celebrated point has not to do with how complicated the parts are, but rather with the specific way they are complicated. He calls this kind of complexity *irreducible*: irreducible complexity.

Muise asks Behe to define this important notion, and he turns to a passage from his own book projected on the screen. The professor is crazy about his laser pointer, and has been shooting its red beam at every exhibit, sometimes even pointing to each word as he reads aloud off the courtroom screen. Now, as he reads his own words from the screen, he underscores each with his laser. It's like one of those bouncing balls in the old Max Fleischer sing-along cartoons from the 1930s and 1940s. "By irreducibly complex, I mean a single system which is necessarily composed of several well-matched interacting parts that contribute to the basic function, and where the removal of any one of the parts causes the system to effectively cease functioning."[3]

In other words, a system is irreducibly complex if you can't remove any of its components without breaking it. Behe's big idea, as he might like it to be remembered, is that if you can find one irreducibly complex molecular machine, you will disprove natural selection. Natural selection can only build a new structure gradually, step by step, selecting for one little change at a time. If each of those individual changes was of no selectable value by itself, then it could never be selected for. The complex machine would never have a chance to evolve.

Darwin was frightfully familiar with the concept of irreducible complexity, though he didn't call it that. In a memorable passage from *On the Origin of Species,* Darwin says, "If it could be demonstrated that any complex organ existed which could not possibly have been formed by numerous successive slight modifications, my theory would absolutely break down. But I can find out no such case."[4]

In his three full days in court (the longest of any witness in the trial) Behe, emboldened by Darwin's challenge, sets about describing three systems that he says are irreducibly complex. His favorite, the one most prominently featured in his book and in the courtroom in Harrisburg, is the bacterial flagellum. This amazing little piece of work is, Behe says, "quite literally an outboard motor that bacteria use to swim."

By the end of this trial, we will all become intimately familiar with the flagellum—its image is put up on the courtroom's projection screen a dozen times or so over the course of testimony. (One of the defense lawyers even suggested that *Kitzmiller* v. *Dover* would go down in history as the "Bacterial Flagellum Trial.") Now Behe is highlighting the image of the single-celled creature with his pointer, explaining how the flagellum works.

Attached to one end of the bacterium, he says, is a long, hair-like appendage called a *filament,* which spins like a propeller and moves the bacterium through its liquid environment. It can spin in both directions with amazing speed and efficiency.[5] The filament is attached to a drive shaft by a kind of a universal joint, transmitting power from the motor, which is inside

the cell membrane, to the filament, which spins outside. Driving the filament is a little rotary motor that is fueled by the flow of acid across the cell
membrane—the way, Behe says, "water flowing over a dam can turn a tur-
bine." The whole thing is kept anchored to the skin of the bacterium by
more protein parts that clamp it the way an outboard is held onto a boat to
prevent the motor from moving around instead of moving the boat forward.
The drive shaft has to pass through the cell membrane so the prop can spin
outside and move the bacterium along. More protein parts act as bushing
materials to allow it to go through the wall and to keep spinning without
letting the cell's innards leak out.

Pointing with his laser to the mechanical drawing on the screen, Behe
explains that it's really much more complex than this cartoon-like charac-
terization. There are at least forty different protein parts, the removal of
any one of which will keep the flagellum from functioning. "Most people
who see this and have the function explained to them," says Behe, "quickly
realize that these parts are ordered for a purpose and, therefore, bespeak
design."

By the end of his first morning of testimony, Behe is looking strong.
He has convinced anyone who wasn't already sure that the biological systems he calls machines are very complex. He's suggested that there is a positive aspect to ID's argument—the detection of purposeful arrangement—
though he hasn't made a definitive case. We'd have to hear a lot more to be
convinced there. He's compared ID to the big bang in an effort to show that
even a theory that can say nothing about its source (in the way that the big
bang says nothing about what came before or caused that original expansion) can still be a subject of scientific study.

Again referring to the big bang, Behe also challenged the idea that ID
necessarily relies on the existence of the supernatural. We don't know what
caused the big bang, he points out truthfully enough, but that doesn't mean

that acceptance of it requires belief in God or any other supernatural actor. Furthermore, even though some scientists do believe it was God who caused the big bang, that doesn't keep it from being taught as science—although, he says, it certainly did keep much of the scientific world from embracing the theory when it was first presented early in the twentieth century.

Behe makes an appeal to common sense by suggesting that although the National Academy of Sciences may subscribe to a particular definition of the word *theory*, scientists, like regular folk, use the word in other ways as well. He defines science a little more broadly: ID is science, Behe says, "because it relies completely on the physical, observable, empirical facts about nature plus logical inferences."

He argues that the subcellular world appears to be designed. Inductively, it is justified to hold that it was designed, unless there is a compelling reason to believe otherwise. It is here that the negative part of the argument takes over. The only reason to believe that complex biological machines are not designed is if Darwin's theory of natural selection, or some other designer-free, materialistic theory, poses a compelling alternative explanation. The negative part of Behe's argument, and ID's argument generally, then, is that natural selection doesn't and can't ever show how these things evolved.

Wait a minute. What Behe portrays this morning is an almost unrecognizable version of ID. Have the plaintiffs' experts been misleading the court? Behe says ID is *not* anti-evolution, *not* based on supernatural explanations, *not* contesting change over time, the multiplication of species, or even common descent. It is *not* religious, let alone evangelical. It is just good, rational observation plus induction. It is a young science, but it holds great promise, he says.

I doubt Behe made any converts on any of these points. But he did raise interesting questions. He may even have raised some fears and hopes that he might be capable of scoring real points for ID as he fills in his sketchy arguments. He seems neither mad, fanatical, nor stupid. And he is holding his own, though his testimony was hardly as lively as Miller's or that of UC

Berkeley paleontologist Padian, who had testified just the day before. Still, Behe gives the impression of an authentic and capable intellectual, an underdog of science burdened with some unpopular but coherent and provocative ideas. Maybe it's not so crazy, I think as I head to the hot dog place for lunch.

I don't know where Behe eats lunch, but when he gets back to the stand in the afternoon, everything changes. The devil is in the details, they say, and it is the details that quickly begin to devil Professor Behe's testimony.

First, it is the details he chooses to present. I can only think that the defense's strategy is to try to demonstrate the seriousness of the ID enterprise by having Behe go over the finer points of his arguments for the irreducibility of not only the flagellum but also the immune system. This is still friendly examination by his own lawyers, but by four o'clock in the afternoon, when the court breaks for the day, defense lawyer Robert Muise looks dazed and is letting Behe ramble on for what seems like ten minutes at a time without posing a question. By the end, a trancelike stupor has fallen over the court, and Behe seems to be talking only to himself. Beat reporters are flummoxed; even the science writers have lost Behe's train of thought by mid-afternoon. The judge clings to his cup of black Starbucks coffee like a lifeline.

Finally, at a little after four, Muise says, "Your Honor, we're about to move into the blood-clotting system, which is really complex." Judge Jones, who's been slumped in his chair, looks stricken. "Really? We've certainly absorbed a lot, haven't we?"

Together they decide that rather than open another can of irreducibly complex worms today, the court will break early and resume with blood clotting tomorrow.

Unfortunately, even a good night's sleep doesn't help.

In the morning, when Judge Jones says, "If it's Tuesday, we must be on the blood clotting," Muise replies portentously: "We will be getting to blood clotting, immunity systems, and many more complex systems, Your Honor."

But it isn't just the details Behe dwells on, overindulges, and stumbles over that bring him down as a witness; it is also the details that emerge in his cross-examination, a withering piece of lawyering by the plaintiffs' chief counsel Eric Rothschild, that begins on that second afternoon, October 18. The attorney comes out slugging.

Rothschild deals Behe, and ID, a public relations blow early on by getting the professor to concede that, under his own definition of science—which Behe had articulated in his pretrial deposition, taken many months before—not only ID but astrology also would fit quite comfortably.

Behe later tries to distance himself from the comment, saying that viewed in full context it was not so bad. He meant, he explains, that astrology "had been" science, by his definition, back in the Middle Ages when it was embraced by scientists. I can tell you, though, even viewed in full context, his admission was as bad as the papers suggested.

"I didn't take that deposition in the 1500s, did I?" asks Rothschild.

"It feels like it," says Behe.

"It feels like it since yesterday," Rothschild shoots back.

And that is just the beginning. After quoting from a National Academy of Sciences report on ID saying that "Creationism, intelligent design, and other claims of supernatural intervention in the origin of life or of species are not science because they are not testable by the methods of science," Rothschild goes on to quote from an American Association for the Advancement of Science report that reads, "The ID movement has failed to offer credible scientific evidence to support their claim that ID undermines the current scientifically accepted theory of evolution." And, "the ID movement has not proposed a scientific means of testing its claims. Therefore be it resolved, that the lack of scientific warrant for so-called intelligent design theory makes it improper to include as a part of science education."[6]

Behe is beginning to get mad: he is rubbing his head with his hand, which Rothschild tells me he and Behe both do when they are getting upset. Behe says, "What scientific paper do you know of that says 'whereas,

135

whereas, whereas, therefore be it resolved?' This is a political document. There are no citations here. There's no marshaling of evidence."

"You're not aware of any major scientific organization that has endorsed the science of intelligent design or the teaching of intelligent design, are you?" asks Rothschild. "In fact," he continues, "this isn't just a big scientific organization's bureaucracy that's taken this position, your own university department has taken a position about intelligent design, hasn't it?"

Now Rothschild projects a copy of the statement from the Lehigh Department of Biological Sciences, which reads, "The department faculty . . . are unequivocal in their support of evolutionary theory, that has its roots in the seminal work of Charles Darwin and has been supported by findings accumulated over 140 years. The sole dissenter from this position, Professor Michael Behe, is a well-known proponent of intelligent design. While we respect Professor Behe's right to express his views, they are his alone and are in no way endorsed by the department. It is our collective position that intelligent design has no basis in science, has not been tested experimentally, and should not be regarded as scientific."

"The department faculty is unequivocal in their support of evolutionary theory," says Behe. "What does that mean? To commit one's self to a theory, to swear allegiance to a theory. *That's* not scientific."

Behe may have a point, but it is eclipsed by the academic insult coming from his own closest colleagues. If he hasn't convinced even one of them of the idea's merit, how can he convince us? It is a serious blow, and the capital "S" for Scientist has just been shifted to the lower case.

As if responding to Behe's protests that all these criticisms are political and rhetorical, not scientific, Rothschild zeros in on Behe's theory of irreducible complexity. He quotes from the professor's expert report submitted to the court prior to his testimony: "'Intelligent design theory focuses exclusively on the proposed mechanism of how complex biological structures arose.'

"Please describe the *mechanism* that intelligent design proposes for how complex biological structures arose," says Rothschild slowly.

Behe hates this. He must. "There is no mechanism, except to say that it must involve intelligence," he answers. "There are many other questions that these theories leave unaddressed, but they do posit some aspect of the cause [that it is intelligent] which is very useful to have and which is supported by the data."

"So intelligent design is about *cause?*" asks Rothschild coyly.

"I'm sorry, could you say that again?" Behe appears not to hear the questions he doesn't like.

"I just want to get it clear here, intelligent design is about cause?" persists Rothschild.

"Well, 'cause' is a broad word. . . . But intelligent design is one reason or one aspect or one cause to explain how the purposeful arrangement of parts that we see did come about," says Behe.

Rothschild repeats his original question: "What is the mechanism that intelligent design proposes?"

Behe says that intelligent design "does not propose a mechanism in the sense of a step-by-step description of how those structures arose. But it can infer that in the mechanism, in the process by which these structures arose, an intelligent cause was involved."

"But it does not propose an actual mechanism?" Rothschild says, hanging on to his question like a fishing line.

"I would not say that there was a mechanism," Behe finally concedes, "I would say we have an aspect of the history of the structure."

"So when you wrote in your report that 'Intelligent design theory focuses exclusively on the proposed mechanism,' you actually meant to say, 'Intelligent design says nothing about the mechanism of how complex biological structures arose'"?

This exchange is riveting. Defense attorney Muise—who probably should have raised an objection here—Rothschild was putting words right into Behe's mouth—just watched, spellbound like the rest of the court.

"Intelligent design does not describe how the design occurred?" asks Rothschild.

Behe admits that it does not, again comparing ID to the big bang theory, which also does not pretend to describe what caused the original bang
itself.

Intelligent design "does not identify when the design occurred?" asks
Rothschild.

"That is correct," concedes Behe.

Rothschild then asks Behe how, exactly, the designer implemented his
design.

Behe says he doesn't know, that there are many things ID does not
tell us.

"Was the design limited to the original blueprint?"

"Well, no," says Behe, "the designer would also have to somehow cause
the plan to, you know, go into effect."

"Did the intelligent designer . . . design every individual flagellum
in every bacteria or just the first lucky one?" and "Did the designer design
every mutation of the flagellum since the first one?"

"Well, that's—that's a very tricky question. But the proper answer is
that, we don't know," says Behe.

Rothschild turns to one of Behe's papers, titled "Reply to My Critics,"
and reads a passage pertaining to the question of whether ID requires a
supernatural actor or cause.[7] The only intelligent designers we know of in
the natural world are humans, says Behe, and they rely on irreducibly complex structures such as the human brain to accomplish their designs. So any
natural designer would itself probably have been designed. "At some point,"
Behe concludes, "a supernatural designer must get into the picture."

In other words, unless the designer is supernatural, He must also be
irreducibly complex and so must have been designed by another intelligent
designer who in turn would have to have been designed. This reminds me
of the ditty, "Little fleas have littler fleas, And littler fleas that bite em, And
littler fleas, have littler fleas, And so on infinitum."

It reminds me, too, of an old joke: An anthropologist asks a Native
American what the world rests on. "A turtle," answers the interviewee. "And
what does that turtle rest on?" asks the anthropologist. "Another turtle," says

the native man. "And that one, I suppose," offers the anthropologist, "sits on still another turtle? Are they turtles all the way down?" The interviewee smiles broadly at this question. "No," he says. "That would be absurd. The turtle is standing on a buffalo. I thought everyone knew that!"

Anyway, Rothschild quotes again from Behe's paper: "'Although possible in a broadly permissive sense, it is not plausible that the original intelligent agent is a natural entity.' So you're saying that it's possible but not plausible that the designer is natural and not supernatural?" asks Rothschild.

"Right," says Behe.

"And you believe the designer to be God, though you acknowledge that's not a scientific opinion."

"Yes."

Then Rothschild reads again from Behe's "Reply to My Critics." "So far I have assumed the existence of God," writes Behe. "But the argument is less plausible to those for whom God's existence is in question, and is much less plausible for those who deny God's existence."

"So the theory is not plausible to those who do not believe in God, or to those who question the existence of God," repeats Rothschild. "It's a God-friendly theory, isn't it, Professor Behe?"

When the court breaks for the day at 4:40, Behe has survived, but barely. He and his movement are severely battered. They had hoped today would be their Battle of Yorktown but it turned out to look more like the Bay of Pigs.

The next morning, the cross-examination resumes, and the emboldened Rothschild takes Behe on in the scientist's own domain. Citing a paper that Behe coauthored with David Snoke, a physicist at the University of Pittsburgh, published in *Protein Science* and titled "Simulating Evolution by Gene Duplication of Protein Features That Requires Multiple Amino Acid Residues," Rothschild questions the work's implications for ID. The paper describes a computer simulation designed to study how long it would take for a kind of selectable gene mutation to occur under various conditions. The paper doesn't mention ID by name, but Behe had already testified that the results were so germane to the debate that he considered it a publication in support of ID. Roughly speaking, the conclusion was that it would take a very large population of microorganisms an inordinately long time to evolve a particular function. Even if the science was pretty opaque to the layperson, the rhetorical effect of this article was crystal clear: mutations occurring at this rate could not accumulate fast enough to drive the kind of change commonly attributed to natural selection.[8]

Rothschild points out that the population sizes considered in the study are huge (10^9), but they are several orders of magnitude smaller than the population of bacteria found in a ton of soil. He also points out that there is more than a ton of soil on earth. Furthermore, he says, Behe's study conspicuously excludes some of the other main, real-world sources of genetic novelty.

"So," asks Rothschild, moving in for the kill, "with much higher populations the time [for sufficient genetic mutation to explain some adaptations] would be . . . ?"

"Much shorter," says Behe.

"Much shorter?" repeats Rothschild.

"Absolutely," confirms Behe.

Behe has challenged biologists to come up with an explanation for the step-by-step evolution of the flagellum, which, of course, he argues is irreducibly complex. If they could do that, he says, his assertion of irreducible complexity would be falsified.[9] But, Behe says, for the irreducibility of the system to be disproved, the function of the allegedly irreducibly complex system must remain intact even as a part is removed.

Rothschild points out that in order to make a challenge to irreducible complexity meaningful you have to leave open all of the various ways by which evolution is known, or thought, to bring about evolutionary adaptations. There is a biological concept known as *exaptation,* for example, which refers to the evolution of a system that accomplishes one function being adopted by a system that accomplishes a different one. For instance, small wings covered with feathers may have served a thermoregulatory function in some early dinosaurs long before they conveyed the advantage of flight. Or in the example of the flagellum, for instance, Kenneth Miller and others have suggested that something called a type three secretory system (TTSS), which shares many protein parts with the flagellum but has fewer of those parts, could have been selected for its effectiveness at secreting things outside the cell. Once the pump and motor were in place, to pump substances out of the cell, the addition of a "propeller" would have converted it into the outboards we see now. Miller shows that you can take away parts of the flagellum and get something very close to a functioning TTSS, which appears to satisfy Behe's challenge.

But Behe disqualifies Miller's answer, saying that Miller would have to show how the smaller set of molecular parts could serve precisely the same function as the larger set. But that's not necessarily how evolution works, says Rothschild. Why would you exclude one of the widely accepted mechanisms of natural selection, exaptation, from your test of natural selection?[10]

In his defense, Behe says he does acknowledge in his paper that it is possible the flagellum might have evolved this way, via exaptation or by some other "indirect" route, but that the probability is just too small. He will not acknowledge that his challenge has been met. Whatever the truth of the matter, the understanding in the courtroom has shifted: Behe now appears to be fixing the rules to ensure the preservation of the flagellum's claim to irreducible complexity. Serious doubt has been cast over the validity of the entire notion.

Taking advantage of Behe's disavowal of, or at least his proclaimed lack of commitment to, the creationist idea of abrupt creation (the idea that the molecular machines or whole species or whatever were made all at once),

Rothschild asks the professor if it is possible that the design, the assembly of purposefully arranged parts, was done slowly, gradually, the way his own kitchen was put together.

Yes, says Behe, that is possible. Whatever his real thoughts on the subject, he has to say that at this point because he's made such a big deal about ID not being fussy about timing.

So, asks Rothschild, both ID and natural selection can tolerate having the parts around that would eventually become a flagellum, but without those parts functioning yet as a motor?

Behe suspiciously acknowledges that an ID scenario, too, could include having non-motor, proto-flagellum parts around that had other functions or no functions at all.

The difference, Rothschild points out, is that while natural selection proposes a mechanism for how those parts could eventually form a flagellum, ID does not? Beyond saying that intelligence was somehow involved, Behe has clearly stated that ID does not suggest an actual mechanism.

❦

Behe also asserts that the flagellum's status as irreducibly complex could be falsified by a simple experiment. "A scientist could go into the laboratory, place a bacterial species lacking a flagellum under some selective pressure (for motility, say), grow it for ten thousand generations, and see if a flagellum—or any equally complex system—was produced. If that happened, my claims would be neatly disproven." Such an experiment would take about two years, he says.

Had Behe tried that himself, asks Rothschild.

No, Behe says. "It's not real likely to be fruitful," he says, because he doesn't think natural selection would come up with anything. And, he adds, he has better things to do.

Rothschild isn't satisfied with that. "It's entirely possible that something that couldn't be produced in the lab in two years or a hundred years, or even in a laboratory that was in operation for all of human existence, could be produced over three and a half billion years," he says. Which is exactly why the age of things, on which ID remains mum, is so important, Rothschild continues. If the earth is ten thousand years old, that presents a whole different collection of problems for evolution than an earth that is many billions of years old.

Now Rothschild is ready to deliver his *coup de grace,* questioning Behe on the evidence for the evolution by natural selection of the human immune system. After a lengthy exchange, he gets Behe to insist that, despite Miller's testimony to the contrary, "the scientific literature has no detailed, testable answers to the question of how the immune system could have arisen by random mutation and natural selection." Recognizing his moment—in a *Miracle on 34th Street* courtroom move he'd planned for months with NCSE's Nick Matzke—Rothschild piles on the witness stand in front of Behe a tall stack of articles and books "proposing, elucidating, testing, and confirming," according to Rothschild, a hypothesis about the evolution of the immune system that Miller had testified about ten days before.

"So these aren't good enough?" Rothschild asks, looking like a caged animal released.

From behind the stack, Behe says that he hasn't read them all, but that nonetheless he is sure they would not satisfy his requirement for showing how natural selection could generate the "irreducibly complex" immune system.

Whatever its truth value, his claim rings as hollow as a bell.[11]

CHAPTER ELEVEN

LIARS FOR CHRIST

Steve Harvey: "Mr. Buckingham, you lied to me at your
deposition on January 3, 2005. Isn't that true?"

eo Strauss, the German-born, mid-century American political
philosopher widely regarded as the father of the neoconservative
movement, is perhaps most famous, or infamous, for endorsing
Plato's idea of the "noble lie," which extended to lying about belief in God
so that the masses, who he felt need religion, might be able to believe.
Highly educated men and women might be able to conduct themselves
peaceably, fairly, and sustainably, Strauss said, while embracing a purely scientific view of the world. But the masses probably couldn't. In his view,
Christianity and Judaism constituted a sort of shorthand for the canons of
Western culture. If you read everything by Plato, Spinoza, Hobbes, and
Machiavelli, then maybe you can be trusted to pilot the airplane of your
own life, and live according to a secular, reasoned understanding of the
world. But if you're too busy, say, earning a living, it's far safer and better

144

for everyone if you just memorize the Ten Commandments and fly commercial, even if the God at the controls is make believe.

I'm sure this caricature of Strauss's idea doesn't do justice to its nuances; but any lie told to convince people of the importance of telling the truth (and obeying the other nine commandments) is too cynical for me to swallow. I have faith (yes, I know it is faith) enough in the virtues of truth to hold that if God doesn't exist, it would be better for us to know that. How can we choose a safe and sensible flight path for ourselves if we leave the controls in the cockpit unattended, assuming God is in there plotting the course?

Strauss was from a different era, and may well have been less enthusiastic about the eccentric, fundamentalist brand of Christianity that has become so influential today, but that just points to one of the noble lie's big problems. If it is made up, it can shift with the political and cultural winds; it's not tethered to the world by truth. It can drift here and there, promoting peace and love in one generation and conquest, terror, and domination in the next. Nonetheless, my new Italian friend Giulio Meotti, the journalist covering Dover for the neocon daily *Il Folio* in Rome, still thinks Strauss and his noble lie are dead on, an antidote to the dangers of cultural relativism. And the noble lie, he says, is represented by the intelligent design movement in the United States.

Someone, I suspect, is lying in the Dover trial, too. Whether it is a noble lie in the Straussian tradition or simply a selfish one is still unclear.

Over the four weeks of the trial so far, it's become clear that *Kitzmiller* v. *Dover* will have two distinct parts. The first is the one in which we are currently immersed, with the testimony of Miller, Behe, and the other scientists and philosophers: a broad-ranging debate over whether ID is science. The second is a narrow one focusing on the question of whether it was always the fundamental intent of the board members to promote a particular religious view—something prohibited by the Establishment Clause of the First Amendment. Whereas the first argument involves philosophical wrangling over the definitions of *science, teaching, religion, theory,* and other big things, the second focuses on a question that is much more down to earth: what actually happened at the meetings leading up to the Dover school board's decision to change its science curriculum.

After so much highfalutin' philosophy, it's a relief to come back down to the real world of evidence.

The reason the court cares about what happened at those board meetings goes back to another Pennsylvania case, *Lemon* v. *Kurtzman*. In 1971, the Supreme Court ruled that private religious schools couldn't be funded by the government without violating the First Amendment. The case established the "*Lemon* test," which outlines the requirements for determining whether or not a government action is inappropriately religious. To pass the *Lemon* test, an action (1) must have "a legitimate secular purpose," (2) "must not have the primary effect of advancing or inhibiting religion," and (3) can't result in government's "excessive entanglement with religion." If any one of those "three prongs" is violated by a government action, it violates the Establishment Clause and is therefore unconstitutional.[1]

Defense counsel Richard Thompson disdains the *Lemon* test. He doesn't much care for the whole Establishment Clause, in fact, and calls constitutional protection of the separation of church and state a "myth." He thinks motives should be legally irrelevant in cases like these. It shouldn't matter why a school board member or a science teacher wants to teach something, he says. What should matter is whether or not what they want to teach is true.

But until the Supreme Court rules otherwise, the law is that if Dover wants to put ID into the classroom, their main reasons for doing so can't be religious. That would violate the first prong of the *Lemon* test.

The plaintiffs' lawyers, of course, are enthusiastic supporters of both the *Lemon* test and the separation of church and state. Shortly after the suit was filed against the school board back in the fall of 2004, the plaintiffs realized it might be possible to get a preliminary injunction on the case without going through a long and costly trial. They could ask the judge to temporarily enjoin the district from reading the ID statement to schoolchildren on the grounds that the board simply had no "legitimate secular purpose," that its motive for introducing ID was to advance a particular brand of Christianity, not to advance science education. If it worked, if they could demonstrate that the board's purposes were religious, not secular, that might have been enough to shut things down without saying anything about whether ID was religion or valid science.

Remember the board's behavior in the months leading up to the suit? First, curriculum committee chair Bill Buckingham delayed the purchase of the Miller-Levine *Biology* textbook because it was "laced with Darwinism." The newspaper reports quoted Buckingham clearly stating that he wanted to balance the teaching of evolution with creationism. "This country wasn't founded on Muslim beliefs or evolution," he'd told one reporter. "This country was founded on Christianity, and our students should be taught as such."

Then at another raucous board meeting, during a heated fight over curriculum, Buckingham had said in frustration, "Two thousand years ago someone died on a cross, can't someone take a stand for Him?"

And former Dover High student Max Pell stood up at a board meeting and warned the townspeople in attendance that teaching creationism as science would only invite a lawsuit. Buckingham told Pell that he had been brainwashed at college.

Finally, Dover High science teachers were told by school administrators about board plans to balance evolution with creationism long before there was any mention of intelligent design. And all of this had been thoroughly reported in the two local dailies.

It should be obvious to all, Rothschild and Harvey thought, that the school board's intention was not to improve science education but to teach creationism, a viewpoint whose religious pedigree was already well established in the courts. The newspaper coverage ought to speak for itself.

But to get a preliminary injunction in time for the start of winter term, when teachers were slated to read the famous statement in biology class, Rothschild's team would have had to act quickly. In two weeks they would have had to assemble a rough-and-ready version of their case. It would have been a scramble, but well worth the effort if it worked. If Jones had granted the injunction, that would have been a clear sign of his inclination to rule in the plaintiffs' favor when the case came to trial. That alone might have convinced the school board to cut its losses and retreat before risking a million dollars or so in legal fees. And if a preliminary injunction from the judge meant that Tammy Kitzmiller's daughter, Jessica, and the rest of the ninth grade biology class at Dover High wouldn't be taught ID, that would be better, too.

An injunction won't necessarily preempt a trial, but it often does, says Nick Matzke at the NCSE, which monitors such cases. He explains that when a judge grants an injunction, it's a kind of endorsement for the merits of the case being brought against a school board. More often than not, in cases like this, the board will settle rather than fight what looks like a losing battle. Of course, this particular board was not too practical in this regard, and for better or worse it was spurred on by a legal team that was on a kind of Holy Crusade of its own and was hoping to take that Crusade to the Supreme Court.

Ironically, while Rothschild and Harvey, the plaintiffs' corporate lawyers, were arguing for the injunction, the team's public interest lawyers, Vic Walczak of the ACLU and Richard Katskee of Americans United, were leaning the other way. When defending someone's civil rights, Walczak and Katskee often have to swoop in and ask for legal action before the offense is committed, the harm is done, and the point is moot. In those cases, explains Katskee, it's often preferable to go into battle sooner, with a preliminary injunction, even if it means going in less well prepared.

But in this case, he recalls, "We still had a lot to learn about both evolution and intelligent design," and the stakes were so high, they didn't want to rush into it. Rothschild and Harvey both felt they had a very good chance of convincing the judge. But, argued Katskee and Walczak, what if the judge denied the preliminary injunction? Then, although they could still take the case to trial, they would have had to fight it with the cloud of that denial hanging over their heads. And this would have put them at a significant disadvantage.

By all accounts, the internal legal debate over whether or not to apply for the injunction was intense. It was "the hardest strategic decision we had to make," states Katskee, and they had to make it fast—before they had earned one another's trust.

Together, though, they devised a compromise strategy. They would depose a few of the board members and administrators central to the case, and then immediately reevaluate their chances for winning a preliminary injunction based on those testimonies. If the depositions revealed a story that was as straightforward as Rothschild and Harvey had reason to believe, then they would file for the injunction.

They requested and got permission from the judge to depose four witnesses: Bill Buckingham, the head of the curriculum committee and the most outrageously strident ID advocate; Sheila Harkins, a board ally of Buckingham's; Alan Bonsell, the board chairman; and Richard Nilsen, the Dover Area school district superintendent.

For Thompson and his defense team, the overtly religious language used by board members, especially Bill Buckingham, posed a big danger. The board's own local solicitor, Steve Russell, had advised caution in a memo sent August 27, 2004. "My concern for Dover," Russell wrote, "is that, in the last several years, there has been a lot of discussion, newsprint, etc., for putting religion back in the schools. In my mind, this would add weight to a lawsuit seeking to enjoin."

For Thompson, an injunction would spell disaster. With a preliminary ruling against them, the board could well get cold feet and pull out.

The night before the preliminary depositions, on January 2, 2005, defense attorneys Richard Thompson and Pat Gillen met for several hours with board members Harkins, Buckingham, and Bonsell, Superintendent Richard Nilsen, and his assistant, Michael Baksa, to prepare. By the next day, when they were deposed, the witnesses' stories had undergone a strange coevolution into something, well, simply unbelievable.

149

Early on the morning of the depositions, January 3, Rothschild and Harvey drove to Dover together from Philadelphia through the cold, gray countryside. They pulled into the high school parking lot, wished each other well, and went their separate ways. Rothschild would be deposing school superintendent Nilsen and board president Bonsell in the school administration building (which used to be the school's bus storage facility), and Harvey would depose Harkins and Buckingham at the high school itself, across the alleyway.

In the morning, Rothschild began with Richard Nilsen, the Ph.D. school superintendent, and was surprised to find his testimony distressingly evasive. Nilsen didn't go so far as to deny that Buckingham, the head of the curriculum committee, had made inflammatory religious remarks, or that he had often mentioned creationism. He just kept saying that he didn't remember, couldn't recall, or hadn't been there. Yes, he was aware of the articles in the paper alleging talk of creationism, and he thought they were inaccurate—at least to his memory. But he didn't have time to try to correct every mistake reporters made. The deposition went on for about two hours, and Nilsen said nothing to confirm reports that members of the board had—at least in the beginning—openly advocated putting creationism into the curriculum.

When it was over, Rothschild called Harvey to report the surprising news. Harvey could sympathize; he had interviewed Sheila Harkins, a super-Christian board member, homemaker, and ally of Alan Bonsell's, and had a similar experience—but worse, he told Rothschild. Unlike the evasive Nilsen, Harkins had directly contradicted the reports in the papers and the numerous other accounts of what had been said in the board meetings. The board had not talked about creationism at all in its meetings, she insisted. And Buckingham had never said anything about the need to balance the teaching of evolution with the teaching of creationism.

Harkins had a bad cold the day of the deposition, and between her sneezing, coughing, and blowing her nose, she was very nearly incoherent. On some subjects, however, she was quite confident: she acknowledged that

Buckingham had made the comment, "Two thousand years ago someone died on a cross for us. Shouldn't we have the courage to stand up for Him?" but said that had happened at an unrelated meeting a full year earlier than reported in the press. He'd made that memorable statement at a discussion over the appropriateness of removing the words "under God" from the Pledge of Allegiance, she said. Nor did she remember Charlotte Buckingham, Bill's wife, reading a passage from Genesis to the board and then making the statements, "How can we allow anything else to be taught in our schools?" and "Evolution teaches nothing but lies."

Harvey was confident that she was not telling him the truth.

That afternoon, Rothschild interviewed Alan Bonsell, who would emerge as a central character in the case. The owner of C. R. Smith Radiator and Auto Repair Shop in Dover, Bonsell presided over the school board. He is a happy-go-lucky, cocksure guy, full of cheerful bravado. His father, Don Bonsell, was on the school board before him, and Barrie Callahan remembers Don announcing back in 1995 that he wanted the Bible displayed at all board meetings.

Alan Bonsell was elected to the board in December 2001 on a platform of fiscal responsibility. There was a big row at the time over the remodeling of the high school, and Bonsell ran on a ticket with Sheila Harkins, Angie Yingling, and Casey Brown on a promise to bring the building project (which they derisively called the "Taj Mahal") to a halt and scale it back to more modest dimensions. Their success at the polls shifted the majority away from the more moderate and, as it happens, more evolution-friendly contingent that had okayed the building project in the first place.

Barrie Callahan, who'd been on the board since 1993, was on the other side of the high school remodeling debate, and she and Bonsell became archrivals, not just on this issue but on pretty much every one that came up. Bonsell represented the ultra-conservative, ultra-Christian, old Dover, which was struggling to reassert itself through civic institutions such as the school board. Callahan represented the elite, over-educated, borrow-and-spend liberals who had somehow snuck local power away from Old Dover, at least in the eyes of Old Dover.

The struggle over the high school was hot enough that two board members resigned over it in the spring of 2002. To fill their seats, the remaining board members could vote to appoint two new members. There were three candidates for the two jobs, Callahan tells me. One was an engineer who was familiar with educational theory and very articulate on the subject. Another candidate was Jane Cleaver, owner of a general store in Dover and a very devout Christian with an eighth-grade education. Finally, there was Bill Buckingham, the ex-cop. The new board consolidated its "moral majority" by forgoing the engineer and appointing Cleaver and Buckingham.

In his deposition, Bonsell, like Supervisor Nilsen and Sheila Harkins, insisted that he had never heard anyone mention creationism in the context of a board meeting, and that Buckingham's statement about Christ two thousand years ago was from an earlier meeting. Like the others, when asked why two competing daily papers would give the same wrong accounts of creationism being discussed at board meetings, Buckingham suggested that the reporters must have compared notes.

When Rothschild called Harvey to find out about the Buckingham deposition, he heard the same tune for a fourth time that day. Only Buckingham's was the most extreme version of all. Not only did he deny having talked about creationism at any of the meetings, he'd also not read any of the newspaper articles about his own alleged indiscretions, nor had he talked to anyone at all about those articles, and no one had ever mentioned to him that they had heard he'd been talking about creationism. He didn't remember anything that had happened at the inflammatory June meetings. But he could confidently say that he and the rest of the board wanted intelligent design in the curriculum only because it was good science, he said, and it was good for students. His interest in ID had nothing to do with his independent interest in creationism. It had nothing to do with his independent interest in religion.

Complete denial.

Here is a synopsis of what Rothschild calls the "parallel universe" described by the board members on that cold January morning:

152

Perhaps it was their own Pennsylvania U.S. Senator Rick Santorum's amendment to the president's 2002 No Child Left Behind bill that piqued their interest, but at some point several members of the cooperative, wholesome, and moderate Dover school board became interested in the scientific theory of intelligent design. In his amendment (which never became law but was adopted into the legislative history of the bill, and may have some influence on its interpretation) Santorum wrote that "Where topics are taught that may generate controversy (such as biological evolution), the curriculum should help students to understand the full range of scientific views that exist, why such topics may generate controversy, and how scientific discoveries can profoundly affect society."[2] Or perhaps it was their own interest in the variety of explanations for the formation of new species. Or their interest in the cutting edge of the biological sciences. But whatever it was that led them there, they had decided that their school would be improved by adding a little more science to the biology curriculum.

In 2003, the board members asked the administrators to float the idea of teaching ID alongside of evolution by the science teachers, who were generally cooperative and open to the idea of enhancing the curriculum in whatever ways their bosses saw fit.

Eventually, in July 2004, they brought it up at a board meeting or two. The community, which had turned out in great numbers at these meetings to discuss an unrelated position in the English department, seemed open to the idea of putting ID into the curriculum. There had been some objections expressed by compulsive complainers, such as Barrie Callahan, but they were addressed in a cooperative spirit.

The school board decided against purchasing *Of Pandas and People* as a textbook, but decided it could be kept on hand as an additional resource for interested students. Fortuitously, miraculously one might even say, the school was granted an anonymous donation of sixty copies of the book. No one had any idea where the donation came from, but they were always happy to receive quality education materials for free.

The school board discussed the possibility of putting ID in their curriculum with both Discovery Institute and Thomas More Law Center, and both organizations concurred that it would be both pedagogically sound and constitutionally safe. If for some reason the board has trouble with the law, they were told by the Law Center's Richard Thompson, the Center would represent them for free. He would defend the school board's right to teach the truth all the way to the Supreme Court if necessary, Thompson said.

Discovery Institute gave the board, through Bill Buckingham, copies of the book *Icons of Evolution,* a documentary DVD of the same name, and another documentary, titled *Unlocking the Mystery of Life*. Buckingham thought these materials might interest the high school biology teachers, and he asked Michael Baksa to pass them on. The teachers found the materials interesting, but reasonably asked that they not be required to teach about "origins of life" or "monkey to man," which the board members took to mean speciation.

Now that the whole community, with the exception of those few compulsive complainers, was in general agreement with the idea of upgrading the biology instruction at Dover High, the board decided to make a minor adjustment to the science curriculum. They would insert the following addition: "Students will be made aware of gaps/problems in Darwin's theory and of other theories of evolution including, but not limited to, intelligent design. Note: *Origins of Life* is not taught."

When they heard about the curriculum change, some of the teachers expressed concern that if there were challenges to its constitutionality, they might be personally liable. Also, not knowing much about ID yet, they requested some specific instructions about how to introduce ID to their students. So, ever responsive to the teaching staff, the board and the administrators composed the four-paragraph statement about how Darwin's theory was a theory and about how there were other good theories, too—ID, for instance—and about how if students wanted to learn more they could read reference books on the subject that would be available in the library. That statement—to be read at the outset of each ninth grade biology class—would be all the discussion of ID required of the teachers. No big deal.

For some reason, probably having to do with the teachers union, even after the administration responded to teachers' worries by writing the statement, the teachers didn't want to read the paragraphs to the students. No problem, said the administrators, we'll read it to the students for you. Nothing to get worked up about, just a short statement about the diversity of scientific theories, they said. It was good pedagogy. Good science.

The board was surprised and dumbfounded when the lawsuit was filed out of the blue by a small group of complainers and the ACLU. The end.

That's the basic story told by all four of the witnesses in their depositions on that freezing January day.

The plaintiffs' legal team was "shocked," says Rothschild. The testimonies were in near perfect alignment with each other but were uniformly out of alignment with the Dover story told by everybody else.

After a brief period of stunned disorientation, during which Rothschild called Max Pell, Barrie Callahan, and others "to see if we were crazy," as Callahan put it—"Are you *sure* you heard them actually use the word *creationism?*" Rothschild asked Callahan. "Yes! Of course!" she said. "Would you be willing to sign an affidavit saying that?" he asked his own client. "Absolutely!" she said—they realized that the witnesses they'd deposed were simply recounting a fairy tale.

It seemed a very shortsighted tactic, says Rothschild. While it might buy the defense a ticket to the trial without the burden of an injunction, it would certainly derail them in the long run if their duplicity were revealed in court. If they were shown to be lying in order to camouflage the creationist roots of their interest in ID, it would drive home the impression that it was religion under cover that fueled the process. The Trojan horse metaphor, applied to the whole ID movement by Barbara Forrest, would seem precisely descriptive of the school board's specific tactics. They had hastily built a silly looking rocking horse out of available bits of scrap just to get themselves in the schoolhouse door.

Furthermore, says Rothschild, their insistence that they couldn't remember ever having discussed creationism effectively locked them out of the effort to characterize or explain that conversation in a way that would make it less objectionable. For example, they were powerless to claim that it was Buckingham alone who cared about creationism, because all of them had denied that the word had even come up.

Who concocted that story? Was it the board members themselves? Their attorneys at the Thomas More Law Center? Only they know what they did at the long meeting the night before the depositions. But it seems reasonable that they may have devised a story that would get them past the preliminary injunction. Was it an elaborate self-deceit, or just old-fashioned but short-sighted lying for a just cause? Maybe the defendants came up with the story on their own, and their lawyers were complicit only in that they didn't sufficiently question their clients. No one wants to accuse the defense lawyers of suborning their witnesses to perjury; certainly the lawyers for the plaintiffs don't want to level such allegations. However it happened, it was a big false first step, and a nice gift for the plaintiffs.

The depositions brought the plaintiffs' lawyers debate about whether to apply for an injunction to an abrupt halt.

After the depositions Eric Rothschild, Steve Harvey, Vic Walczak, Richard Katskee, and Paula Knudsen (another ACLU lawyer from the Pittsburg office) ate dinner together at the mahogany-paneled downtown Harrisburg restaurant, Stocks on 2nd.

"At that dinner our team really came together for the first time," Harvey says. "We coalesced."

"Our entire team was back in agreement at that point," says Katzkee. The judge would never grant a preliminary injunction, not without some agreement between the parties on what had happened at those board meetings. They'd crossed their Rubicon; they were going to trial and their preparations—which now would include revealing the lies told at the depositions, as well as deconstructing intelligent design—began in earnest.

❧

When the teachers heard that the possibility of a preliminary injunction was dead, they decided to protest the board's action and announced that they would not read the ID statement to their students. Later in January, when school reconvened, administrators Michael Baksa and Richard Nilsen took on the role themselves and went into each of the ninth-grade biology classes and read the statement aloud to the students. When Baksa and Nilsen came to Jennifer Miller's classroom, Miller and her student Jessica Kitzmiller excused themselves and waited in the hallway while the statement was recited.

CHAPTER TWELVE

THE UNRAVELING

BILL BUCKINGHAM: "I had it in my mind to make sure, make double
sure nobody talks about creationism, we're talking intelligent design. I had
it on my mind, I was like a deer in the headlights of a car, and I misspoke.
Pure and simple, I made a human mistake."
STEVE HARVEY: "Freudian slip, right, Mr. Buckingham?"

T hose pretrial depositions were ten months ago. Over that time,
the plaintiffs' lawyers have immersed themselves in the broad
fields of evolutionary biology and intelligent design. They have
also learned a lot about the local characters and events that put ID into the
Dover classroom. Rothschild and his colleagues believe they know enough
now to prove that Buckingham, Bonsell, Harkins, and Nilsen were lying at
those January pretrial depositions.

A lot of what they've learned centers around Bill Buckingham. In the
midst of this controversy, in August 2005, a month before the trial opened,
Buckingham resigned from the school board and moved to North Carolina,
allegedly for health reasons. So although he was at the center of the most
inflammatory allegations and stories, I have never seen him. In my mind at
least, he'd begun to take on mythical proportions. I imagined he would be

the trial's Billy Graham–like character, robust and strident, a master of Christian apologetics, confident in Word and deed.

But to my disappointment, the defense isn't planning to call Bill Buckingham up at all; he will only be brought up later as a hostile witness by the plaintiffs. First we'll hear testimony from the mouths of the school administrators, the paid executors of the school's policy: Superintendent Richard Nilsen and his assistant, Michael Baksa.

By the time of their testimonies, several important bits of information have surfaced. One of the most interesting is the source of the miracle that brought those sixty copies of *Pandas* to the high school. Lawyers for the plaintiffs got hold of the check that had paid for the books and found—lo and behold!—that it had been written by Bill Buckingham, who had raised the money from his congregation one Sunday morning at Harmony Grove Community Church. The check was made out to Donald Bonsell, father of school board president Alan Bonsell. Buckingham had given the money to Alan, who passed it on to his dad, who purchased the books. It was not a very sophisticated scheme; in the check's subject line was written: "For *Pandas and People*."[1] Remember, in his deposition Buckingham had denied any knowledge of where the books had come from.

This does not look good for the defendants. The money was surreptitiously raised in a church by a member of the board, laundered through the board president, and given to a former board president, himself known for his activism in bringing religion into the schools, who secretly bought the books. If you were trying to prove a covert religious intent, you couldn't find a better story than this one to illustrate it.

The court has also heard testimony from several Dover science teachers, who all told a very different story than the one in those January depositions.

Bertha Spahr, the plucky forty-one-year veteran teacher at the school and the head of the science department, insisted that none of the teachers had been at all comfortable with the idea of putting ID into the school's science curriculum. She said that about a year before the curriculum change,

Baksa had given her a "heads up" that a member of the school board was interested in having creationism share equal time with evolution. Spahr asked Baksa which board member that was. "Alan Bonsell," he said.

Spahr testified that she'd had numerous meetings with administrators and board members at which the word *creationism* was used. But it wasn't just the use of the word that the board members had misrepresented, Spahr said. They'd told an unrecognizable story about the role of the teachers in the whole process.

Jennifer Miller, a fourteen-year veteran Dover High biology teacher, echoed that sentiment. "We never liked the statement. We never wanted to put ID into the curriculum. We never wanted to be or appear to be in cahoots with the board in making the statements. We never wanted to use *Of Pandas and People*." Although board members and administrators were asking for the advice of teachers, Miller said in an interview, they were not listening to it. Certainly they weren't heeding it.

I had asked Miller if she felt supported by Nilsen and Baksa when the curriculum change was still in the works, before the suit was filed. "No," she said. "I'd asked several times point blank for them to stand up and say 'This is not right.' But they didn't. In fact, at one point Mr. Baksa came to talk to me and said, 'If you do this [refuse to support the policy], then the board can get you for insubordination, and I can't stand up for you.'"[2]

The cats are streaming out of the bag. Defendants have lied about where the copies of *Of Pandas and People* came from, about whether or not they had discussed putting creationism into the curriculum, and about the role the science teachers (the only ones on the staff or the board with any science expertise at all) had played in the decision to adopt ID. All this deception is apparent to the court. By the time Superintendent Nilsen takes the stand on October 20, we—the science writers, the reporters, and public observers in the courtroom—are all asking the same questions: How will he handle it now? Will he continue to toe the party line, to pretend he knew nothing of the motivations and plans of his bosses? Will the fact that he has already been dishonest lock him into a fabulous story the way a child sometimes gets locked into a lie, no matter how absurd?

Nilsen has frequently been in court in the days before his own testimony, and I've been watching him closely. Though he often sits next to Bonsell, his affect is at the other extreme. Where Bonsell chews gum and lounges, arms outstretched, in his pew, Nilsen is reserved and sits up straight, his hands folded in his lap. He is tall, mustached, and rakish, handsome even, and dressed carefully in a blue blazer, pressed trousers, and conservative ties.

But once on the stand, he also looks pained and anxious. Local columnist Mike Argento, who covered the trial closely for the *York Daily Record*, later wrote that Nilsen wore the expression of "a man on his way to a prostate examination."

Now Nilsen is saying that he remembers Buckingham and the student Max Pell having a heated exchange, but he can't remember what they talked about. He remembers Bill Buckingham's wife, Charlotte, standing up before the board and reading from the Bible for fifteen minutes (an account that everyone else said was a plea for teaching a literal Biblical understanding of creation), but, "to this day I have no idea what she was trying to present," he says.

Nilsen says he does not remember anyone using the expression *creationism* at all. He does remember getting a memo from the high school principal warning him that the senior science teacher, Bertha Spahr, had told her she was being pressured by Buckingham to bring creationism into the science class, but Nilsen dismissed the memo because the principal was known as an alarmist prone to exaggerate. He'd read the reports in the newspaper about Buckingham's statements, and though he didn't think they were accurate, he hadn't tried to correct them. He even went on to say that the crowded, red-hot July meeting in the summer, just before the curriculum change was adopted, had drawn so many people, as far as he knew, not because of the science curriculum but because the board was considering eliminating a high school English position.

Rothschild is unfazed. Over and over again, he brings up events at which ID and evolution and creationism had been discussed, at which teachers had voiced concerns about creationism entering the curriculum, and time and again Nilsen says he can't remember.

Then Rothschild floats the idea that the defense witnesses, during that original set of pretrial depositions ten long months ago, had colluded. He reads a memo from Nilsen to the board members: "The time and effort put in over the holidays"—this would be the Christmas holidays before the January 2 depositions—"has produced a positive impact. The plaintiffs, ACLU, could not find anything to file an injunction on our biology curriculum. In conjunction with the Thomas More lawyers, Mr. Baksa, Mr. Buckingham, Mr. Bonsell, and Mrs. Harkins did a great job. The ACLU is doing a great job of putting a 'positive spin,' on the situation, but I cannot help but feel gratified that they could not stop the implementation [that is, get the injunction], and you know if they could, they would have."

Everyone is looking at Nilsen for some sign of contrition or any emotion at all. His face remains impassive.

❧

Barrie Callahan is in the courtroom for part of Nilsen's testimony. Her son had a successful emergency appendectomy the night before, and her husband, Fred, another plaintiff, has melanoma surgery scheduled for later today. So instead of pacing around and worrying about their son in recovery, or Fred's upcoming cuts, husband and wife decide to step into the court to see Nilsen testify.

"It was so painful to witness," she says later. "I like Dr. Nilsen." Callahan pauses. "It was excruciatingly uncomfortable. I wanted to scream, 'What are you doing?'"

Instead, she whispers. Callahan is sitting in the front row of the observation pews, right behind the bar, and "whispers" to her husband, "I can't believe he's covering up for them!" But the whisper carries across the courtroom, and Vic Walczak swings around in his seat on the far side of the bar and glares at her.

At the end of his cross-examination, Rothschild asks Nilsen about the e-mail that Steve Russell, the board's own local lawyer, had sent recounting a conversation he'd had with Richard Thompson. Russell wrote in the e-mail "they [Thomas More lawyers] refer to the creationism issue as 'intelligent design.'" Indicting enough to suggest that they need a translation from their real concern, creationism, to the updated lingo, ID, but Russell goes on to warn his client "it could be difficult to win a case. I say this because one of the common themes in some of the U.S. Supreme Court decisions, especially dealing with silent meditation, is that even though something is voluntary, it still causes a problem because the practice, whatever it may be, was initiated for religious reasons." Russell points out that if the school board were to lose the case, even though Thompson's firm was representing them for free, they would have to pay the legal fees for the prevailing plaintiffs. "And you think our fees are high . . . ," he writes.

Finally, the Russell memo concludes, "My concern for Dover is that, in the last several years, there has been a lot of discussion, newsprint, etc., for putting religion back in the schools. In my mind, this would add weight to a lawsuit seeking to enjoin, whatever the practice might be."

Rothschild asks Nilsen, "That's what Mr. Russell told you, giving his legal advice in this e-mail he sent to you?"

"Yes," says Nilsen.

"And you knew exactly what he meant, didn't you?" says Rothschild.

"Yes."

It is a touching moment. Rothschild has given Nilsen, the child locked into his story, a way of indirectly acknowledging the truth. It seemed a very decent and humane thing to do.[3]

"This would be a good time to break, Your Honor," says Rothschild.

Bill Buckingham is an odd character to find at one of the two centers of this binary star–system of a trial. As it turns out, he is in no visible way a powerful person. Presumably he was once somewhat imposing, at least when in his police uniform. But not anymore. By the time he is sworn in on

October 27, Buckingham appears weak in mind and body. He walks with a cane because of knee problems, and every limp expresses a weary kind of bitterness.

If Buckingham is pathetic, it is a pathos that is hard to sympathize with for long. He displays the kind of confidence that only the ignorant can wear in public without embarrassment. A retired cop and prison guard supervisor, he acts above the law, as though too sly to worry about any government bureaucracy like the federal courts or "liberal" lawyers—such as the Republican Steve Harvey, who has him on the stand.

Buckingham is also a recovering drug addict. Several years ago, after knee surgery, Buckingham was prescribed, and became addicted to, Oxy-Contin, the addictive painkiller—sometimes called "hillbilly heroin"—that took Rush Limbaugh out of service for a couple of months in 2003. And it was his OxyContin addiction that prompted Buckingham to resign from the board in August 2005 and move to North Carolina.

Before they moved south, Buckingham and his wife had lived in Dover for twenty-eight years. They have three grown kids, all of whom went to Dover High. They attended Harmony Grove Community Church, probably the most conservative of the dozens of local evangelical churches in Dover. (Out of curiosity, I went to a Fourth of July service at the church and found the fusion of Christian and patriotic military symbolism—crosses and fighter jets projected onto the giant video screen—chilling.)

Buckingham is to this part of the trial what Behe was to the scientific debate. Everyone covering the event has been waiting to see him take the stand. But unlike Behe, whom the defense team was proud to present, Buckingham has not been called forth by his own lawyers. Rather, he's been subpoenaed to testify as a hostile witness by the plaintiffs' lawyers and was flown here from North Carolina for the occasion. In fact, it occurs to me during Gillen's presumably friendly examination of Buckingham that the most effective defense strategy for them now might be to just throw Buckingham to the sharks, act as if he were just one rogue ultra-Christian creationist on an otherwise science-oriented curriculum committee. If only he hadn't been the chair of that committee. And if only he hadn't been so inextricably tied to the board's president and its two remaining members. And if only Harkins and Bonsell hadn't also pretended Buckingham never pushed teaching creationism in the first place. Anyway, the sharks would never be satisfied with Buckingham alone.

Although Alan Bonsell seems to have been the first Dover board member in the modern era to have made creationism an issue for the district (at his first board retreat back in January 2002 he listed "creationism" as a priority for the coming year), it was Buckingham, appointed to head the district's curriculum committee by Bonsell, who pursued creationism, then ID, with a very public vengeance.

But from the moment Buckingham takes the stand, it is clear that his interest in ID isn't driven by the irreducible complexity of the bacterial flagellum, nor by irksome doubts about the inability of natural selection to account for the pace of speciation in the Cambrian explosion. It is clear, in fact, that where an interest in evolution might reside, Buckingham has only prejudiced reflexes. And they are good enough for him.

When asked to explain intelligent design, he says, "Scientists, a lot of scientists, don't ask me the names, I can't tell you where it came from, a lot of scientists believe that back through time something, molecules, amoeba, whatever, evolved into the complexities of life we have now."

Did the head of the curriculum committee want to add anything to that? Rothschild asks. Sure. Buckingham adds, "Plus the fact that I felt that life was too complex to have randomly happened without a design of some sort."

His testimony borders on bathos. Harvey asks him whether he had read the newspaper accounts describing his own creationism quotes at board meetings. Buckingham says that he stopped reading the paper long ago. They never get anything right anyway. Harvey asks if he gets the papers delivered to his home. Buckingham says, "My father did, when he came to live with us after my mother passed away, and he liked getting both the papers, and he was with us for almost seven years before he died of lung cancer."

When did your father die? asks Harvey. In 2003, says Buckingham. But you kept getting the papers, says Harvey, trying to stay on topic. "They came," admits Buckingham, "but I didn't read them."

This was the man assigned by Bonsell to govern the school district's curriculum.

As it happens, those two daily papers play a central role in this part of the trial. To support their story that there was no board meeting talk about creationism, board members had to contend that the newspaper stories reporting such conversations were made up. And the board members and administrators also had to explain why none of them had objected to the alleged inaccuracies of the reporting at the time. It is an implausible story to maintain, but because they committed to it in the pretrial depositions, as their price of admission to the trial, they have to try.

"Now," Harvey counters, "it's your testimony that at neither [June] meeting no one on the board ever mentioned creationism, isn't that right?"

"That's true."

"You're very clear on that point, correct?"

"Absolutely, because it's just something we didn't do."

At least they *tried* to stop doing it after they were told it was unconstitutional. But Buckingham couldn't help himself. At the end of his testimony, Harvey runs a video of a local television news report that showed Buckingham wearing the same Christian cross wrapped in an American flag that he has stuck in his lapel today. In the news clip, which was shot in June, Buckingham told the interviewer, "My opinion [is that] it's okay to teach Darwin, but you have to balance it with something else, such as creationism."

Asked to explain how he came to make that remark, he says, "I had it in my mind to make sure, make double sure nobody talks about creationism, we're talking intelligent design. I had it on my mind, I was like a deer in the headlights of a car, and I misspoke. Pure and simple, I made a human mistake."

"Freudian slip, right, Mr. Buckingham?" asks Harvey.

"I won't say a Freudian slip. I'll say I made a human mistake," says Buckingham.

By this point Judge Jones must know, as everyone in the courtroom must, that the story told in the pretrial depositions was a fabrication. And his impatience is beginning to simmer. In place of his benign equanimity that impatience grows visible in his displeased expression and his reddening face. He keeps the lid on it through Buckingham's testimony, however.

Jones preserves his controlled demeanor through Michael Baksa's testimony, too. Baksa is the assistant superintendent in charge of curriculum. He was the go-between charged with the awful task of trying to impose what he knew to be a bad board policy on a good teaching staff. While still evasive, compared with Nilsen's and Buckingham's, Baksa's testimony is refreshingly frank. He appears to be struggling to let the truth out without completely giving up the board's charade. I assume this is a reflection of his character, but it may also be due to the fact that he was not deposed in January like the others, so he is not as bound by his own early testimony.

In any case, Baksa acknowledges that Buckingham talked about creationism at the June meetings, just like the reporters said he did. Everyone already knows that, but it is an important moment just the same because Baksa is testifying for the defense. He is one of them, and he is acknowledging the real world. After a year of denying that fact, and forcing reporters to defend their work, the truth is confirmed by the defendants' own witness.

The judge even retains his composure through the testimony of board member Heather Geesey, a caricature of the hapless creationist. While Geesey maintains that she thinks it's important to inform students of the "gaps and problems" with evolution, she clearly has no idea what those gaps and problems are. Nor does she know what is covered in *Of Pandas and People*. Nor does she know anything about what she refers to as "intelligence design." In fact, she tells the court, no one has ever explained ID to her, she was just relying on the experts, Buckingham and Bonsell, to make the right decision regarding the science curriculum. She trusted them, she says, and cites Buckingham's experience in law enforcement as evidence for his scientific authority.

Who will play these people in the movie? I wonder.

However, John Jones III—who says he would rather be portrayed by Tom Hanks than Alec Baldwin—can stand what he stands, but he can't stand

no more, as Popeye used to say. The judge finally loses his composure during board chairman Alan Bonsell's evasive testimony. For several hours Bonsell dissembles on questions about his use of the word *creationism*, about why
he'd not tried to correct any of the supposedly fabricated stories in the local
press, and whether or not the board ever intended to put creationism into
the curriculum. As with the other board members, it becomes pretty clear
that Bonsell hasn't taken the time to actually learn much about either evolution or intelligent design.

Gillen asks Bonsell if he thinks ID is creationism and Bonsell says
absolutely not, that creationism is "the creation as recounted in the Bible,"
and ID is "a theory made up by scientists."

Asked what problems he has with teaching the theory of evolution
alone, he says, "What runs in my mind is basically the, when you're teaching, this is a theory that they're teaching, and when they don't include, you
know, problems with it or gaps in a theory I mean, and you teach it, it
almost sounds like they're teaching it as fact, and that's what, you know, I
was sort of concerned about and was just asking questions about."

But when he is cross-examined by Harvey, the subject finally comes
back to the question of where the money was raised and how it made its
way to the publishers of *Of Pandas and People*.

In his testimony Buckingham has already admitted, in contradiction
to his January 3 deposition, that he had raised the money for the books at
his church and that he had written out a check for $850 to Bonsell, who had
given that check to his father, Don, who had sent it to the publishers of *Of
Pandas and People*. So the facts of the matter are already established. It was
also clearly established that Bonsell, like Buckingham, had originally denied
this account of things. But now, on the stand in the courtroom, he is unwilling to acknowledge that he lied in his sworn deposition. The judge has finally
had enough and exercises his prerogative to step into the examination and
dress Bonsell down.

"Why," Judge Jones intones at Bonsell, "did you say in your deposition
that you didn't know who was involved with the donation of the books?"

It is like the scene in *The Wizard of Oz* when the frightful, bulbous-headed image on the screen turns out to be a mere Frank Morgan. Only it is reversed. In this case, the mild-mannered, fair, and funny John Jones transforms from a mere Tom Hanks into a frightening figure lording over the courtroom with a red face and distended arteries pounding on his neck.

Bonsell's cocksure posture crumbles. He tries to answer, but like the Cowardly Lion he is worse than speechless. A strange arrangement of barely related words emerges, and buried within them is an acknowledgment of his perjury: "Then I misspoke," he says, "because I was still under—from behind—wait a second. I—well, I'm going back here—and so, yeah, that's my fault, Your Honor, because that's not—in that case, I would have—I should have said [in answer to the question, Who was involved with the donation?], Mr. Buckingham."

Wan, deflated, and trembling, Bonsell, and the board's self-image as honorable Christians fighting for truth and honor, are dismissed from the stand as the court adjourns for the day.

CHAPTER THIRTEEN

THE FORTIETH DAY

SCOTT MINNICH: "So you have this most sophisticated information storage
system coupled with macromolecular machines that are also highly
sophisticated, with ordered parts that we by definition call
irreducibly complex. It's appropriate to go back and ask,
Is a Darwinian mechanism sufficient to account for the appearance of these?"

uddenly, somehow incredibly, the trial has come down to its last
day. But before the closing arguments can commence, the defense will present its final witness, what it hopes will be its
knight in shining lab coat: an academic microbiologist from the University
of Idaho, and another fellow at Discovery Institute, Scott Minnich.

The final designated scientist turns out to be a likeable, middle-aged
guy with thinning bangs and a nice smile who can say, "Molecular genetics
is my bread and butter," without smugness. Under direct examination by
Robert Muise, the young Kennnedyesque defense lawyer with Thomas
More, he admits that he has not studied evolutionary biology beyond the
introductory undergraduate level. But then, why would he need to? Frankly,
he says, as microbiologists, he and his colleagues don't pay much attention
to evolution. The theory of natural selection, while interesting and valuable

as far as it goes, is mostly irrelevant as a tool in their work and hardly a cornerstone of the sort of modern biology that he practices from day to day.

Plaintiffs' attorney Steve Harvey makes the mistake, at least he swears it's a mistake, of twice calling Minnich "Dr. Behe," but it has the rhetorical impact of reducing two ID scientists down to one. The testimonies of Behe and Minnich are, to put it gently, reflective.

"We're clones," jokes Minnich.

Judge Jones smiles and raises his eyebrows.

It borders on parody when Minnich chooses to illustrate the concept of irreducible complexity with our old friend the bacterial flagellum. "We've seen that," the judge quips dryly when the image appears on the display screen.

"I kind of feel like Zsa Zsa's fifth husband, you know? I know what to do but I just can't make it exciting," Minnich jokes back, provoking a little sympathetic laughter.

Although he promises to try to buck the odds and to make his testimony interesting, alas, it really isn't much different than Behe's: a bacterial flagellum, with its remarkable tail, is just way too complex, and complex in way too complex a way, to be explained away by natural selection. It looks like a machine—and every machine has a designer (and also a creator, Steve Harvey slyly points out in his cross-examination).

He is not anti-evolution, Minnich assures the court; it's just that he has profound doubts about the ability of natural selection to explain the diversity of life we see around us. "The cell is now recognized as being orders of magnitude more complex and sophisticated than Darwin envisaged," Minnich testifies. "It's reasonable . . . to revisit the question as to whether natural selection is sufficiently up to the task of design engineering this recognized sophistication we find in even the simplest of cells."

When Muise asks Minnich why this isn't just an argument from incredulity, he answers that it is just the opposite. As a scientist, he says, he is called to be relentlessly skeptical. But when it comes to accepting that there is an evolutionary pathway that explains incredibly complex, and irreducibly complex, molecular machines such as the flagellum, he's just supposed to operate on faith, to suppress his skepticism. Well "darn it," he says, raising his voice a little, it's unfair that we are then "accused of suffering from incredulity because we can't imagine how these came about.

"As a scientist I am supposed to accept without blinking that this is a product of a Darwinian mechanism, and I'm sorry, these are highly sophisticated systems, and I know from experience that when you see a machine, a rotary engine, in any other context, you would assume that there's an engineer around."

Muise seems to sense that this latest appearance of the flagellum in Judge Jones's courtroom has been one too many, and changes gears. He gives Minnich the same series of questions he had asked Behe: Is ID science? Yes. Does it make testable claims? Yes. Does it require the action of a supernatural creator? No. Is Darwin's theory a fact? No. Are there gaps and problems with Darwin's theory? Yes. Does making students aware that Darwin's theory is not a fact promote good science education? Yes. Examination concluded.

Steve Harvey, the intense forty-seven-year-old Pepper Hamilton lawyer, rises to cross. Even if natural selection is inadequate to the task of explaining the origins of life and the evolution of the complex machinery we see, he asks, how, from that, can we conclude the existence of intelligent design? Is there a positive argument for design?

"Inference," says Minnich. It looks a lot like things we know are designed so without a better explanation we can infer it is so.

Then Harvey pulls a rabbit out of his hat, a rabbit with a tail that could spin at the rate of 100,000 rpm. A flagellar rabbit in the form of an article, predating by three years the publication of *Darwin's Black Box,* the book by Michael Behe in which the idea of "irreducible complexity" was allegedly hammered out and from which the bacterial flagellum became the molecular poster child for both irreducible complexity and intelligent design.

The article, titled "Not So Blind a Watchmaker," is in a journal called *Creation Research Society Quarterly*, an overtly creationist journal published by the Creation Research Society.

And there, on page 19, is a picture of none other than our now old friend the bacterial flagellum, accompanied by text that calls it a "nanomachine," which sounds a lot like biological machine, and a description that is a pretty good summary statement for Behe's and Minnich's claim for the flagellum's irreducible complexity: "However, it is clear from the details of [the flagellum's] operation that nothing about them works unless every one of their complexly fashioned and integrated components are in place."

And a little further along in the article, he reads, "In terms of biophysical complexity, the bacterial rotor flagellum is without precedent in the living world. . . . To evolutionists the system presents an enigma. To creationists it offers clear and compelling evidence of purposeful intelligent design."

"I'd like you to agree with me, Dr. Behe," said Harvey, getting the name wrong again, "that that is essentially the same argument . . ."

"Minnich," says Minnich, this time without humor.

"I did it again," says Harvey, "I'm sorry. . . . I'd like you to agree with me, to know whether you agree with me that that is the same argument that you have advanced here today in your direct testimony."

"Right, I mean in terms of—I don't have any problem with that statement."

Minnich remains calm, but the betrayal is evident. The flagellum has already been a poster child! For the Creation Research Society!

Pressing on, Harvey lists other Discovery Institute fellows who happen to think that the intelligent designer is the Christian God of the Bible: Nancy Pearcey, Phillip Johnson, Michael Behe, William Dembski, Dean Kenyon, and Charles Thaxton.

Yes, that's true, Minnich acknowledges, but their reasons for believing in the Christian God are not scientific; they are religious. He himself is predisposed to believe that the intelligence behind the magnificent cellular structures he works with every day is the Christian God, too. But as a scientist, he can't say that. All he can say is that it's something.

But, Harvey wants to know, why some *thing*, singular? There's no scientific reason not to believe that there are lots of intelligent designers, or competing intelligent designers, or evil intelligent designers. The philosopher David Hume had asked a version of this question more than two centuries ago: Even if you are convinced of divine creativity, he'd said, how do you know that God is working alone and not as part of a committee, or that He is not incompetent, or an infant God, or just an experimenter who has long ago abandoned His invention? Minnich agrees, we do not know.

And on that ambiguous note, the testimony for the trial of the century comes to an end.

❧

All that remains are the closing arguments.

Opposing counsel will be addressing an audience of one, Judge Jones, so there will be no off-the-cuff oratorical flourishes, no folksy anecdotes, no ad hominem scriptural exegesis. It will be lawyer talking to lawyer, and in the defense's effort to persuade the judge not to rule on the science, it will revolve around that most common legal concept: standing. Pat Gillen has to convince the judge that he is in no position to evaluate the merits of what is at root a dispute among scientists, and that it would be a case of judicial overreach for a nonscientist to deny Dover students the right to hear a theory that credible scientists support. With all due respect, who are you, Your Honor, to decide what is science and what is not?

On the matter of the defendants and their intentions when it came to putting ID in the science curriculum, that is another thing. All the defense can do is plead no contest; the board members were religious people, yes, but they were also justified in thinking that ID would be good for their science students. And that justification speaks for itself. They cannot be blamed for their religious beliefs and interests, surely.

The plaintiffs, alternatively, have to successfully argue that the judge is being asked only to do what judges are specifically empowered to do: separate truth from deception.

Rothschild goes first. Capable and self-assured, he never appears arrogant. But he ran along the river this morning and has a spring in his step now as he walks toward the podium. He wishes he'd had a chance to memorize it, but he will have to read the closing to the judge just as he read it to his colleagues, tweaking and polishing it, the night before. It came together naturally over the previous week, bits occurring to him on his morning runs, others while watching his colleague Harvey do the heavy lifting in court in the second half of the trial.

With a brief glance back to his wife and two children in the gallery, Rothschild begins with a quote from the testimony of plaintiff Fred Callahan, the paper company president. "What am I supposed to tolerate? A small encroachment on my First Amendment rights? Well, I'm not going to. I think it is clear what these people have done, and it outrages me."

Callahan, Rothschild says, "is standing up to the wedge that has been driven into his community and his daughter's high school by the Dover school board's anti-evolution, pro-intelligent-design policy," referencing the now infamous Wedge document that promised to take down the tree of naturalistic science and the relativistic, permissive moral culture that it has shaded.

Rothschild goes on to track the origins of the case to the school board retreat in 2004, during which Bonsell expressed his commitment to bringing creationism into the science classroom. When the board was manipulated and whittled down to Bonsell's supporters, the institution set out on a path that brought them to this courtroom. Despite the efforts of Thomas More Law Center and assorted fellows of the Discovery Institute to obfuscate the issue, the law is clear: the teaching of creationism in the public schools is unconstitutional. The board intended to promote teaching creationism, and ID is creationism.

"What I am about to say is not easy to say, and there's no way to say it subtly," Rothschild goes on. "Many of the witnesses for the defendants did not tell the truth. They did not tell the truth at their depositions, and they have not told the truth in this courtroom."

Referring to the defendants' unwillingness to acknowledge their early discussion of creationism, Rothschild mentions Heidi Bernhard-Bubb and Joe Maldonado, "two hard-working freelance reporters [who] had their integrity impugned and were dragged into a legal case solely because the board members would not own up to what they had said."

But the most poignant and vivid example of the defendants' deception, Rothschild continues, was Bill Buckingham's appearance on the TV news, in which he advocated balancing evolution with creationism. It was footage shown on the very day that he swore in court that he had not even used the word.

"That was no deer in the headlights," says Rothschild. "That deer was wearing shades and was totally at ease."

All of the lies, Rothschild suggests, were calculated and tactical. The board was "trying to conceal an improper purpose for the policy they approved and implemented, namely an explicitly religious purpose."

He then moves on to the larger picture. "The board's behavior," he asserts, "mimics the intelligent design movement at large. The Dover board discussed teaching creationism, switched to the term *intelligent design* to carry out the same objective, and then pretended they had never talked about creationism.

"This trial has established that intelligent design is unconstitutional because it is an inherently religious proposition, a modern form of creationism," Rothschild continues. "It is not just a product of religious people, it does not just have religious implications, it is, in its essence, religious. Its central religious nature does not change whether it is called creation science or intelligent design or sudden emergence theory. The shell game has to stop."

ID is not science, he stresses, and to say it is would undermine some of science's greatest intellectual and humanitarian contributions.

"The board is delivering Michael Behe's message. Don't bother studying the development of the immune system, you're just doomed to failure. In science class, they are promoting the unchanging certainty of religion in place of the adventure of open-ended scientific discovery. . . .

"Thankfully," he concludes, "there are scientists who do search for answers to the question of the origin of the immune system. . . . It's our defense against debilitating and fatal diseases. The scientists who wrote those books and articles [that Rothschild piled on Behe's witness stand] toil in obscurity, without book royalties or speaking engagements. Their efforts help us combat and cure serious medical conditions. By contrast, Professor Behe and the entire intelligent design movement are doing nothing to advance scientific or medical knowledge and are telling future generations of scientists, don't bother.

"How dare they," he says, looking out in the audience to see Tammy Kitzmiller and her daughters. "How dare they stifle these children's education, how dare they restrict their opportunities, how dare they place a ceiling on their aspirations and on their dreams. Griffin Sneath [the son of plaintiff Cyndi Sneath] can become anything right now. He could become a science teacher like Bert Spahr or Jen Miller or Bryan Rehm or Steve Stough, turning students on to the wonders of the natural world and the satisfaction of scientific discovery, perhaps in Dover or perhaps some other lucky community.

"He could become a college professor and renowned scientist like Ken Miller or Kevin Padian. He might solve mysteries about the immune system because he refused to quit. He might even figure out something that changes the whole world, like Charles Darwin."

A big part of the rationale behind the Establishment Clause in the Constitution is to guard against the civil divisiveness that results when the government meddles in religious issues, says Rothschild.

"We've seen that divisiveness in Dover," he says. "School board member pitted against school board member. Administrators and board members no longer on common ground with the schoolteachers. Julie Smith's daughter asking [her mother], 'what kind of Christian are you?' because her mother believes in evolution."

Finally, in a touch he later acknowledges was suggested by Steve Harvey the night before, Rothschild invokes Pennsylvania's tradition of religious freedom. "This colony was founded on religious liberty. For much of the eighteenth century, Pennsylvania was the only place under British rule where Catholics could legally worship in public," he says.

And "in his declaration of rights, William Penn stated, 'All men have a natural and indefeasible right to worship Almighty God according to the dictates of their own consciences. No man can of right be compelled to attend, erect, or support any place of worship or to maintain any ministry against his consent. No human authority can, in any case whatever, control or interfere with the rights of conscience, and no preference shall ever be given by law to any religious establishment or modes of worship.'

"In defiance of these principles which have served this state and this country so well, this board imposed their religious views on the students in Dover High School and the Dover community. You have met the parents who have brought this lawsuit. The love and respect they have for their children spilled out of that witness stand and filled this courtroom.

"They don't need Alan Bonsell, William Buckingham, Heather Geesey, Jane Cleaver, and Sheila Harkins to teach their children right from wrong. They did not agree that this board could commandeer the religious education of their children, and the constitutions of this country and this commonwealth do not permit it."

He thanks the judge, the judge thanks him, and with that, the plaintiffs rest their case.

Now it's Pat Gillen's turn.

He summarizes his argument neatly in the first minutes of his statement. "I am confident that upon a full deliberation and reflection on the evidence of record, not rhetoric . . . you will find that the plaintiffs have failed to prove that the predominant purpose or primary effect of the curriculum change which was approved by the Dover Area School District on October 18, 2004, is to advance religion. Quite the contrary, the evidence of record demonstrates that the curriculum change at issue here had, as its primary purpose and has as its primary effect, science education."

Sure, Alan Bonsell might be "interested" in creationism. That's a personal religious view that he has a First Amendment right to hold. Sure, he believes that the separation of church and state is a myth, but so did William

Rehnquist, and so do lots of legal scholars. Anyway, it's not what Bonsell is interested in that matters, it's what he does.

The purpose of the school board's policy, Gillen said, was not to promote a religious view but to improve the science education for the students at Dover High School. They thought that introducing students to the idea that there are other credible approaches to explaining the history of life than Darwinian evolution would be good for those students, would broaden their minds, strengthen their critical thinking skills. And they were not alone. There are bona fide biologists, such as Michael Behe and Scott Minnich, for instance, who agree. Obviously, there is debate on the subject, and that debate should be encouraged, not squelched.

Intelligent design is not the majority view in science, Gillen concedes. But that no more justifies making it illegal to mention in school than it would have justified some time ago outlawing talking about the big bang theory or the theory that the sun rather than the earth is at the center of the solar system.

It's the plaintiffs, and their witnesses, who want to eliminate any mention of intelligent design because of their own ideology. The defendants are not trying to impose any dogma. They are merely advocating a free exchange of scientific ideas. They don't want to lock evolution out of the classroom; they want to teach more about it, they want to teach about its strengths as well as its weaknesses, they want to teach about evolution and intelligent design.

The "four-paragraph statement, an informational statement . . . does not detail the claims of intelligent design." It does not advance religion, but it "may serve to prompt the curiosity of students, may lead them to the library." How can a policy that has simply brought more books into the library be construed as bad? asks Gillen, adding that in addition to placing the sixty *Pandas* books in the library, it also added several other books, including one by Robert Pennock, and even Kenneth Miller's book, *Finding Darwin's God*, a book about faith and evolution.

"The evidence shows that intelligent design is science," says Gillen, circling back to the heart of his argument. "[It's] a theory advanced in terms of empirical evidence and technical knowledge proper to scientific and academic specialties. It is not religion." The fact that ID relies on causal explanations "which some might classify as supernatural, at least in light of current knowledge, does not place intelligent design theory beyond the bounds of science. Quite the contrary, intelligent design theory's refusal to rule out this possibility represents the essence of scientific inquiry, precisely because the hypothesis is advanced by means of reasoned argument, based not on the Bible but on empirical evidence and existing knowledge.

"This Court must eschew the plaintiffs' invitation to declare the laws of science from the bench if only because history demonstrates that all such efforts are doomed to failure," Gillen says.

"Your Honor, I respectfully submit that the evidence of record shows that the plaintiffs have failed to prove that the primary purpose or primary effect of the reading of a four-paragraph statement to make the students aware of intelligent design, explaining that it's an explanation for the origins of life different from Darwin's theory, letting students know there are books in the library on this subject, does not, by any reasonable measure, threaten the harm which the Establishment Clause of the First Amendment to the United States Constitution prohibits, but, instead, the evidence shows that the defendants' policy has the primary purpose and primary effect of advancing science education by making students aware of a new scientific theory, one which . . . may well open a fascinating prospect to a new scientific paradigm."

After Gillen sits down, Judge Jones briskly wraps up the proceeding. He thanks observers and the press for their good behavior and the lawyers for theirs. "I am struck," he says, "by the solemnity, the dignity, the appropriateness that all of you had, and I'm talking about parties and spectators. And I appreciate that deeply. It was befitting a court of law where important issues are being discussed, and I thank you again for that."

Jones has high praise for the lawyers. "Those of you who have sat through this trial, parties and spectators, have seen, by each and every one of the lawyers, some of the best presentations, some of the finest lawyering that you will ever have the privilege to see."

When the judge asks whether anyone has anything further to say, Gillen pipes up.

"Your Honor," he says, "I have one question, and that's this: by my reckoning, this is the fortieth day since the trial began and tonight will be the fortieth night, and I would like to know if you did that on purpose."

"Mr. Gillen," replies Judge Jones, "that is an interesting coincidence, but it was not by design."

❦

The fortieth day of the trial falls on November 4, Tammy Kitzmiller's forty-first birthday. The plaintiffs and their legal team take over a restaurant, Fisaga, with a big outdoor courtyard on State and North 2nd Streets in downtown Harrisburg. Rothschild and the other lawyers loosen their ties and even smoke cigars. By the end of the night several of the party are still standing out on the curb, unwilling to let the occasion end, exchanging hugs and thank you's and promising to stay in close touch over the long weeks of waiting to come.

Kitzmiller is convinced they have won. She doesn't see how the judge could possibly rule against them. But as the days after the trial go by her confidence flags. Anything can happen; who knows what really drives Judge Jones? She and her new friends Cyndi Sneath and Bryan and Christy Rehm throw themselves completely into activity surrounding the upcoming school board election. Because so many members have quit over the past term, eight of the board's nine seats are being contested in the election. Though there are candidates who say otherwise, there is only one issue on the ballot, intelligent design, and the sixteen candidates are split right down the middle on the issue: the eight incumbents are for keeping ID in the science curriculum and the eight challengers are against it. The election is going to be the democratic doppelganger of the trial, and the result, for this community, could be at least as profound.

CHAPTER FOURTEEN

THE PEOPLE'S COURT AND THE GOSPEL ACCORDING TO JOHN JONES

ERIC ROTHSCHILD: "Hopefully we won't be back in a couple
of years for the 'sudden emergence' trial."
JOHN JONES: "Not on my docket, let me tell you."

ight of the nine seats on the Dover school board are up for grabs in a campaign that is as close as it is combative. If the challengers win, the trustees who brought intelligent design to Dover could be out on their ears by the time Judge Jones hands down his decision. If the incumbents win, their pro-ID activism will gain a new mandate not only in Dover but nationwide.

"We led emotionally and physically exhausting parallel lives during the trial; we spent days in court and nights at CARES meetings," says Tammy Kitzmiller. "They were equally important to us."

Dover CARES, which stands for Dover Citizens Actively Reviewing Educational Strategies, is an ad hoc group promoting a slate of candidates to oppose Alan Bonsell and his pro-ID allies. Once the courtroom phase of the trial is over, Kitzmiller and her pals throw themselves into the election campaign completely.

Canvassing for any Dover school board election would give a revealing peek into the homes, hearts, and heads of middle-Americans, but this particular campaign also gives canvassers a glimpse into the heart of darkness.

Bernie Reinking, a retired nurse running for the board on the Dover CARES ticket, is campaigning for a seat and is met by everything from people jumping around taunting her with monkey noises to doors slammed in her face.

Unlike Dover school board elections past, mellow affairs which took place pretty much in the background, this election is hot and heavy; evidence of it is everywhere. Lawn signs and billboards pepper the landscape. The incumbents published pamphlets linking their opponents, including Reinking, to the ACLU—which, the pamphlets said, also supports the North American Man-Boy Love Association's right to instruct men on how to lure young children into having sex with them. For Reinking, a conservative Catholic, the idea of that association is as painful as it is absurd.

"Every one of us on the CARES ticket believed in God, so no one could say we weren't religious," she says. "But they said just about everything else."

Six months ago, in the school board's primary elections—held on May 17, 2005, half a year after *Kitzmiller* had been filed but long before it had gone to court—Dover area voters had a record number of school board candidates to choose from. They narrowed a field of eighteen down to sixteen: eight incumbents, many of whom had been appointed to fill positions left open by members resigning during all of the ID controversy, and eight CARES candidates.

One of the CARES candidates chosen in that primary was Bryan Rehm, the stocky, six-foot four-inch high school physics teacher who fled Dover High for a position in another district rather than contend with Bill Buckingham and Alan Bonsell as bosses. Rehm and his wife were also plaintiffs in the *Kitzmiller* case, and he had the strange distinction of both suing the board and running for a place on it at exactly the same time.

Today, in addition to the Rehms, plaintiffs Kitzmiller, Cyndi Sneath, Deborah Fenimore, Joel Leib, Steve Stough, Barrie Callahan, and Julie Smith are all also working hard to oust the same board regime they are suing. The twisted potential consequence of this is that if they prevail in getting Alan Bonsell, Sheila Harkins, and their allies off the board, and if Judge Jones rules against the pro-ID defendants, then the new ID-free board will have to suffer the consequences of the old board's actions. In Bryan Rehm's case, since he's actually campaigning for a seat, that could mean figuring out how to pay, as a trustee, the attorney fees for the lawyers (and now friends) who prevailed in his own representation. It will also mean helping to decide whether to accept the ruling or appeal the judge's opinion to a higher court. Suddenly his own attorneys, Rothschild, Harvey, Walczak, and Katskee, will also be his opponents, sort of. If that happens, though, the new board will likely accept the judge's ruling against it, and the case will be put to rest. Of course that new board will still have to come up with a big pot of money to pay legal fees for Pepper Hamilton, the ACLU, and Americans United.

If, alternatively, the incumbents are reelected in sufficient numbers to keep their majority, but they lose the legal case, the narrative will continue along its current path; the board that invented and implemented the ID policy will deal with the legal consequences of it themselves. In that scenario, the election is just a bump in the Bonsell board's road to the Supreme Court, or as far as it can go in that direction.

It's also possible that the pro-ID school board can lose its majority in the election but win the court case. While the ID policy might be reversed by a new board in Dover, at least temporarily, other school districts around the country will feel legally free to put ID into their own curriculums.

Finally, if the pro-ID incumbents on the board win both the election and the legal case, the plaintiffs will still appeal, if they can; but while they are doing so school boards across the nation will not only feel legally free to adopt ID curriculums, but also feel politically emboldened to do so. It is that possibility that keeps Kitzmiller and her friends awake at night. For the

ACLU, Americans United for Separation of Church and State, and the National Center for Science Education, such a double loss is the doomsday scenario.

⬤

On November 8, only four days after the doors to Courtroom 2 on the ninth floor of the Federal Building were closed, and as Judge Jones is toiling away on his decision back in Philadelphia, the voters of the district come out to settle their case. That night, the results show a clean sweep for the Dover CARES candidates.¹ They take every one of the eight contested seats, though some by a very narrow margin. The entire Bonsell-led board, with the exception of Heather Geesey, whose seat was not in contest, is thrown out. Alan Bonsell and Sheila Harkins, the only members named in the *Kitzmiller* suit besides Geesey, get fewer votes than any other candidates.

"I didn't expect a sweep," says Cyndi Sneath. "I was conservatively hoping for four seats, five, which would have been a majority, would have been nice, but I would have been grateful for whatever we got.

"There was sheer jubilation at the CARES camp that night," she says. "But we were all still very cognizant of the trial."

High school teacher, plaintiff, and coach Steve Stough says that Bonsell's, and the pro-ID board's, vote numbers were heavily influenced by the dressing down Judge Jones gave Bonsell on the stand a few days earlier. "People at the polling places were saying, 'We don't vote for liars.'" Stough says. "And they didn't."

⬤

In the old days, legal decisions would literally be handed down from the judge's elevated bench. Today we still say that a judge's ruling is "handed down," though a more precise term in a case like *Kitzmiller* would be *spread across,* as in spread across the country via the Internet. After six weeks of deliberation and writing, Judge Jones's decision is spread across at 10:30 in the morning on Tuesday, December 20, a typically crisp and vivid mid-Pennsylvania winter's day with big dark clouds suspended in a bright blue sky.

Kate Henson, Eric Rothschild's legal assistant, woke up early this morning. The week before, the court had warned that the decision would likely be handed down today, and no one on the plaintiffs' team could think or talk about much of anything else. Over and over again, Henson ran through the possibilities in her mind. When her hopes soared, she tethered them down with the knowledge that Judge Jones was a Bush appointee, a personal friend of former Pennsylvania governor and current Homeland Security czar Tom Ridge. It was only a few months before that President Bush had publicly said that he thought "both sides" of the ID issue should be taught in public schools. Henson is smart, but she is also known for her heart, and she, maybe more than anyone else on the plaintiffs' team, had personalized the case. When she imagined a negative decision, she worried above all about the plaintiffs' disappointment, about all the time and spirit they'd given to the case. The idea of having to call them with bad news made her heartsick.

But then they couldn't lose, she told herself; their case was so strong, the judge would have to be a radical activist to rule against them. And Jones seemed anything but. They would win, Steve Harvey, her boss, had consoled her. It was just a matter of how much they would win.

The legal team for the case assembles for the occasion at Pepper Hamilton's Harrisburg office. Rothschild, Harvey, legal assistant Hedya Aryani, Walczak, Pepper Hamilton lawyers Alfred Wilcox and Tom Schmidt, Richard Katskee, Kevin Padian, and Genie Scott are all there.

They know the decision is coming, but they don't know when, and they sit around anxiously awaiting the "ding" of the e-mail announcing the availability of the decision online. To distract themselves, they place bets on when the news will come. At 10:30, Steve Harvey walks solemnly out from an office into the crowded hallway and reports that he won the bet; the decision has just been handed down, just at the time he's predicted.

"We scattered like roaches," says Henson later, each running to a computer where he or she could pull up the decision off of PACER, a federal Website where court documents can be filed and accessed. Rothschild had already begun printing the decision and is reading it off his computer screen. Henson is so impatient, she tugs on the pages as the printer spits them out. On page three she catches sight of the words "For the reasons that follow, we hold that the ID Policy is unconstitutional," which she reads aloud, to cheers from around the office.

The decision, which is 139 pages long, takes a long time just to print, and longer still to read.

Rothschild, Walczak, and Wilcox are all in the big conference room reading the decision to themselves quietly, with periodic outbursts: "Have you read page 64, 'ID is not science!'?" One of the lawyers skips to the end: "Breathtaking inanity!" he cries out.

Rothschild, knowing Henson would love the job, asks her to call the plaintiffs and give them the good news: They have won. They won everything. In Judge Jones's binding opinion the school board policy is a violation of the First Amendment, as is teaching ID in science class generally. And ID is not science, in Judge Jones's view, it is religion.

Calling the plaintiffs "was the greatest thing I could have been asked to do," says Henson, and she relishes the job, telling each of them to head on up to the Harrisburg office.

First she calls Tammy Kitzmiller.

"I was alone when I got the call from Kate Henson," Kitzmiller says later. "I was at work. When I hung up, I cried."

Kitzmiller text messages her daughter, Jessica, at school: "WE WON."

By the time Henson gets through to Barrie Callahan, the former school board member has already heard from Cyndi Sneath. Sneath's call came just as an NBC camera crew was walking up Callahan's stairs.

"As I was hearing the decision on the phone, they were walking into my house. I had cookies in the oven and my dog was running all around and the reporters in my house were asking me questions. It was loony. As surreal as it gets," says Callahan. Then comes the call from Kate, and before she knows it Callahan is leaving the bedlam in her house behind, reporters and all, and speeding north to Harrisburg with her husband, Fred.

That afternoon, with most of the plaintiffs assembled, the team holds a conference in Pepper Hamilton's biggest conference room, which seems pretty small when crammed wall-to-wall with reporters, camera crews, and radio journalists from around the world. Rothschild, Harvey, Walczak, Katzkee, Kitzmiller, and Scott all give prepared statements and then take turns answering questions. It is a circus, but it is a perfect circus from the victors' point of view. Nothing can be wrong. Ever again.

Meanwhile, in Seattle, it is "just another day at the office," when Casey Luskin gets an e-mail from a law professor acquaintance with Jones's decision attached. It is like a deep ocean earthquake recorded by a seismograph, and the geologist in Luskin knows that a tsunami of press calls will hit him soon. He reads as fast as he can to be ready when it comes.

He was not surprised that the defendants lost, he says later. "There was pretty strong evidence that they were religiously motivated," and he expected the judge to rule against them on that. But he was surprised and disappointed that Jones went so far as to define science, and to define ID as standing outside of it. As he speed reads the ruling he sees that "some very black-and-white issues were wrong," he says.

"For instance, the judge's saying that there were no ID peer-reviewed papers. That is just patently untrue. And I was very surprised that he said that if you believe that evolution is antithetical to belief in a supreme being, that that belief is 'utterly false.' I couldn't believe that he traipsed into such controversial areas," Luskin says.

Everyone is surprised by the decision. It is 139 pages long, a mammoth work even for a trial of this length and complexity. It is beautifully written, for a court document anyway. And, finally, it is unequivocal, ruthless, and trenchant in its condemnation of the defendants and their case.

The judge, in his conclusion, writes that it is "abundantly clear that the Board's ID Policy violates the Establishment Clause" of the First Amendment. "In making this determination," he goes on, "we have addressed the seminal question of whether ID is science. We have concluded that it is not, and moreover that ID cannot uncouple itself from its creationist, and thus religious, antecedents."

There has been an ocean of analysis, and we will take a dip there, but really, those two points say it all. One, the school board's decision to put ID in the curriculum intended to, and did, have the effect of promoting a particular religious view, namely creationism. And two, ID is not science.

Let's take them one at a time. First, to determine whether the board's policy violated the First Amendment, the judge applied both the *Lemon* and endorsement tests. Remember, the *Lemon* test has three main aspects or "prongs": A government action is considered religious if (1) it does not have a secular purpose, (2) its principal or primary effect advances or inhibits religion, or (3) it creates an excessive entanglement of the government with religion. The endorsement test requires the court to determine what message a challenged governmental policy or enactment conveys to a reasonable, objective observer who knows what's going on.

If an action fails any one of the *Lemon* test's three prongs, or if a reasonable and objective person would interpret the action as an effort to promote religion, and thus flunk it on the endorsement test, then the action can be judged unconstitutional.

For all of the reasons argued by the plaintiffs' lawyers, the Dover school board failed both the *Lemon* and endorsement tests with flying colors, writes the judge. A reasonable and "objective" person would recognize the language that stresses the "gaps" and "problems" in evolution, in both the curriculum change and the statement read to ninth graders, as a tell-tale mark of an old creationist tactic for promoting a particular religious view, namely creationism.

For the "intent" to promote religion, the judge noted that Bonsell and others on the board, starting in 2002, talked about wanting to bring religion back into the school, and specifically about promoting creationism. They delayed purchasing the Miller-Levine textbook because they objected to its emphasis on evolution. They pressured teachers to minimize teaching evolution and to introduce creationist concepts. They ignored their own solicitor's warning that what they were doing would be interpreted as religious advocacy. The curriculum committee forced *Pandas* on teachers, who didn't want it, as a reference text. The newsletter the board sent out to everyone in the district was an effort to promote ID, in other words, creationism.

Furthermore, the judge concludes that there was no evidence that the board had a valid secular motivation. Though they claimed to be moved by a desire to improve science education and critical thinking skills, the evidence doesn't show that at all, the judge says. "Their asserted purposes are a sham," he concludes.

If they were really trying to improve science education and promote critical thinking, they would have asked the advice of scientists or scientific organizations, whereas they didn't even listen to their own experts, the science teachers in the district, writes Jones. They relied only on advice from Discovery Institute and Thomas More Law Center, both organizations with religious missions. Plus, the coup de grace: most, if not all, of the "board members admittedly had no comprehension whatsoever of ID. . . . To assert a secular purpose against this backdrop," he wrote, "is ludicrous."

Sham. Ludicrous. These are not words often found in a legal judgment.

The secular purposes claimed by the board, the judge writes, "amount to a pretext for the Board's real purpose, which was to promote religion in the public school classroom, in violation of the Establishment Clause."

It's enough that the board's actions fail the endorsement test and the purpose prong of the *Lemon* test; there really isn't need to look further, writes the judge. You only need to violate one of the *Lemon* prongs, fail the endorsement test, or both, and you're out on your unconstitutional ear. But for completeness, Jones said, let's take a look, too, at the "effect" prong of the *Lemon* test.

It is like the Passover ritual, in which, while thanking God, you go through a list of His blessings and after each one repeat, *Dianu,* Hebrew for "it would have been enough." It would be enough if God brought us out of Egypt and had not divided the sea for us; Dianu. It would have been enough had God divided the sea and not let us cross on dry land; Dianu. And on and on.

To apply the effect prong of *Lemon,* the judge had to consider whether government had placed its "prestige, coercive authority, or resources behind a single religious faith or behind religious belief in general, compelling non-adherents to support the practices or proselytizing of favored religious organizations and conveying the message that those who do not contribute gladly are less than full members of the community."

The judge says that the school board's policy gets punctured by the effect prong, too. The statement read to students discredits evolution and bolsters ID, which is creationism, which is a particular religious view. Juxtaposing the disavowal of evolution with the encouraging of students to look at alternative religious concepts, as presented in *Pandas,* implies the school board's approval of the religious principles promoted by ID.

"The effect of Defendants' actions in adopting the curriculum change," Jones concludes, "was to impose a religious view of biological origins into the biology course, in violation of the Establishment Clause."

Judge Jones rules that intelligent design is not science for three reasons. First, he says, it relies on supernatural causation, which defies the very definition of science. Second, the central ID argument from irreducible complexity is nothing new, but rather an old staple argument of the creationist movement, and a bogus one. And finally, intelligent design's negative attacks on evolution have been disproved. Anyway, writes the judge, to think that an argument against evolution is an argument for ID is "at bottom premised upon a false dichotomy that is no more compelling today than when it was employed to justify creation science two decades ago."

The judge critiques the "positive argument" for ID, what Michael Behe calls the "inference from the purposeful arrangement of parts." The analogy between the human ability to recognize artifacts and to detect design in natural objects, such as the bacterial flagellum, is just an analogy, and not a very good one, says the judge. What's missing, he says, is recognition that unlike human artifacts, biological systems live and reproduce over time, are replicable, undergo genetic recombination, and are driven by natural selection.

The inference to design based upon the appearance of a "purposeful arrangement of parts" is completely subjective, writes the judge. And both Behe and Scott Minnich acknowledged in cross-examination, the judge writes, that there is no quantitative criterion for determining the degree of complexity or number of parts that suggest that a designer, rather than a natural process, is responsible. Behe did point out though, that you are much more likely to find design a plausible explanation if you already believe in God.

Judge Jones writes that ID distorts the paleontological evidence, that it fails to produce peer-reviewed publications, that it is, ultimately, "grounded in theology, not science."

He even goes out of his way to preempt what will likely be the next evolutionary stage of the anti-evolution movement by saying that the approach of "teaching the controversy" about evolution, but not ID itself, "is at best disingenuous, and at worst a canard. The goal of the IDM [intelligent design movement] is not to encourage critical thought, but to foment a revolution which would supplant evolutionary theory with ID."

Since the scientific revolution, writes Jones, "science has been limited to the search for natural causes to explain natural phenomena. This revolution entailed the rejection of the appeal to authority, and by extension, revelation, in favor of empirical evidence. Since that time period, science has been a discipline in which testability, rather than any ecclesiastical authority or philosophical coherence, has been the measure of a scientific ideas worth."

Judge Jones also draws attention to what he calls ID's "complete absence of peer-reviewed publications supporting the theory." The process of scientific review is "exquisitely important" in the scientific process, permitting scientists to test, criticize, and study one another's work. If an idea does not produce published papers, it cannot be considered credible.

The judge concludes that ID is not science, but he goes further, concurring with Kenneth Miller that "attributing unsolved problems about nature to causes and forces that lie outside the natural world is a 'science stopper.'"

"As Dr. Miller explained," says the judge, "once you attribute a cause to an untestable supernatural force, a proposition that cannot be disproved, there is no reason to continue seeking natural explanations as we have our answer. ID."

So ID is not a scientific idea, but a religious one, Jones rules. He goes through a list of notable ID proponents who've said this or that connecting ID to its religious and cultural fuel sources. The quotes, mostly entered into the record by philosopher Barbara Forrest's testimony, include Phillip Johnson calling ID "theistic realism," which, Johnson explains, means "that God is objectively real as Creator and recorded in the biological evidence." And that "Darwinian theory of evolution contradicts not just the Book of Genesis, but every word in the Bible from beginning to end. It contradicts the idea that we are here because a creator brought about our existence for a purpose."

He cites Discovery Institute mathematician William Dembski, who had, you'll remember, wished to remain out of this trial, claiming that ID is a "ground-clearing operation" conducted to allow Christianity to receive serious consideration, and "Christ is never an addendum to a scientific theory but always a completion."

"Although proponents of the intelligent design movement occasionally suggest that the designer could be a space alien or a time-traveling cell biologist," writes the judge, "no serious alternative to God as the designer has been proposed. . . . In fact, an explicit concession that the intelligent designer works outside the laws of nature and science and a direct reference to religion is *Pandas'* rhetorical statement, 'What kind of intelligent agent was it [the designer]?' and answer: 'On its own science cannot answer this question. It must leave it to religion and philosophy.'"

193

I feel vindicated by this observation. As I've said, it seems to me that the IDers' insistence that nothing could ever be said about the intelligent designer was stronger evidence of a theological grounding than the claim that there is evidence of an intelligent designer in the first place.

Although the judge refuses to say anything at all about the "ultimate veracity" of ID, he reaches "the inescapable conclusion that ID is an interesting theological argument, but that it is not science."

In summary, on the matter of ID's status, he says "the overwhelming evidence at trial established that ID is a religious view, a mere re-labeling of creationism, and not a scientific theory."

To be sure, he says, "Darwin's theory of evolution is imperfect. However, the fact that a scientific theory cannot yet render an explanation on every point should not be used as a pretext to thrust an untestable alternative hypothesis grounded in religion into the science classroom or to misrepresent well-established scientific propositions."

Jones is clearly peeved about the lies told in court. "It is ironic," he says, "that several of these individuals, who so staunchly and proudly touted their religious convictions in public, would time and again lie to cover their tracks and disguise the real purpose behind the ID Policy."

While the lawyers for the pro-ID defense may have been braced to hear that their case had failed to show sufficient secular reason for the Dover school board's curriculum change, Jones's description of ID as "nothing more than the progeny of creationism" is a blow to the solar plexus of the entire ID community.

The judge reserves some special ridicule for Thomas More Law Center. He asserts that "this case came to us as the result of the activism of an ill-informed faction on a school board, aided by a national public interest law firm [TMLC] eager to find a constitutional test case on ID, who in combination drove the Board to adopt an imprudent and ultimately unconstitutional policy."

The judge hits lower even than the solar plexus on the body of Discovery Institute's Center for Science and Culture, whose *raison d'être* is to advance the scientific status of ID. In addition to writing that ID is a theological theory, not a scientific one, Jones also calls Discovery a religious organization, citing the Wedge document, which he says "represents from an institutional standpoint the intelligent design movement's goals and objectives, much as writings from the Institute for Creation Research did for the earlier creation-science movement."

For the NCSE's Nick Matzke, however, this double victory was a dream come true. "It was the best evidence I'd seen of the existence of a God . . , I mean, an intelligent designer," he jokes.

Judge Jones's decision is eloquent and thorough, but it is also blunt, especially in its condemnation of the school board's efforts to disguise its religious motives. The board made a decision of "breathtaking inanity," he writes, and it "dragged" its community into a "legal maelstrom with its resulting utter waste of monetary and personal resources."

❦

Because of the school board sweep a month before, there will in all likelihood be no appeal of this decision. The new board, now hostile to the idea of teaching ID in science class, will cooperate with the judge's order to permanently halt implementation of the ID curriculum policy throughout the Dover Area School District, to stop requiring teachers to "denigrate or disparage" evolution, and to "stop requiring teachers to refer to the religious alternative theory known as ID."

Because the plaintiffs' civil rights under the Establishment Clause were violated, the defendants will have to pay "injunctive and declaratory relief, but also for nominal damages and the reasonable value of Plaintiffs' attorneys' services and costs incurred in vindicating Plaintiffs' constitutional rights." In other words, the loser, the school board, will have to pay for the winners' case.

Although the decision will have the force of law only in the middle of Pennsylvania's three federal judicial districts, legally ID still has a clean slate in the rest of the country. But practically speaking, the decision should give pause, or halt in its tracks, any school district thinking of instituting a similar policy. The decision is so thorough in its analysis of constitutional precedent that other courts simply will not be able to ignore it.

It is an audacious decision. It goes as far as a legal document possibly can to blow intelligent design to Kingdom Come. It concedes virtually every one of the plaintiffs' legal points, and gives the defendants nothing, not even their good names. Going far beyond the limits of the case at hand, the judge stigmatizes the very notion of ID, unequivocally branding it the "progeny of creationism." It is an act that will further polarize the country, further alienate those many millions of Americans who are already convinced of the Darwinian conspiracy to wipe out religion and moral certainty. Even if the ruling does put a damper on the effort to advance intelligent design, its ultimate effect may be to make martyrs of its proponents and thus to promote the cause.

Just as Judge Jones predicted they would, the staunch supporters of ID, after a brief period of stunned Christmas silence, come out fighting mad and accuse the judge of courtroom activism. Judge Jones's conservative pedigree is like Teflon, though, making it much harder to make the accusation stick, though his critics keep trying.

Within only a few months, Casey Luskin and a few of his colleagues at Discovery Institute will self-publish a rough-and-ready response to the ruling called *Traipsing into Evolution: Intelligent Design and the Kitzmiller* vs. *Dover Decision*. The book's first rhetorical task is to distance Discovery from the case. "In many respects *Kitzmiller* was wholly unsuited to serve the function of a worthy 'test case' for ID."

But exceeding even Discovery Institute's dislike for the *Kitzmiller* case is their dislike for Judge Jones's opinion. They describe the Jones decision as an instance of extreme judicial overreach. It is wrong, absurd even, that a judge with no scientific authority can decide once and for all whether or not a field of research is a science, they say. Beyond that, though, Luskin and colleagues' book has four main objections to the *Kitzmiller* ruling. It says that the plaintiffs' witnesses and Jones got the history of ID all wrong; that he got the science all wrong; that he had a one-sided and biased treatment of the religious implications of scientific theories; and finally that his ruling was, in effect, an effort to dictate a particular theological view known as naturalistic materialism, the scientific pillar of which is evolution. The authors argue that Jones is the one breaching the First Amendment because he is defending evolution by saying that it is compatible with certain kinds of theism, namely his kind.

❧

After the press conference, at which the plaintiffs' lawyers, NCSE's Eugenie Scott, and Tammy Kitzmiller all give prepared statements and then, along with other plaintiffs, answer questions, most of the reporters and cameramen go off to write, file, or edit their stories. Some of the long-form magazine writers and others not on deadline follow the plaintiffs and their legal team to Max's, an Italian restaurant on North 2nd Street, where they are met by a second wave of TV crews. The plaintiffs and their lawyers order drinks and watch one another being interviewed on the two big flat-screen TVs over the bar. One of the lawyers or plaintiffs would go outside and do a live interview, legal assistant Kate Henson says later, "and the rest of us would point and cheer and yell at the TV inside."

There are a couple of "arrogant jerks" at the bar who hadn't come in with the happy Kitzmiller crowd, Henson says. They've been drinking for a while, it was obvious, and try to pick a fight with her about ID and evolution. "What is the world coming to," one guy asks, "when the court tells a school board what its teachers can and can't say?"

"They're just liberals and atheists trying to kick God out of the schools. Afraid of the truth! Of course intelligent design is a fact."

"It was obvious they didn't know what they were talking about," says Henson. But really, where was an argument like that going to go?

Henson, who has big innocent blue eyes, levels a calm and cheerful gaze at the men and says, "Well, a federal judge appointed by George W. Bush disagreed with you today, didn't he?"

CHAPTER FIFTEEN

AFTERWORD

The philosopher Thomas Kuhn became famous in 1962 with his publication of *The Structure of Scientific Revolutions*. No twentieth-century work of philosophy had greater impact on popular culture than Kuhn's book; though Kuhn was not himself a deconstructionist or a relativist, his book arguably set both of those movements on their way. Into the mainstream lexicon, he introduced the expression "paradigm shift."

A scientific paradigm, Kuhn said, is "a universally recognized set of scientific achievements that for a time provide model problems and solutions to a community of practitioners." Evolution, for example, represents the dominant paradigm in the biological sciences today. While a scientific paradigm may do a lot of good work for a long time, eventually, especially if it is focused on the frontiers of knowledge, it will reach the limits of its explanatory power. As those limits are exceeded, the number of "anomalies" may grow even as the number of unexplained phenomena in the field remains constant or continues to shrink. An anomaly, according to Kuhn, is data that seem to contradict a paradigm. Eventually, as happened most famously with Ptolemaic astronomy and Newtonian physics, the weight of the anomalies becomes too great and the old paradigm begins to rattle even when driven at the speed limit.

When this happens, Kuhn wrote, when a paradigm gets old and shaky, all kinds of mischief occurs. You get self-aggrandizing people promoting rival theories to replace the tried-and-true, but now aging and besieged, paradigm. Some may be reasonable, others may be nuts.

It is always culturally traumatic to endure the overthrow of a paradigm; its roots can extend deep into the culture, the mainstream culture as well as the culture of science. The traditionalists circle the wagons, insisting that nothing is wrong, and prepare to fight off the revolutionaries, many of whom will be true believers in their new theories and ready to kill and die for them.

Phillip Johnson calls on Kuhn's explanations, explicitly marshalling the forces for an overthrow of the Darwinian paradigm. The anomalies in evolution have reached that critical mass, the IDers say, and they have begun to leave the theory untenable. It's a coherent claim, and an exciting one for many, especially those, like my father, who like both revolutions and religion—and it is almost surely wrong. There *are* anomalies within evolutionary biology, but the theory is humming along smoothly at very high speeds.

Another attempted Kuhnian coup is going on here, too, and it reaches far beyond the labs and universities and science classrooms. It is centuries old. Kuhn talked about the difficulties of living in periods of overlapping paradigms, and even of rare occasions when two paradigms can coexist peacefully . . . for a while. Peaceful coexistence is much rarer in the rigorous environment of science than it is in the broader, sloppier world of ideas at large. Today we see coexistent and competing paradigms in a tense struggle for hegemony over the human mind.

But the forces so engaged are much broader than scientific paradigms. They are what I'd call "theories of everything." Kuhn said that in extreme

200

cases of paradigm revolution, those working in different paradigms might be said to actually "live in different worlds." In the case of modern America, one world is materialistic and the other theistic. Most of us live most of the time in one or the other. Most of us are also able to some degree to navigate both. But we switch back and forth as if looking at the famous illusion of a goblet that with a shift of glance turns into two inward-looking profiles. Each depiction is clear, but only one can be seen at a time. Each world seems internally consistent right up to its edge; but from within each one the other appears incoherent. That's why, to materialists, teaching a theistic metaphysics in science class is absurd. And that's why, to theists embracing a strictly Biblical view of the world, the Darwinian narrative appears equally absurd, no matter how much scientific evidence supports it.

We are part of a centuries-long battle of the worlds, the theistic and the materialistic. It is such a slow revolution that it is often not even clear who the insurrectionists are. Are they the materialists, with their four-century-old scientific method, or are they the theists with the millennia-old narrative authority? The battle is punctuated by bursts of territory loss and gain, but lately it is the materialists who have been taking the most ground. At any given time, the human realms are divided up into provinces overseen by one or both, and truces are sworn. Science, for example, promises not to venture into the realm of the meaning of life, if religion promises not to touch human origins and speciation. Peacemakers on both sides, like Stephen Gould, E. O. Wilson, and the Templeton Foundation (which promotes research on the compatibility of science and religion) help try to keep the truce. But they don't last; both views of the world have temporarily repressible, but ultimately undeniable, hegemonic ambitions. And maybe the compromises come at too high a cost; the cost of living a double life.

The intelligent design debate at Dover was in one sense a battle over which of these two worlds can claim primacy in the science classroom— the place where each generation gets to hear the previous generation's consensus about that which is considered objective truth. But in another way, it was a battle over who gets to define the truth itself, over who gets to say which of the worlds is the real one. The really real one. Not just which one is logically possible and socially acceptable to believe in, but which one is true with a capital T.

❦

On November 7, 2006, U.S. Senator Rick Santorum was defeated in his bid for the Pennsylvania seat he'd held for two terms. Santorum, the conservative evangelical Christian who sat on the governing board of the Thomas More Law Center, was a friend of the Discovery Institute and sponsored the language in President Bush's No Child Left Behind bill cited by the Dover school board as justification for its ID policy.[1] Many religious conservatives regarded Santorum as a strong, perhaps the strongest, Republican candidate for the presidency in 2008; had he kept his Senate seat that would have been a very real possibility. Now it isn't.

The electorate's change of heart about Santorum and his brand of Christian nationalism had several factors, but the defeat of ID, and the disgrace of its promoters in Dover, was surely a part. It was not so much Santorum's association with a scientifically dubious religion-friendly hypothesis that influenced conservative Pennsylvania voters; more important was the fact, clearly spelled out in detail by Judge Jones, that the pro-ID forces were deceptive. From the lowest local school board to the highest national political and intellectual think-tanks they were spinning, manipulating, redefining, and re-creating the truth.

And what was that truth? In Dover, it was that the school board's religious and increasingly powerful pro-creationist core wanted Dover schools to teach science that was confirming of its own creationist religious view of the world. They settled on intelligent design, and camouflaged their true opinions and hopes, because it seemed the best legal way to pursue that aim.

Dover's truth is a reflection of the broader national truth about the intelligent design movement; it is driven by a group of religiously motivated scientists, politicians, and cultural reformers who hope—and believe—their view of the world will give rise to a bona fide science. That's fine. The problem arises when they lie about the status of the work they've done so far and the integrity of the work done by the thousands of evolutionary biologists and other scientists who devote their lives to progress in scientific fields, from virology and immunology to paleontology and genetics. The irony is that they have adopted the very postmodern relativistic ethic that they avowedly loathe; say loudly enough and often enough that something is so and it will be so. Well, in the measurable world, the real world, it doesn't work like that. The truth is less fashionable.

And the truth, at least so far according to the vast majority of authorities in the relevant fields, is that as science, ID has produced only "a bag of intuitions and a handful of notions," to quote Discovery's own fellow Paul Nelson. At this time, it is a view of the world with ambitions to become a science. (Evolution, alternatively, is a science that has, for better or worse, also given rise to a view of the world.)

The problem manifested, for the school board and the national ID movement, when deception (self-deception or intentional political deception) became the tool of implementation.

I don't think there's any doubt that the ID debate, and *Kitzmiller* in particular, influenced many of the 2006 mid-term elections across the nation. In addition to Santorum, several others come to mind. One, for example, would be the gubernatorial race in Michigan, where Republican candidate Dick DeVos—a supporter of the Thomas More Law Center and a conservative Christian—said that he approved of teaching intelligent design along with evolution in science classes. The statement provoked a storm of controversy and a much closer look at DeVos's radical religious and cultural conservatism, which had been camouflaged behind his largely state-budget-oriented campaign. Once voters saw what DeVos was really all about, the race then swung in favor of his Democratic adversary, Jennifer Granholm, an opponent of giving intelligent design time in the science classroom.

In Kansas, one-time Republican candidate Cindy Neighbor switched parties in her race for the Kansas House of Representatives, explaining to her constituents that she could no longer stomach a Republican platform that included support for teaching ID and opposition to stem cell research. The ethic in the Republican Party has become "if you don't agree with us, you're not one of us," she told *Salon.com* reporter Nadia Pflaum. That sounds like the old Dover school board all over.

I think it is fair to say that that antideception (noble or otherwise) sentiment colored the entire 2006 election. All lies and liars took a hit, especially antiscience lies: from fabricated justifications for the war in Iraq to suppressed intelligence on nuclear threats elsewhere and bowdlerized EPA reports about clean air and global warming. The antideception ethic hit Republicans especially hard; from Mark Foley and his homoerotic e-mail hypocrisies to the Dover school board and the lies they told to get God and patriots back in the schools.

As Dover plaintiff, science teacher, coach, and Republican Steve Stough said, "We don't vote for liars."

A paradoxical by-product of the Dover debate was the emergence of a much broader national discussion of science and religion. Specifically, the ID movement's insistence that science could speak to the question of the existence of an intelligent designer made way for a debate over God's existence. Before ID, that question was discussed only gingerly, and indirectly, if at all. Groups such as the Templeton Foundation, which began sponsoring discussions among scientists about science and religion in the late 1980s, never stooped to asking directly about God's existence. The ID movement's claim to have found strong scientific evidence for the existence of God (or a being with a very God-like résumé, anyway) opened the door for direct debate in the widest possible forums: TV, radio, the blogosphere, books, journals, and lectures.

Suddenly, after Dover, atheism is everywhere. Oxford biologist and poster-child of scientific atheism Richard Dawkins published *The God Delusion* in the fall of 2006, and it took no time at all climbing onto the bestseller list, where it joined neurobiologist Sam Harris's *Letter to a Christian Nation* and Daniel Dennett's *Breaking the Spell*. One week in November, the cover of the *New York Times* book review section was illustrated with the word God made of neon lights. The "o" in the middle of the word was fashioned into a question mark. Does God exist? The question was everywhere.

Dawkins is unapologetically antireligion; his book is a literary by-product of his BBC TV series *The Root of All Evil*. That root would be, in Dawkins's view, of course, religion. In 2005, when I interviewed him for *Salon.com*, I asked Dawkins if he thought the existence of God was a question science could address. "Absolutely," he said, agreeing on that point with Phillip Johnson and William Dembski. "And it is one of the most important questions to ask right now. If there is no God, then we'd better start acting like it and start taking responsibility for what we do."

Dawkins shared the cover of *Time* magazine in November 2006 with genome-pioneer and evangelical Christian Francis Collins, whose new book *The Language of God: A Scientist Presents Evidence for Belief* is an explanation of his faith. The debate between Dawkins and Collins addresses the question of God's existence straight on, and readers responded with an avalanche of letters to the editor.

Wired magazine ran a cover story called "The New Atheism," and editorial and opinion pages around the country were crowded with debates about the costs and benefits of religion, the existence or nonexistence of God. Wherever you look today, the question, once held at a polite and denial-permitting distance, is in your face.

In the months following his ruling, Judge Jones became the judicial equivalent of a rock star. He was on the cover of *Time* as one of America's one hundred most influential people, and *Wired*, that bastion of techno-hipness, named him one of America's ten "Sexiest Geeks" for 2005. Attacked as an activist in a black robe by Anne Coulter in her book *Godless: The Church of Liberalism,* Jones countered with measured reasonableness. As the anniversary of his decision came around he was still keeping up an impressive schedule of talks, at which he stressed the importance of preserving judicial independence. Computer geek and NCSE Public Information Project Director Nick Matzke became something of a celebrity, too. *Seed* magazine profiled him as one of the year's revolutionary thinkers. He deserves the attention, but it's a little disturbing to think of defending evolution in 2006 as a revolutionary act.

Back in Dover, the impact of the trial and its decision is both greater and less than elsewhere. On one hand, the newly elected anti-ID-in-science-classroom board had to pay $1,000,011 out of the district's general fund. A million of that was to be divided by the ACLU, Americans United, and Pepper Hamilton for attorney fees and litigation costs.[2] The remaining eleven dollars was to be distributed evenly among the plaintiffs.

"It is a lot of money," says Bernie Reinking, the board's new president, voted in with the Dover CARES ticket in November 2005. But that million comes out of a $37,000,000 overall budget. "It won't bankrupt the district," she says. The general feeling among current board members is, "let's be done with it," says Reinking. "In fact," she says, "while other districts across the country may still have to deal with intelligent design and evolution controversies, we've gotten it out of our systems. Completely out. We're done with it."

I saw many of the plaintiffs again at Tammy Kitzmiller's house in early November 2006, exactly one year after the courtroom phase of the trial ended. They are all getting on with their lives, which, in their middle ages, seem marked more by their children's progress than their own. Barrie and Fred Callahan are enjoying being out of the limelight.[3] Tammy Kitzmiller and her neighbor Cyndi Sneath are concentrating on their jobs and their kids again—though they still pay very close attention to local politics—and are trying to make enough money to put a little in their kids' college funds each month. Bryan and Christy Rehm are both in graduate programs at a local university now, and Bryan's position on the Dover school board keeps them about 50 percent too busy for their liking. Steve Stough is back at the Racehorse most evenings, hanging out with his friends, shooting the breeze, and drinking beer. Ordinary people, ordinary lives.

Except that when they get together now, as they did in early November, it becomes clear to anyone observing that the Dover plaintiffs are not ordinary at all. Their willingness to stand up to the bullying, mendacious, and self-righteous zealots on their school board was heroic. And it had ramifications extending far beyond their community, from sea to shining sea.

Bill Buckingham and his wife have moved back to Dover from North Carolina. He is bitter about the trial and insists, "It wasn't lost. It was stolen." He calls Judge Jones "a liar and an idiot" and says of today's America, "It's like we're living in Nazi Germany and they're persecuting the Christians. All we wanted to do was mention ID! Kids I grew up with, who were Christian, who went to church, went to college and came back atheist because of teachers leaning toward evolutionary biology."

"Suppose we're right," he warns me. "When you die do you want to take that chance? I would rather lean on Somebody who's going to be there for me when I cross over than turn my back on Him."

As for me, in my journey through the trial of the century, I found neither compelling scientific evidence of the big Father nor any profound understanding of my own lower-cased version, whose conversion to evangelical Christianity a couple of decades ago catalyzed our own creationism-evolution debate.

My father is a theist. I am a materialist. It is painful to acknowledge that we live in different worlds. Both have their roots deep in Western culture. Both describe essential aspects of the American identity. Our struggle to connect with each other across the divide, to make sense of the differences, and to stand by our convictions, reflects a broader effort at the top of our species' agenda. What kind of species will we be? Will we be driven by a hypothetical God, about which we agree the world itself can say nothing? Or will we muster up our courage, open our eyes, and try our hardest to become our own intelligent designers?

Prologue

    1. In 2006, IVC Press ("Evangelically Rooted, Critically Engaged" is their motto) published *Darwin's Nemesis: Phillip Johnson and the Intelligent Design Movement,* edited by William Dembski. This collection of essays celebrates the life and accomplishments of "the architect of the ID movement." Johnson is, in other words, the ID movement's own intelligent designer.

    2. Several years ago I interviewed two dozen top scientists from around the world who described themselves as religious. Many of these interviews appear in a book I coedited with Mark Richardson, *Faith in Science: Scientists Search for Truth* (New York: Routledge, 2001).

Chapter One: The Takeover

    1. Darwin discovered twelve new species of finches on his voyage to the Galápagos Islands in the 1830s. Although he didn't recognize it until he got back to England, they were all closely related. Darwin realized that they were all descended from a common ancestor that must have flown to the islands from mainland South America many generations before. This set him thinking about how the different conditions on the different islands had encouraged changes in the beak

sizes and other characteristics of the birds. The combination of their isolation (from their mainland ancestors and, to some degree, from each other) and natural selection led them to adopt different adaptive strategies and develop different traits over time. Darwin's insights into the relationships between the Galápagos finches, or "Darwin's finches," as they are called, marks an important moment in the development of the theory of natural selection and also marks the beginning of biogeography, the study of the evolutionary and geographical relationships among living things around the world. Intelligent design advocates generally admit the kind of "minor" or "micro" adaptation found in Darwin's finches, but say such small changes could never lead to the evolution of entirely new types of animals.

2. Voting in favor of the measure were Sheila Harkins, Bill Buckingham, Alan Bonsell, Jane Cleaver, Heather Geesey, and Angie Yingling. Voting against it were Noel Wenrich, Casey Brown, and Jeff Brown.

Chapter Two: The Train to Dover

1. Richard Dawkins, *The Blind Watchmaker: Why the Evidence of Evolution Reveals a Universe Without Design* (New York: W. W. Norton, 1986).

Chapter Three: The Theory Is Not a Fact

1. A friend of mine, Ashley Schannauer, who graduated with Jones from Dickinson School of Law at Penn State, says of his former classmate, "He had a lot of common sense, was empathic (especially for a rich kid from a small town), and was never afraid to speak his mind, all qualities that make for a good judge."

2. Charles Darwin, *On the Origin of Species by Means of Natural Selection, or The Preservation of Favored Races in the Struggle for Life* (London: John Murray, 1859), p. 490.

3. Darwin, *On the Origin of Species,* p. 189.

4. Theodosius Dobzhansky, "Nothing in Biology Makes Sense Except in the Light of Evolution." *American Biology Teacher,* 1973, *35,* 125–129.

Chapter Four: Assembling Goliath

1. In 1999, the Kansas State Board of Education removed evolutionary theory from its statewide standardized tests and left to local school districts the decision of whether or not to teach evolution, creationism, or both. The action prompted the electoral overthrow of the pro-creationist members, and evolution was reintroduced to the schools' standards in 2001.

2. That famous case, immortalized in the play and movie *Inherit the Wind,* pitted teacher John Scopes against the State of Tennessee. The ACLU defended John Scopes, who tried teaching evolution to his students in defiance of a Tennessee law prohibiting the teaching of any theory that "denies the story of the Divine Creation of man as taught in the Bible, to teach instead that man has descended from a lower order of animals." Scopes and the ACLU lost, but the case made the teaching of evolution a cause celebre and made famous the then-seminal ACLU.

3. During Kitzmiller's deposition, Pat Gillen tried to question Kitzmiller about her religious beliefs but, she says, Rothschild "threw a million objections in his path insisting again and again that [her] religious beliefs could not possibly bear on the case. He was like a guard dog keeping me safe," she says, petting her own giant, blind puppy.

Chapter Five: Thomas More and ID Lite

1. The "opinion" Tennessee was trying to impose was that only Biblically compatible science should be taught to high school students.

2. The Website, called the Nuremberg Files, was eventually shut down by a ruling of the Supreme Court in 2001.

3. This chapter is modified from a profile I wrote of Thompson for *Salon.com.* In a weird postmodern twist, a section of the story, including the four paragraphs about relativism preceding this note, was read to the court by plaintiffs' counsel to demonstrate Thompson's unabashed radicalism.

211

4. Discovery distributed a book titled *Intelligent Design in Public School Science Curricula: A Legal Guidebook,* by David K. DeWolf, (Discovery's own) Stephen C. Meyer, and Mark E. DeForrest.

5. Specified complexity, Dembski says, is what you find in a Shakespearean sonnet; every letter in the sonnet plays a specific, determinate role, and yet the whole thing is very complex. Algorithms can be applied, says Dembski, to calculate the degree of specified complexity embodied by something, say a string of DNA or a bacterial flagellum. High levels of specified complexity, he maintains, indicate design. Dembski's mathematical arguments are highly controversial and are dismissed by many mathematicians and evolutionary biologists; nevertheless, he is seen as the leading intellect of the ID movement.

6. During the trial, on October 21, Thompson traveled to Washington, D.C., to participate in an American Enterprise Institute–sponsored forum titled "Science Wars." The director of Discovery Institute's Washington, D.C., office, Mark Ryland, told the audience that Discovery "never set out to have school boards teach intelligent design." Thompson says he "called Ryland's bluff" by holding up a copy of a Discovery-distributed publication, *Intelligent Design in Public School Science Curriculum: A Guidebook,* and reading a passage from the volume's conclusion: "School boards have the authority to permit, and even encourage, teaching about design theory as an alternative to Darwinian evolution—and this includes the use of textbooks such as *Of Pandas and People* that present evidence for the theory of intelligent design."

Chapter Six: ID Heavy and the Wedge

1. This "signature" is Dembski's "specified complexity."

Chapter Seven: Down by Law

1. "The Wedge document really gave me the creeps when I first read it," Tammy Kitzmiller told me. "The idea that they have this agenda with a time line . . . It reminds me of George Orwell's *1984*." So with

the dueling worldviews we also have dueling dystopian visions of dehumanization summarized by Orwell and Huxley, both written not all that long after the Scopes trial.

Chapter Eight: Search and Replace

1. Philosophical naturalism, also called philosophical materialism, is the view that nature is all there is. This is opposed to methodological materialism, which only says that when you're doing science, or otherwise trying to interact with the material world in a practical way, it's best to act as if nature is all there is.

2. Creation science applied the rhetoric, methods, and empirical practices of science to try to validate creationism. Basic tenets included young-earth flood geology (explaining the ordering of the fossil record, for instance, in terms of the Noachic flood and the belief that the earth is less than ten thousand years old), rejection of evolution, embrace of the sudden occurrence of species, and Biblical inerrancy.

3. The introduction to the twenty-page *in limine* brief supporting the motion to exclude Forrest reads "Dr. Barbara Forrest ('Forrest') has no scientific, technical, or other specialized knowledge that will assist the trier of fact. A close inspection of her 'expertise' and proffered testimony reveals that she is little more than a conspiracy theorist and a web-surfing, 'cyber-stalker' of the Discovery Institute ('DI') and its supporters and allies—none of whom are affiliated with DASD [Dover Area School District]. Through her testimony, Plaintiffs seek to introduce immaterial and impertinent matter masquerading as expert opinion. It is Plaintiffs' attempt at achieving 'guilt by association' without the association. This court should exclude such matters." The reference to "'guilt by association' without the association" is an effort to say that even if Forrest does discredit Discovery Institute, that says nothing about the Dover school board. However, through overlapping staff, mission, and founders with the Foundation of Thought and Ethics, DI is tightly wrapped up in the development

of *Pandas* and in the evolution of ID generally, the integrity of both of which are central to this case, so the argument held very little water.

4. John Perry, "Courtly Combatant," *World Magazine,* Dec. 13, 2003, *18*(48), 34–38.

5. Phillip E. Johnson, "Starting a Conversation About Evolution," Access Research Network, August 31, 1996. Available at www.arn.org/docs/johnson/ratzsch.htm.

6. William Dembski, "Signs of Intelligence, A Primer on the Discernment of Intelligent Design," *Touchstone,* July-Aug. 1999, pp. 76–84. "Information theory" is a field within applied mathematics that studies and tries to maximize efficiency of the flow and storage of data. But Dembski may be referring specifically to the study of his idea of "specified complexity" as it pertains to the broader field of information theory.

7. *Edwards* v. *Aguillard,* when it reached the Supreme Court, was decided by summary judgment, and so never went to a full trial, and so Kenyon never actually testified. Nevertheless, in written briefs and in his oral arguments, the counsel defending Louisiana's law leaned heavily on the expert witness affidavit written by Kenyon. In it Kenyon insisted that creation science was the only possible alternative to natural selection.

8. The Foundation for Thought and Ethics insisted that it was not a religious organization but, when shown its own tax forms and mission statement with explicitly religious language in them, it had to shuffle off with its tail between its legs. Judge Jones refused to allow the organization to be party to the case.

9. The hunch was Nick Matzke's at NCSE. He'd heard that there were earlier versions of *Pandas* that predated the popularity of ID, and it occurred to him that they might be indicting. He fired off an e-mail to the Pepper Hamilton lawyers saying, "I am reasonably sure that the word 'creation' would be substituted for 'design' or 'intelligent design' at many points within that manuscript. This would prove our point in many ways."

10. The version produced later in 1987, after *Edwards,* was identifiable because it had a footnote referring to the decision. The older 1987 version did not.

11. The plaintiff's attorneys, after much discussion, decided not to use that page as evidence. "It would have rubbed salt into the wound, when the wound was a decapitation," says Matzke.

Chapter Nine: The Varieties of Materialistic Experience

1. "The *Kitzmiller* Decision," Daniel Dennett reaction, Butterflies and Wheels.com. Available at www.butterfliesandwheels.com/articleprint.php?num=162. Accessed January 10, 2007.

2. Cornelia Dean, "Scientists Speak Up on Mix of God and Science," *New York Times,* Aug. 23, 2005.

3. Stephen J. Gould, *Rocks of Ages: Science and Religion in the Fullness of Life* (New York: Ballantine, 1999).

4. Gordy Slack and Mark Richardson (eds.), *Faith in Science: Scientists Search for Truth* (New York: Routledge, 2001).

5. William A. Dembski, *Intelligent Design: The Bridge Between Science and Theology* (Downers Grove, Ill.: InterVarsity, 1999), p. 224.

6. William A. Dembski, "What Every Theologian Should Know About Creation, Evolution and Design," Leadership University, the Virtual Office of William A. Dembski, July 2002. Available at www.leaderu.com/offices/dembski/docs/bd-theologn.html.

Chapter Ten: The Flagellar Fandango

1. These correspond roughly to Kenneth Miller's three parts of evolution, though what Miller calls "natural selection" also includes Meyer's multiplication of species and gradualism.

2. This was the book Phillip Johnson saw in the British bookstore window that catalyzed his conversion, too.

3. M. J. Behe, "Reply to My Critics: A Response to Reviews of *Darwin's Black Box: The Biochemical Challenge to Evolution,*" *Biology and Philosophy,* Nov. 2001, *16*(5), 683–707.

4. Charles Darwin, *The Origin of Species: A Facsimile of the First Edition* (Boston: Harvard University Press, 1964), p. 189.

5. In the familiar *E. Coli* bacterium, the shaft can spin at 18,000 rpm, thrusting the cell ahead at 30 microns per second. The fastest recorded flagellum turns at rates exceeding 100,000 rpm and can move cells at hundreds of micrometers per second. If the slower one, *E. Coli,* were the length of a ten-foot-long car, traveling at proportional speed, it would be driving at over two thousand miles per hour. That's one speedy pathogen and one effective motor.

6. National Academy of Sciences, *Science and Creationism: A View from the National Academy of Sciences,* 2nd ed., 1999. Available at http:// books.nap.edu/html/creationism/index.html; American Association for the Advancement of Science, *AAAS Board Resolution on Intelligent Design Theory,* approved by the AAAS board of directors on October 18, 2002. Available at www.aaas.org/news/releases/2002/ 1106id2.shtml.

7. Behe, "Reply to My Critics."

8. The introduction of random gene mutations is one big source of gene variation that gives natural selection new material to select from. The great majority of gene mutations will convey no advantage to the organisms in which they occur and will lead to either negative or neutral outcomes. How many negative and neutral mutations you'd need to get just one that conveyed an advantage is a debated subject in biology. IDers regularly claim that the kind and pace of adaptation claimed by evolution would require far more mutations than the available time permits.

9. It would only be falsified for that one case, however, and ID theorists could always come up with many more such challenges; for example, "OK, maybe we were wrong about the flagellum, but we're more confident about the blood-clotting cascade." The enterprise of disproving irreducible complexity could occupy biologists forever.

10. To use Behe's example, exaptation might explain how a mousetrap, without its holdbar, or its base, could still be valuable, and thus

selectable, for some function other than killing mice. As noted earlier, Kenneth Miller wore to court a tie clip made out of a deconstructed mousetrap.

11. Afterward, Behe accused Rothschild of "theatrics." "Damn right!" Rothschild wrote to me later. "Ken Miller had already discussed the substantive scientific points in the articles; they hardly required repetition by a lawyer. I was shooting at Behe's assertion that there were no peer-reviewed articles explaining the evolution of the immune system. Sixty articles show that *Darwin's Black Box* is misleading, and is a vivid contrast to the nonproduction by Behe and ID."

Chapter Eleven: Liars for Christ

1. Another relevant legal measure of whether a government action amounts to an endorsement of religion is known as the "endorsement test." Proposed by Supreme Court Justice Sandra Day O'Connor in the 1984 case of *Lynch* v. *Donne,* it holds that a government action is invalid if it creates a perception in the mind of a reasonable observer that the government is either endorsing or disapproving of religion.

2. It was a bit of irony that Ted Kennedy proposed the vote to adopt Santorum's legislation, not realizing that it was designed specifically to promote the teaching of intelligent design.

Chapter Twelve: The Unraveling

1. Donald Bonsell's role in the acquisition of the sixty copies of *Pandas* was revealed in early 2005 when Pepper Hamilton associate Joe Farber took the elder Bonsell's deposition. At the end of that important deposition Farber had a seizure, ending up in the arms of his opponent Pat Gillen, the gentle Modiglianiesque lawyer for Thomas More. That sad day signaled the recurrence of a brain tumor Farber had had treated years before. He died late in the spring of 2006 at the age of thirty-four.

2. Regarding the teachers' role, says Nick Matzke at NCSE, which deals with many cases of teacher intimidation every year, "It is by far

the most common, though rarely reported, anti-evolution problem in the U.S." In this case, he says, it is being "exposed in all its ugly glory, in open court, for everyone to see."

3. There is some evidence that Nilsen, though locked into his original story, wanted to let the truth be known. Nilsen had stumbled on notes from a board retreat from 2003 with the word *creationism* written next to Bonsell's name. He never admitted remembering why *creationism* was written there, but he did turn those notes in to Gillen, who dutifully gave them to Rothschild.

Chapter Fourteen: The People's Court and the Gospel According to John Jones

1. Bryan Rehm's district required a recount because of a broken voting machine. When the recount was taken in early January, Rehm was declared the winner.

Chapter Fifteen: Afterword

1. A Santorum-sponsored amendment was adopted into the legislative history of President Bush's 2002 No Child Left Behind bill. It says that "Where topics are taught that may generate controversy (such as biological evolution), the curriculum should help students to understand the full range of scientific views that exist, why such topics may generate controversy, and how scientific discoveries can profoundly affect society."

2. The billable cost was more like two million dollars, says Eric Rothschild. While they didn't want to harm the students of Dover, it was important to let other school boards know the potential consequences of such a lawsuit, so they reduced their bill to one million dollars.

3. Barrie and Fred's daughter, Arrie, is writing a master's thesis at NYU about the ID statement the school-board-mandated school administrators read to ninth-grade biology students.

ACKNOWLEDGMENTS

First of all, I want to thank my father, Charles William Slack, who more than a decade ago led me into the fascinating thicket of argument surrounding evolution and creationism and who has been happy to spend hundreds of hours locked with me in no-holds-barred debate. We are father and son, made of the same stuff, yet we live in different worlds; he is a creationist with a rich and meaningful life, and I am an evolutionist who loves his life, too. The effort to understand and come to terms with our differences led to this work.

I also want to thank Kevin Berger, my editor at *Salon.com,* who assigned me to cover *Kitzmiller* v. *Dover* and who gave me enough editorial rope to hang myself—and to dangle for a while over the courtroom in a way that permitted me to follow one of the most wide-ranging and fascinating trials in American history.

I was in Harrisburg for the first week-and-a-half of the six-week trial and then made two trips back, one in the summer of 2006 and another in the fall. I owe a great deal to the many people on both sides of the case who tolerated my poking around in their business at those times and who then collectively spent several hundred hours talking with me on the phone.

I'm very grateful to Richard Thompson, chief counsel for the defense, who gave me several interviews though it was clear to him that he and I did not see eye-to-eye on many of the big questions addressed in the book.

Lawyers Richard Katskee, Eric Rothschild, Steve Harvey, and Vic Walczak helped me tell their stories and comprehend the legal nuances of the trial and their strategy. Pepper Hamilton legal assistants Kate Henson and Hedya Aryani, both natural storytellers with great eyes for detail, never showed any signs of impatience, though they must have tired of my relentless questions. Their behind-the-scenes descriptions add leavening to the sometimes heavy issues at the heart of the trial.

Defendant Bill Buckingham, the former head of curriculum on the Dover Area School Board, was also generous with his time.

The *Kitzmiller* plaintiffs were an extraordinary, and extraordinarily helpful, group of sources. They were generous with their time and their stories. In particular I want to thank Barrie and Fred Callahan, Christy and Bryan Rehm, Tammy Kitzmiller, Cynthia Sneath, Steve Stough, Joel Lieb, and Deborah Fenimore.

Dover schoolteachers Robert Eshbach, Bert Spahr, and Jennifer Miller helped me to understand the educational issues in Dover and to get a sense of what it is like to be a science teacher in a district run by a pro-ID board.

I got a lot of help and information from Nick Matzke, Glenn Branch, and Eugenie Scott at the National Center for Science Education and from Casey Luskin, Rob Crowther, and Stephen Meyer at Discovery Institute.

I want to thank, too, my very competent and delightful editor on this project, Naomi Lucks, for her authoritative yet light-handed shepherding; my agent, Giles Anderson, who worked hard to find the perfect home for this project; Julianna Gustafson and the team at Jossey-Bass who made that house the perfect home; and David Horne, who took great care in the copy-editing of the manuscript.

I am deeply grateful to my editor, friend, and brother-in-law John Raeside, who read early and late versions of the book and was a high-fidelity sounding board on issues big and small. I also want to thank my office mates Molly Bentley and Peter Williams and my friend Ben Wurgaft for their contributions. If they grew weary of my obsession with this trial, they never let it show. Their puns and needles kept me alert and hopeful through the rough patches and often even made them fun.

Finally, and most of all, I want to thank my wife, Adriana Taranta, for her great ideas and her constant love and encouragement. Without Adriana, I couldn't have begun this book, let alone finished it. I will never be able to thank her enough, though I look forward to trying.

ABOUT THE AUTHOR

GORDY SLACK is a science writer specializing in evolutionary biology and the relationship between science and religion. He has written for *Mother Jones, Wired,* and *Salon.com* and is a regular contributor to KQED Radio, San Francisco. He was formerly a columnist and senior editor at *California Wild* magazine. He is coeditor of *Faith in Science,* a collection of interviews with religious scientists. Slack lives in Oakland, California, with his wife and two sons.

INDEX